Place
20¢
Stamp
Here

VISICALC MODELS FOR BUSINESS
P.O. Box 50507
Indianapolis, Indiana 46250

NOW AVAILABLE!

The models in this book are *also* available on disk. Now, without the delay and inconvenience of entering them manually, these helpful financial tools can be put to use immediately. To order, check the disk(s) you want and return this card.

_____ copy(s) of diskette #1 @ $39.95 each = $ _______
(models in chapters 1, 2, 3 and 4)

_____ copy(s) of diskette #2 @ $39.95 each = $ _______
(models in chapters 5, 6, and 7)

Shipping & Handling = $ 2.50

TOTAL = $ _______

Method of Payment: ☐ Check ☐ MasterCard ☐ Visa

Credit Card Number: _______________

Exp. Date: _______________

Check Program: ☐ SuperCalc ☐ VisiCalc
SuperCalc format requires version 1.06 or later.

Check Format:
- ☐ IBM PC (PC DOS 1.1)
- ☐ IBM PC (CP/M-86)
- ☐ 8″ SS/SD
- ☐ Osborne I
- ☐ Apple II (with SoftCard)
- ☐ Apple III

Name: _______________

Address: _______________

____

City, State, Zip: _______________

VisiCalc Models for Business

Douglas Ford Cobb
Gena Berg Cobb

Que Corporation
Indianapolis

VisiCalc is a registered trademark of VisiCorp.

Library of Congress Catalog No.: 82-42767
ISBN 0-88022-017-1

Cover art: Dick Held
Design: Paul Mangin
Typeset in Helvetica by Alexander Typesetting, Inc.
Manufactured in the United States of America
Published by Que Corporation
7960 Castleway Drive
Indianapolis, Indiana 46250

First Printing, March, 1983
Second Printing, June, 1983

About the Authors

DOUGLAS FORD COBB

General Manager—Software Products, Que Corporation

Mr. Cobb received his B.A. degree, magna cum laude, from Williams College and his M.S. in accounting from New York University's Graduate School of Business Administration. After graduation, he worked for the firm of Arthur Andersen & Co. Before joining Que, he was president of Cobb Associates, Inc., a Boston-based microcomputer consulting firm.

In addition to this book, Mr. Cobb was the writer of the article on interactive spreadsheeting in Que's *IBM PC Expansion and Software Guide* and was one of the contributors to *IBM's Personal Computer* by Que.

GENA BERG COBB

Mrs. Cobb received her B.S. degree in marketing from the McIntire School of Commerce of the University of Virginia. After graduation, she held market research and marketing management positions with American Digital Systems, Inc., and John Wiley & Sons, Publishers. She is currently a second-year student at the Harvard School of Business.

Editorial Director

David F. Noble, Ph.D.

Editors

Diane F. Brown, M.A.
Virginia D. Noble, M.L.S.
Jean White, B.A.

Technical Editor

Thomas B. Henderson

Managing Editor

Paul L. Mangin

Que Microcomputer Products

BOOKS:	ISBN No.	Date Available
Apple II Word Processing	0-88022-005-8	Currently
C Programming Guide	0-88022-022-8	Spring, '83
CP/M Compatible Software Catalog 2nd Ed.	0-88022-018-X	Currently
CP/M Word Processing	0-88022-006-6	Currently
IBM PC Expansion & Software Guide	0-88022-019-8	Currently
IBM PC Pocket Dictionary	0-88022-024-4	Spring, '83
IBM's Personal Computer-hbk.	0-88022-101-1	Currently
IBM's Personal Computer-pbk.	0-88022-100-3	Currently
The Osborne Portable Computer	0-88022-015-5	Currently
Personal Computers for Managers	0-88022-031-7	May, '83
SuperCalc SuperModels for Business	0-88022-007-4	Currently
Timex/Sinclair 1000 User's Guide, Vol. 1	0-88022-016-3	Currently
Timex/Sinclair 1000 User's Guide, Vol. 2	0-88022-029-5	Currently
Timex/Sinclair 1000 Pocket Dictionary	0-88022-028-7	Spring, '83

SOFTWARE:

CalcSheets for Business	1100 Series	Currently

"CalcSheets for Business" is a series of VisiCalc and SuperCalc models to assist businesspeople in cash management, debt management, fixed asset management, working capital management, and other business management. These models run on the IBM Personal Computer, Apple II computer and other popular personal computers.

Table of Contents

Preface

VisiCalc® Models for Business is a book of models, or templates, for the electronic spreadsheet program VisiCalc. The book presents over 20 models that show you creative ways to use your computer and VisiCalc to help you run your business.

This book could be titled *Managing Your Business with VisiCalc*. Business concepts behind each model are explained in the text so that you can learn new management techniques while you learn to use VisiCalc. For example, some of the concepts covered by the text are net present value, internal rate of return, ratio analysis, and cash flow management.

The models in this book range from fairly simple to very complex and cover topics from budgeting and financial statement preparation to managing accounts receivable. The text contains easy-to-follow instructions on how to set up and use the models. Foldouts illustrating the model formats are included so that you can follow along with the text.

Many of these models can be applied to your own business problems without modification, but some may need slight adaptation. Each model includes a section describing how the model can be modified to fit your needs.

Throughout *VisiCalc Models for Business,* you will find innovative and creative techniques that can be used in your own models to "bend" VisiCalc to fit your needs. Note that these innovations are not limited to business applications for VisiCalc. Personal and home users as well can benefit from them. The models in this book were created, tested, and documented to help you obtain maximum benefit from the VisiCalc program. All VisiCalc commands and functions are explained in the models so that even a novice can use them. In addition, a number of "tricks" are introduced, which you can use to make VisiCalc more powerful and flexible.

Because these features are provided, you will not have to spend time to develop them yourself. This book gives you sophisticated, adaptable models that you can use immediately. It will also give you new insights into the capabilities of VisiCalc and help you become a VisiCalc "pro" in a matter of days instead of the weeks it might take you on your own.

Introducing CalcSheets for Business

If you would like these and other templates for your personal use, but don't have the time to key them into your computer, you need QUE's new product, *CalcSheets™ for Business.* The first series of CalcSheets presents on diskette the models in this book, ready to be loaded into your computer and run.

You can buy *CalcSheets for Business* at your local computer store, or directly from Que Corporation by using the order card in the front of this book. Calcsheets are available in disk formats for most popular microcomputers.

Future series of CalcSheets will include templates for personal financial planning; tax planning; and for banking, insurance, accounting, and other professions.

Introduction

What Can I Do with VisiCalc?

Spreadsheet programs like VisiCalc are electronic replacements for the traditional financial modeling tools: the accountant's columnar pad, the pencil, and the calculator. In some ways, spreadsheet programs are to those tools what word processors are to typewriters. They offer dramatic improvements in ease of setting up and using financial models.

Because the computer's memory holds the spreadsheet programs while you set up the model, you are not bound by the physical limitations of the printed page. Are some of your formulas repeated across time? Use the spreadsheet's replicate function to project quickly your assumptions from one cell to another. Did you forget a row or a column? Simply insert it at the appropriate point. Is one of your assumptions or formulas incorrect, or is there a typographical error in one of your headings? Correct the error instantly with the edit command.

The act of building a spreadsheet model defines all the mathematical relationships in the model. Until you decide to change them, every sum, product, division, subtraction, average, and net present value will remain the same. Every time you enter data into the model, computations will be made at your command with no effort on your part. All of the computations will be calculated without math errors. Then next month, should you decide to use the model again, the formulas will still be set, ready to calculate at your command.

Even more important, spreadsheet software allows you to ask "What if . . . ?" after your model has been developed. If you use paper, pencil, and calculator to build your models, then every change will require recalculating every relationship in the model. If the model has 100 formulas, and you change the first one, you must make 100 calculations by hand to flow the change through the entire model. When you use VisiCalc, however, the same change requires pressing only a few keys! The program does the rest. This feature makes extensive "what if" analysis possible. The versatility of VisiCalc, SuperCalc™, and the other visible numeric processors makes them important tools for both small and large businesses. More and more companies of all sizes are using VisiCalc and other spreadsheets to help speed and simplify financial analysis.

Spreadsheet programs are sometimes called planning tools, and one of their major uses is business planning. But thinking of spreadsheet programs only in this way ignores the spectacular power they have to solve other kinds of problems. VisiCalc can be configured to solve almost any problem that used to be attacked with a pad and pencil. It can be an auditing tool to assist accountants in the preparation of reports and financial statements, or it can analyze collections on accounts receivable, evaluate inventory stock level, and record employee performance. A well-designed spreadsheet program can function even as a limited accounting system for a small business, helping track disbursements into budget categories and monitor collections of accounts receivable.

Spreadsheet software can solve far more business problems than most people think. This book demonstrates the use of VisiCalc for such diverse tasks as balancing a checkbook, evaluating investments in fixed assets, calculating depreciation, prepaying a loan, monitoring the activity of a line of credit, generating quotes, and preparing financial statements, as well as budgeting and forecasting.

The Table of Contents illustrates the broad range of models in this book. The models are grouped under seven categories: Cash Management, Debt Management, Fixed Asset Management, Working Capital Management, Financial Statements, and Planning and Budgeting. These chapters cover the most important areas of financial business management.

Some of these sophisticated and flexible models can be combined with other models to form *Super*Models if your computer has sufficient RAM. For example, the Ratio Analyzer in Chapter 5 can be combined with the Interactive Income Statement and Balance Sheet in the same chapter, or with one of your own income statement/balance sheet models, to form a complete financial analysis system. The ACRS Depreciation Calculator can be combined with the Internal Rate of Return Calculator in Chapter 3 to create a lease evaluator model. The Cash Disbursements Spreadsheet in Chapter 1 can be combined with the Checkbook Balancer template in that chapter to build a comprehensive checkbook management model. In fact, the possibilities for combination are virtually limitless. Look for other ways to use these models with each other or with some of your own applications.

Who Should Use This Book?

VisiCalc Models for Business should be used by anyone who owns, or is considering purchasing, the VisiCalc program. Whether you are an experienced VisiCalc user or a novice, this book will help you be more productive in your use of VisiCalc.

A Note to Beginners

If you are just starting out with VisiCalc, you will appreciate the book's thorough, easy-to-understand explanations of VisiCalc commands and concepts. For example, the Managing Cash Flow section in Chapter 1 includes a discussion of "what if" analysis that will familiarize you with the technique that makes spreadsheet programs so popular and powerful.

The Statistics Calculator model, in Chapter 6, explains the built-in VisiCalc functions @MAX, @MIN, @AVERAGE, and @COUNT. Also in this chapter, VisiCalc's @IF function is demonstrated and explained in the Budgeting for a New Ventures section. This simple example will prepare you for more advanced uses of the function in other models.

The concept of *forward references* is illustrated in the Interactive Income Statement and Balance Sheet in Chapter 5. This model shows you how to use forward references to make your own models more flexible.

VisiCalc Models for Business will quickly bring you up to speed on VisiCalc. While you are learning about the program, you will be building VisiCalc models that will help you manage your business. Once you've learned the basics, *VisiCalc Models for Business* will carry you on to more advanced concepts.

For Experienced Users

Professional users will appreciate *VisiCalc Models for Business*'s explanations of the more advanced VisiCalc features. For example, the ACRS Depreciation Calculator in Chapter 3 contains a complex @LOOKUP table that uses conditional statements. This feature should suggest new ways that you can incorporate @LOOKUP tables in your models.

Another sophisticated @LOOKUP table is used in the Internal Rate of Return Calculator in the same chapter. This table combines the @LOOKUP function with the @NPV function to compute efficiently internal rate of return.

You may know that VisiCalc does not include a looping function. The Loan Payoff Calculator in Chapter 2 uses a tool that helps overcome this problem and shows you how to avoid extra keystrokes when solving long and complex problems.

A technique for automatically posting data to different columns is demonstrated in the Cash Disbursements Spreadsheet in Chapter 1. This posting technique can be applied to many types of models.

Only a few features of *VisiCalc Models for Business* are mentioned above. Almost every model includes a twist that will help you make better use of VisiCalc.

What Do You Need to Use the Models in This Book?

The models in this book were developed on an IBM PC microcomputer with 64K of RAM memory and two disk drives. Many of the models can be used on systems with less memory. If your computer has at least 48K, you will be able to use most of the models. Two disk drives are recommended, but only one is required.

Some models will barely fit on a 64K microcomputer. If you are fortunate enough to own a computer with more RAM, you will be able to expand the models to make use of that extra memory.

Although *VisiCalc Models for Business* discusses many VisiCalc functions, it is not a substitute for the VisiCalc manual. Before you begin using the models in this book, take the time to read through the manual and use the program until you are familiar with its basic functions. The explanations in this book assume that you are familiar with the concepts of rows, columns, and cells; the use of addition, subtraction, multiplication, and division in VisiCalc; the concept of formulas between cells; and the commands SAVE, LOAD, OUTPUT, REPLICATE, FORMAT, DELETE, and INSERT.

Even if you don't own a computer, *VisiCalc Models for Business* can show you some of the ways you could apply one. It can help you to begin thinking about how to use a computer in your business.

Conventions Used in VisiCalc Models

A number of conventions, or standards, are introduced in *VisiCalc Models for Business* to help you use the models. Some of the more important conventions are discussed below. The models in each chapter are arranged in order of difficulty—from simple to complex.

You will notice that each model is divided into sections. Typically, a model will have four sections: ASSUMPTIONS, SOLUTIONS, INSTRUCTIONS, and CONTENTS. Each section is labeled with a header and a sheet number.

A table of contents appears at the top of most models. In a few models the table of contents appears at the bottom for formatting reasons. Each listing contains the symbol ">" and a cell reference. The symbol is an indication to execute the GOTO command to jump to the cell noted with the symbol. Each model also has a brief set of instructions, usually located at the bottom. You can leave these sections out of your models if you wish. The model explanations do not mention the contents or instructions sections. However, these sections can be valuable aids in building and using the models. If you "lock" the screen at the bottom of the contents section (usually around row 9) with the command `/TH`, this section of the model will always be visible on the screen, giving you a permanent point of reference that will help you find your way through the models.

The explanation of each model is also divided into sections. The first section explains the business PRINCIPLES that lie behind the model; the second is a tour through THE MODEL; the third explains the steps that must be taken in USING THE MODEL; and the last suggests possible MODIFICATIONS to the basic model. This structure should help you find the information you need.

The cell references in the text are presented in the same format that VisiCalc uses when you print the contents of a model. For example, look at this formula:

A5 /FI (V) A1*100

The first symbol, A5, is the reference of the cell that contains the formula. The phrase /FI indicates a cell format—in this case, `I` stands for Integer. Sometimes, the symbol **$** (Dollar format) is used. The `(V)` indicates that the cell has been defined as a value, or numeric entry. Some cells are defined as labels, and the definitions of these cells contain the symbol `(L)`. The final part of the formula represents the cell's contents.

Whenever you are asked to enter any information or type any commands, the text to be typed is shown in `a distinctive typeface.` Each command is presented exactly as it is to be typed, although the command may appear differently on the screen. The symbol `(CR)` in a command tells you to press the RETURN key on your keyboard. This key may be labeled ENTER, or RETURN, or it may be marked by a symbol like this: ↵. Some typed letters will appear as a whole word, followed by a comma.

After you learn these conventions, the only thing that should keep you from realizing the full potential of VisiCalc in your own business is a lack of imagination. Experiment with VisiCalc to find new ways to use the program in your own environment. *VisiCalc Models for Business* can be your springboard to even more imaginative applications for VisiCalc.

If you create a model that you think is unique and especially useful, QUE would like to hear from you. Call us at (317) 842-7162 and let us know what you are doing. We would also welcome any comments and suggestions that you have about *VisiCalc Models for Business.*

Happy Modeling!

CHAPTER 1
Cash Management

Balancing the Checkbook
Tracking Cash Disbursements
Managing Cash Flow
Projecting Cash Flow

Balancing the Checkbook

When was the last time you opened your monthly bank statement and found that the ending balance agreed with your checkbook balance? Maybe never? Every business faces the frustrating chore of reconciling its checkbook to a bank statement at least once a month. Many businesses must reconcile more than one account. This boring and repetitive job always seems to require more time than it is worth. But, because the bank statement serves as the only check against in-house records, the job must be done. Let's see how VisiCalc can help streamline the checkbook-balancing process.

Principles

The disparity between your balance according to the bank and your checkbook balance can occur for one of three primary reasons. The most common one is that either you or the bank made a mistake in recording a check or a deposit, or in computing the balance, or both. Whatever your situation, the error must be corrected so that both sets of records are accurate and in agreement.

A second possible difference arises from bank-initiated charges or credits, such as a monthly service charge. If your cash is in a NOW account, you will also show a credit for interest earned on your monthly statement. These charges and credits must be entered into your records before the books will balance.

The third common cause of discrepancies is time. Often a delay of one or more days occurs between the date you write a check and the date it is charged against your account. Some banks will not credit your account until a deposit has cleared at another bank, which may take several days. These timing differences have specific names: outstanding checks and deposits in transit. You must identify these items and make adjustments for them before your checkbook will agree with the bank statement. This can be a time-consuming task, but the Checkbook Balancer can make it much easier.

The Model

This model has four sections: CHECK DATA, CODING DATA, PREVIOUSLY OUTSTANDING ITEMS, and RECONCILIATION. The CHECK DATA section begins at cell A8. Column A displays the dates of all checks entered in the period. The check numbers are recorded in column B. Notice that cell B15 is defined as 1+B14, cell B16 as 1+B15, and so on. With this arrangement, the model can number the checks on a spreadsheet automatically, saving input time.

Columns C, D, and E provide space for a description of each check. Column F contains the check amounts, and column G shows the amounts of any deposits made.

The running balance in the account is computed in column H. The formula in cell H15,

```
H15 /F$ (V) +H14-F15+G15
```

is typical of the cells in this column.

CODING DATA, the second section of the model, begins at cell I8. Columns I and J code outstanding checks and deposits in transit for adjustment. If a check listed at the left is not reflected in the bank statement, it should be recorded as outstanding by inserting a 1 in column I. To code a deposit as outstanding at the end of the period, insert a 1 in column J. Check or deposit amounts coded in this manner will automatically appear in column K or L after the model has been recalculated. This automatic entry is achieved by using an @IF statement in the cells in columns K and L. For example, the formula for cell K15 is:

```
K15 /F$ (V) @IF(I15=1,F15,0)
```

The same relationship is used for the other cells in these two columns. Take the time to become familiar with this method of coding. It can be very useful in models where certain items in a series must be isolated for special treatment. Automatic entry is also used in the Cash Disbursements Spreadsheet model.

PREVIOUSLY OUTSTANDING ITEMS, the third section of the model, begins at cell A59. This section accounts for checks that are outstanding for more than one month.

RECONCILIATION, the fourth part of the model, begins at cell A73.

Notice that its components are the same as those discussed above: bank initiated charges and credits, outstanding checks and deposits in transit, and adjustments to the bank balance. Cells G80 and G81 total the outstanding checks and deposits in columns H and I, using the formulas:

```
G80 /F$ (V) @SUM(K15...K72)
G81 /F$ (V) @SUM(L15...L72)
```

Cell G76 is an input cell. You supply the proper amounts for bank credits and charges when the bank statement is received. Cell G81 will be used infrequently, but it is needed for error adjustment.

Using the Model

Begin by calling the model from disk. Move the cursor to cell B15 and input the first check number for the new month. If the last check written for the preceding month was number 1004, then 1005 should be entered in cell B15. Now, recalculate by typing ! and note how the check numbers are replicated down column B in ascending numerical order.

Move the cursor to cell H14 and input the last period's closing balance according to your checkbook. If you have not yet reconciled the account for last month, you may leave this cell blank for now and fill it in after the reconciliation is completed. Note, however, that until it is filled in, the running balance column will not be up-to-date. If you post your unreconciled balance to this cell, you may need to make an adjustment to it after completing the prior month's reconciliation.

When you receive the bank statement for the prior month's activity, fill in the PREVIOUSLY OUTSTANDING section of the model. Examine the statement, looking for outstanding checks and deposits. Move the cursor to cell A59 and post each outstanding item, just as you would a newly written check. Be aware, however, that these items are not included in the running total. This part of the model only holds the checks and deposits until they clear on a subsequent statement.

The model is now configured for a new month. As you write checks, input the information as you would in a manual checkbook—amount, date, and description. If a check is voided, type `VOID` into the amount column for that check number. Post deposits in column G as you make them throughout the month.

At the end of the month, be sure to save the just-completed worksheet by typing `/SSFilename (CR)`. A descriptive file name will help you remember where you stored your data. For example, April's check register may be saved as `Chkbk482`, an abbreviation for "Checkbook 4/82."

When you receive a bank statement, call up from disk the checkbook file for the month covered by the statement. Compare the statement with the check register and code any outstanding checks or deposits in transit, using a "1" in column I for checks, and a "1" in column J for deposits. Note whether any items in the PREVIOUSLY OUTSTANDING section are still outstanding on this statement and code them as explained above. Be sure to blank the cells that contain information about any checks that did clear. Finally, move the cursor to cell G76 and enter the net amount of any bank-initiated charges or credits for the period.

Position the cursor to display the entire reconciliation box on the screen. Recalculate the worksheet by typing ! Cells G80 and G81 will display the total amount of any outstanding items, and cell G84 will show the computed bank balance. Compare this amount with the balance on your bank statement. If the two numbers agree, fine. If they don't, review the worksheet, making sure that all check amounts have been input correctly, that all outstanding items (and only outstanding items) are properly coded, and that the bank charges have been computed properly. If no errors are found, check again, then consider whether there may be an error in the bank statement. If you find an error, enter the adjusting amount in cell G82 and call the bank to have an official correction made.

After the checkbook and the bank balance are reconciled, save the sheet by typing /SSFilename (CR), then print it by typing >A8 (CR) /PPM85 (CR). You can use the completed worksheet to update the model for the following month, which should be partially complete by this time. Post the ending book balance from the old model to cell H14 in the new one and record any checks outstanding at the end of the prior period in the PREVIOUSLY OUTSTANDING area of the current model. The cycle is now complete, and you're ready for the next end of month, the next statement, and so on.

Modifications

The Checkbook Balancer model can be easily expanded to accommodate more checks and deposits or previously outstanding items, by inserting rows as needed and replicating the relevant formulas into the new rows.

This model and the Cash Disbursements Spreadsheet can work well together. Take the time to review that model, then consider expanding the check register by adding the spreader to it. This modification will create the VisiCalc equivalent of a one-write cash management system, with the added advantage of simplifying your month-end reconciliations.

Tracking Cash Disbursements

Many small companies do not have enough accounting activity to justify the time and expense required to maintain a complete general ledger system. They do, however, need financial records. It is particularly important that these businesses monitor their expenditures because reliable budgets are almost impossible to develop and maintain without accurate expense information.

Spreading the checkbook is a technique used by many businesses to provide expense information quickly and easily. The term "spreading the checkbook" is derived from the use of accountants' spreadsheet paper to do the job. With this method, each check written in a period of time is assigned to one of several "accounts." The accounts summarize the disbursements in that period for different types of expense activity (e.g., salaries, rent, or supplies).

Each spreadsheet column represents one account. Check amounts are posted in the appropriate column. When all the checks are posted, each column is totaled to arrive at the balance for each account. The spreadsheet is essentially a simple general ledger.

One of the primary assumptions of VisiCalc Models is that what can be done with a manual spreadsheet can be done better with VisiCalc. Let's see what VisiCalc can do with a checkbook-spreading model.

Principles

Spreading the checkbook with traditional tools (pencil, paper, and calculator) is a fairly simple job. Each check is listed at the left on the spreadsheet paper. The check is then assigned to an account, and the check amount is written in the appropriate column.

The problem comes at the end, when the columns must be totaled. If a number of checks have been processed, computing the total in each column is sure to be a time-consuming task. At best, the addition will have to be performed only once. If there is any discrepancy between the original total of the checks and the sum of the totals of the spreading columns, however, the entire process must be repeated, taking far more time than such a simple operation deserves.

Using VisiCalc to spread the checkbook eliminates all of this addition and ensures that every column has been properly totaled.

The Model

The model has two sections: CHECK DATA and SPREADING TABLE. Unlike most of the models in this book, the sections in this model are arranged from side to side, rather than from top to bottom. The CHECK DATA section begins at cell A10. Columns A, B, C, D, E, and F record the number, date, description, and amount of each check. This part of the model should be used the same way you use your check register or check stubs.

In the SPREADING TABLE section, which begins at cell I10 and continues at cell P10, columns I through U contain the "accounts" established to summarize the period's activity. Column V totals the amount spread in each row in columns I through U.

Column G, labeled Code, is one of the time savers in this model. Study the example. You will notice that each check has been assigned a code that matches the number of one of the 13 spreading account columns. The amount of the check appears in the column that matches the code. These codes serve as automatic spreaders, eliminating the need to scroll left and right with the cursor to spread the checks. Checks are spread through the use of conditional statements in each cell in the posting range. For example, cell I18 is defined as:

```
I18 /F$ (V) @IF(G18=I13,F18,0)
```

Similarly, the following formula can be found in cell J25:

```
J25 /F$ (V) @IF(G25=J13,F25,0)
```

This formula means: if the code in cell G25 is the same as column J's code, found in cell J13, then post the value of the check found in cell F25 into cell J25; otherwise, set cell J25 to equal 0. This technique saves much time during posting.

The cells in row 42 total the amounts posted in each spreading column. Figures in these cells are determined through simple addition. The formula in cell F42 is an example:

```
F42 /F$ (V) @SUM(F17...F41)
```

A Note on Summing Ranges

You will notice that cell F41 in the example contains a dashed line. The inclusion of this line in the summing range allows the model to be expanded without modifications to the formulas in row 42. To add one more check to the model, type:

```
>A41 (CR) /IR
```

After the row is inserted, look at the cells in what is now row 43. You will see that the formulas in those cells have been altered to include the new row 42. For example, cell F43 is now defined as:

```
F43 /F$ (V) @SUM(F17...F42)
```

The model is ready for you to enter new check data. This technique can save a lot of time, especially in models you expand frequently.

Finally, look at column V. The cells in this column total the amounts posted in columns I through U, using formulas similar to the one in cell V30:

```
V30 /F$ (V) @SUM(I30...U30)
```

The totals in column V serve as error checks. Compare the amounts in column V with those in column F. You will see that the two columns are identical, indicating that the checks in column F have been spread completely. This error-checking feature is particularly valuable when checks are posted manually.

Using the Model

At the beginning of a new period, call up a blank copy of the model from disk. Each day, as you write checks, enter the requested data (check number, date, description, and amount) in columns A through F. If any checks are void, type `Void` in the cell next to the number. Be sure to save the model under a descriptive file name at the end of the day by typing `/SSFilename (CR)`.

At the end of the month, load the model again and move the cursor to cell G17. Move down the worksheet, coding each check in the appropriate category. When this task has been completed, recalculate the model by typing ! Each check amount should be posted to the cell you have indicated, and all totals should be computed automatically.

Sometimes a check must be posted to more than one column. For example, loan repayments usually include principal and interest, and the two amounts must be separated for accounting purposes. When you come to a check like this in your posting process, do not enter a code for the check in column G. Instead, move the cursor across the sheet to the appropriate columns and type in the correct amounts. When the sheet is recalculated, column V will total the amounts posted to the various columns. Be sure to check the total in column V against the check amount in column F. If they do not agree, review your entries to find the error. After you check for errors, save the worksheet and print it by typing `>A10 (CR) /PPV43 (CR)`.

You can edit a spreadsheet after it has been saved by calling it up from disk. Move the cursor to the cell, or cells, to be corrected and enter the new information. After the changes are made, recalculate, save, and print the sheet again.

Modifications

The simplest modification you can make to this model is to add more rows and columns to the spreadsheet. Depending on the memory capacity of your computer, you may be able to build a sheet that spreads 100 checks across 50 columns. This modification requires the use of the Insert and Replicate commands.

You may also want to merge this model with one of the other models in this book, such as Balancing the Checkbook, or with one of your own models.

Managing Cash Flow

If you are like most business people, managing cash flow is one of the most important financial planning activities you perform. This is especially true for managers in small businesses, where growth can strain cash balances to the limit. Even the treasurers of Fortune 500 companies, however, must keep tight control over cash. Every business person would like to know weeks or months in advance when cash crunches will occur, or when cash will be available for discretionary expenditures.

This model is designed to help the business, professional, or personal VisiCalc user manage cash. By tracking cash balances on a day-to-day basis, the model may help you avoid nerve-shattering cash lows, and may even help you put excess funds to work earning interest.

Principles

Cash flow activities can be divided into two broad categories: disbursements and receipts. The task of cash flow management is to match these outflows and inflows as closely as possible so that a given cash balance is maintained. Managing cash flows also requires the ability to predict periods of unacceptably low and high cash balances so that corrective action can be taken. The problem with cash flow planning is that it requires predicting the future—something people still don't have the knack of, after centuries of trying. The trick of cash flow planning, then, is to estimate accurately the timing of future receipts and disbursements.

Cash receipts are usually generated by sales, although receipts may also be either refunds for merchandise exchanged or inflows of borrowed money. Receipts are difficult to time precisely, because the payment decision comes from someone else. Estimating exactly when an overdue invoice will be paid is probably the toughest part of planning cash flows. Most business people, however, can estimate to within a week or two when their customers will pay. Such an estimate will be sufficient for this model. Predicting when borrowed cash will be repaid is generally easier because borrowing is usually a discretionary activity.

Cash disbursements are typically easier to plan. Regular disbursements, such as rent and payroll payments, occur at the same time every month (or week, as the case may be). These payments can easily be assigned a payment date. Payments for merchandise or other goods purchased on credit can also be planned fairly accurately. These bills usually carry terms (e.g., Net 30 Days) that provide a range of acceptable payment dates. Purely discretionary disbursements, such as dividend payments, offer more flexibility because they have no due date.

One type of disbursement—emergency expenditures—is not easy to forecast. When an important machine breaks down, there is no time to be concerned with the cash flow implications of the repair. The machine must be fixed. In fact, the possibility of emergency expenditures is one of the strongest arguments in favor of cash flow planning. A company with a planned cash reserve is more likely to weather such a crisis.

After all disbursements and receipts have been assigned a planned activity date, you have the beginnings of a cash flow model. All that remains is to arrange the various activities in chronological order and to add or subtract them from the previous balance. None of these procedures requires the power of VisiCalc.

One factor has not been fully considered, however. Because each planned activity date is a prediction, it involves some uncertainty. If even a few dates are wrong, the model's results can be seriously flawed. VisiCalc has the power to help you manage that uncertainty, through the use of "what if" analysis.

A Note on "What If" Analysis

"What if" analysis is useful for factoring away uncertainty in models that make predictions. In this kind of analysis, different versions of a model are developed, each based on a different revised set of assumptions. A worst-case scenario would include the most pessimistic assumptions, and a best-case version would illustrate the most optimistic outcome. Between these two cases lies one that illustrates the most likely outcome. Each case can be thought of as the answer to a different "what if" question, such as: What if bill XYZ isn't paid as rapidly as planned? What if an emergency expenditure is required? Analyzing the problem with "what if" analysis lets you see how changes in your assumptions affect the expected outcome. Even though "what if" analysis does not eliminate the risk of erroneous estimates, it does help you evaluate the consequences of errors and decide if the risk can be absorbed.

The obvious problem with "what if" analysis is that it takes a great deal of time to develop successive versions of a model when traditional computing tools like paper, pencils, and calculators are used. VisiCalc, however, can compute each version of a model in a matter of seconds, letting you develop as many "what if" cases as you wish.

The Model

This model has only one section, DAILY ACTIVITY, which begins at cell A9. Side-to-side scrolling is not necessary to view your results because the model is exactly one CRT screen wide.

The far left column, labeled Date, contains the days of the month for the month selected, in this case April. Cell A18 contains the first day of the month, entered as a label:

A18 /FR (V) "4-1

Cell A20 contains the second day of the month, entered as a number:

A20 /FI (V) -2

Each date cell below row 20 in column A is defined by subtracting one from the immediately preceding date. For example, cell A26 is defined as:

A26 /FI (V) +A24-1

Moving from left to right, notice that columns B, C, and D are labeled Receipts, with the subheadings Description and Amount. These three columns are used to enter actual and estimated cash inflows. Similarly, columns E, F, and G, labeled Disbursements, are used for cash outflows. The final column, H, shows the balance after each day, which is calculated as the previous balance, plus receipts, less disbursements. Cell H18 is therefore defined as:

H18 (V) +H17+D18-G18

This relationship is repeated in each cell in column H.

Using the Model

Move the cursor to cell B11 and input the name of the month to be planned. Next, move to A18 and change the label in that cell to the first day of the month in MM-DD format.

Cell D17 shows the beginning cash balance for the period. This amount should equal your reconciled closing checkbook balance for the previous month. Every balance in the model builds on this amount; therefore, it is very important that the amount be correct.

After recalculating the sheet by typing !, you will be ready to begin. If no entries have been posted, your opening balance should appear in every cell from H17 to H80. The proper dates should also appear in column A. Move the cursor to an entry cell in column E. Enter a description, then move the cursor to column G, same row, and enter an amount. Recalculate the sheet by typing ! Notice that every cell in column H below the row you just defined equals the beginning balance less the application you posted. All entries are posted to the model this way.

Once you feel ready to solo, begin entering your own data into the model. Start with your regular disbursements, such as rent and payroll. Next, enter any payments on accounts you know will come due in the current month. Finally, post your estimated receipts. Be certain that every entry is posted to the proper date.

Move the cursor up and down along column H. Does your cash balance become negative at any point? Does it soar above a level of reasonable reserves? If so, then you are ready to do some "what if" analysis. If your payment on invoice XYZ is delayed 10 days, what happens to your cash balance? If you hold payment on bill ABC for 15 days, will you avoid a cash crunch? Can you make a discretionary expenditure that you've been wanting to make? Be sure to consider what will happen if a major receipt is delayed for a few days. Would such a delay be a problem?

Juggle your estimates until you are satisfied that the best balance has been reached. Then save the model to disk under an appropriate name by typing `/SSFilename (CR)` and print it by typing `>A9 (CR) /PPH84 (CR)`. You now have a cash budget for the month.

You can also use this model to track your actual cash inflows and outflows. As each day ends, call the model back up. If all activity for the day went according to plan, move the actual line down and resave the model. If any disbursements or receipts were made that were not in accordance with the budget, adjust the day's activity to reflect those changes so that your running balance will be correct. Finally, consider whether any changes must be made to the forecast for the rest of the month. If so, revise your budget accordingly.

Notice the repeating text line at cell A34. This line separates the month's actual activity from the planned activity for the rest of that month. As time passes, move this row down the worksheet to indicate the current status of the month's activity. You can move the line by moving its row with the MOVE command. For example, to move the line from its current location at row 34 to row 36, use the command:

>A34 (CR) /M.A37 (CR)

Modifications

This model has two rows for each day of the month so that two receipts and two disbursements can be posted each day. If you need more space, add a row and replicate the formula for the previous cell into that row and down the rest of the worksheet. For example, the commands to insert a row between the current rows 27 and 28 (to create more entry space for the date 4-5) would be:

>A28 (CR) /IR
>H27 (CR) /R (CR) H28 (CR) RRR

Larger companies can use this model for cash flow management on a wider scale. Rather than showing day-by-day activity, the model can be used as a weekly or monthly budget. The scale in column A, currently showing days, can be set to months. Instead of showing each transaction separately, one entry can summarize all results from operations for the period. Other entries can then represent capital or various discretionary expenditures.

Projecting Cash Flow

For many businesses, cash flow is as important as profitability. This is especially true of start-up companies, rapidly growing firms, and companies that have seasonal sales. Often a new or fast-growing company has a product that sells, but has a difficult time meeting expenses between the time the product is made and the time the actual payment from the sale is received.

Companies with seasonal sales must build inventories during the off-season in order to have sufficient products to sell during the peak period. Off-season production means that materials must be purchased, workers paid, and other expenses met several months before any sales revenue is received. These obligations are often covered by a line of bank credit that is used several months each year and paid off the rest of the year.

This model requires a full 64K of RAM to operate. If your computer has less than 64K of user-available memory, you will have to condense the model to make it fit. One solution is to omit the Table of Contents and the Instructions sections from the model itself and refer to them in the book when necessary.

Principles

With VisiCalc, a business manager can project future cash flows using assumed sales, collections, and disbursements to indicate how much financing will be needed and when. This forecast can be valuable when a company is uncertain of its ability to meet its needs with its current short-term credit, or where conditions of a line of credit are difficult to meet. For example, a company may have a $50,000 line of credit that must be fully paid off for 120 days each year. Will this amount meet peak borrowing needs? Will the company be able to keep a zero balance for four months? These questions can be answered with a cash projection model.

A cash projection model can also be used to analyze and manage a cash account. With today's high interest rates, any company should limit its debt financing and invest its excess cash in interest-bearing securities. Knowing what the future pattern of borrowing and excess cash will be can facilitate this kind of management. Often a firm that experiences seasonal cash lows also experiences seasonal cash gluts.

This VisiCalc model is designed to project cash flows for a firm with seasonal sales. Projections for one year are made based on sales, collections, inventory build-up, disbursements for expenses, and loan repayments. A minimum cash balance is assumed. If this balance cannot be met in a given month, then the difference between the cash minimum and the available cash is borrowed on a line of credit.

The Model

The model shows a twelve-month cash requirement forecast for a mythical company. It has five sections: ASSUMPTIONS, CASH RECEIPTS DETAIL, CASH DISBURSEMENTS DETAIL, ANALYSIS OF CASH REQUIREMENTS, and BALANCES IN KEY ACCOUNTS.

The ASSUMPTIONS section includes data about sales, collections, purchases, and debt, used in later sections to build the cash requirements projection. This section begins at cell A8 and continues at cell A23. Labels for each assumption appear in cells 11 through 34.

Row 11 contains the total dollar sales for the period. Cells in rows 13, 14, and 15 show the estimated collection pattern for each month's sales. It is assumed that a certain portion of total sales will be made for cash, and that the rest will be collected in 30 to 60 days. For example, for February, 10% of the sales are for cash, 40% will be collected in 30 days, and 50% in 60 days.

The model is designed so that the only input you need is the percentages for cash sales and sales that will be collected in 30 days. The 60-day collection percentage is computed automatically by subtracting the total of the cash and 30 day sales from 100 (percent). For example, the formula in cell H15 is:

H15 (V) 100-H13-H14

Cells F17 and G17 show the dollar amount of November's sales to be collected in December and January. This data is used to compute January's cash receipts detail.

Row 19 displays the average gross margin percentage that will be earned on sales. You must supply this data for each month in the projection.

The total purchases on credit for each period are shown in row 25. This data is used to compute monthly cash disbursements.

Rows 27 and 28 hold data concerning the company's line of credit. The interest rate for line-of-credit borrowings each month is in row 27, and the line-of-credit balance for December is in cell F28.

Long-term debt information is in rows 30 through 32. Cell F30 contains the interest rate, which we assume does not vary from month to month. Cell F31 shows the balance in the long-term debt account in December, and Cell F32 shows the monthly payment on the debt.

Row 34 contains the company's minimum acceptable cash balance for each month. This balance can be thought of as the company's cash "safety margin." The minimum acceptable balance is used to compute monthly cash requirements.

The CASH RECEIPTS DETAIL section begins at cell A38. Cash receipts consist of cash sales, collection of receivables, and other receipts, which may be interest received, proceeds from an insurance claim, or any other source of cash not derived from the ordinary line of business.

The cash sales figure is computed by multiplying total dollar sales in a given month by the assumed cash sales percentage.

For example, cash sales for March, shown in cell I41, are calculated by the formula:

I41 (V) (I11*I13)/100

Collections of receivables are computed by totaling the sales from the previous two months which will be collected in the current month. For example, for March, collections are equal to the sum of February's 30-day collections and January's 60-day collections. This number is displayed in cell I42 by the formula:

I42 (V) ((G11*G15)+(H11*H14))/100

Any other cash receipts are input in row 43. The total cash receipts for each month are displayed in row 45. These totals are obtained by adding all the receipts for the month. For example, in March, total receipts are displayed in cell I45 using the formula:

I45 (V) @SUM(I41...I44)

The next section of the model, CASH DISBURSEMENTS DETAIL, begins at cell A53. Some of the amounts in this section, such as operating expenses, income taxes, and other, are entered by you; others are calculated by VisiCalc.

Payment for credit purchases equals the total credit purchases for the previous month. This equation is based on the assumption that suppliers offer 30-day credit terms. For each month, a reference is made to the cell that contains the previous month's credit purchases. For example, the March payment for purchases is displayed in cell I56, which is defined as:

I56 (V) +H25

Debt service cash flows are computed from information you input in rows 27 through 32. The monthly long-term debt interest expense is computed by multiplying the long-term interest rate by the outstanding principal balance. In January, the interest expense is computed by the formula:

G58 /FI (V) +F30/100/12*F31

The monthly principal payment is computed by subtracting the monthly interest payment from the total monthly payment. The principal payment for January is computed in cell G59 by the formula:

G59 /FI (V) +G32-G58

The following month, the interest payment is calculated by the formula:

H58 /FI (V) +F30/100/12*(F31-@SUM(G59...G59))

This formula takes into account the previous month's principal payment. In March, for example, the formula for the monthly interest expense is:

I58 /FI (V) +F30/100/12*(F31-@SUM(G59...H59))

Row 60 shows the monthly interest payments on the company's line of credit. The payment for March is computed in cell I60 by the formula:

I60 /FI (V) +I27/12/100*H92

Line 64 displays each month's total cash disbursements. The @SUM function is used to calculate the figures in cells G64 through R64. For example, the total cash disbursements figure for March appears in cell I64:

I64 /FI (V) @SUM(I56...I63)

The ANALYSIS OF CASH REQUIREMENTS section begins at cell A69. This part of the model analyzes the monthly cash balance and line-of-credit activity based on the cash receipts and disbursements figures computed earlier. First, the net cash generated in the month is computed in row 71 by subtracting total disbursements from total receipts. In April, for example, net cash receipts are displayed in cell J71:

J71 /FI (V) +J45-J64

This figure may be negative, indicating that more cash was paid out than received. To get the beginning cash balance for the month, refer to the ending cash balance for the previous month. The beginning cash balance for April is displayed in cell J72, which contains a reference to March's ending cash balance:

J72 (V) +I87

The cash balance before borrowings, shown in row 74, is the sum of the net cash generated this period and the previous cash balance. For example, the formula in cell J74 is:

```
J74 /FI (V) +J71+J72
```

The amount below the minimum acceptable balance, shown in row 75, represents the difference between the cash balance before borrowing and the minimum cash balance entered in row 34. For April, the cash deficit is computed by subtracting the $20,000 minimum from the cash balance before the borrowing of -$39481. This deficit is displayed in cell J75 by the formula:

```
J75 /FI (V) +J74-J34
```

VisiCalc next examines the cash deficit or surplus, and either increases or decreases borrowing against the line of credit. This change in borrowings appears in row 77 and is calculated by a complicated formula. For example, the formula for the April increase in borrowings, as displayed in cell J77, is:

```
J77 /FI (V) @IF(J75<0,@ABS(J75),
            @IF(@AND(J75>=0,I92>0),
            @IF(I92>@ABS(J75),-J75,-I78),0))
```

This formula is complicated because it must take into account situations where a cash surplus allows a repayment of funds borrowed on the line of credit, as occurs in the month of May. For this calculation, the program must evaluate the cash generated in the current period and the overall level of indebtedness at the end of the previous month.

Row 78 shows the total borrowings at the end of each month. This total is the sum of borrowings for the previous period and any increase or decrease in borrowings in the current month. For example, total borrowings in April are displayed in cell J78 by the formula:

```
J78 /FI (V) +I78+J77
```

The ending cash balance for each month is in row 80. It is calculated by adding the cash balance before borrowings to the increase or decrease in borrowings for the month. The ending cash balance for April, as displayed in cell J80, is $20,000. This balance is calculated by the formula:

```
J80 /FI (V) +J77+J74
```

The last section of the model, BALANCES IN KEY ACCOUNTS, begins at cell A84. This section summarizes the calculations made in the previous sections and displays the information in terms of account balances. The first account balance given is cash, which is taken directly from the ending cash balance figure in row 80. In March, for example, the cash account balance shown in cell I87 refers to cell I80:

```
I87 /FI (V) +I80
```

The accounts receivable balance is computed by adding the dollar amounts of all credit sales made in the current month to those made the month before which have not been collected (the 60-day sales). For April, this balance is displayed in cell J88, using the formula:

```
J88 /FI (V) ((I11*I14)+((J14+J15)*J11))/100
```

Inventory is computed by adding the balance for the previous month to the dollar amount of the net change for the current month. The net change is computed by subtracting the cost of the units sold in a given month from the cost of the units purchased in that month. The cost of units sold is computed by multiplying the total dollar sales in row 11 by the gross margin percentage in row 19. For example, the formula in cell J89 is

```
J89 /FI (V) (J25-((J19/100)*J11))+I89
```

Accounts payable equals the credit purchases for the current month. Each cell in row 91 refers to the corresponding figure in row 25. In April, for example, the accounts payable balance is obtained by the reference:

```
J91 /FI (V) +J25
```

The outstanding balance in the line of credit equals the total borrowings at the end of the current month as computed in row 78.

For example, in March the line-of-credit balance is displayed in cell I92 by the reference:

I92 /FI (V) +I78

Net working capital is calculated by subtracting current liabilities—in this model, line of credit and accounts payable—from current assets, which are cash, accounts receivable, and inventory. For example, March's net working capital is shown in cell I94, which contains the formula:

I94 /FI (V) +I87+I88+I89-I91-I92

Notice that December cash and inventory balances must be entered manually. The model uses these balances to compute some of the January balances.

Using the Model

Because of its complexity, this model is more difficult to use than some of the others in this book. The first step in using the model is to collect the data about sales, purchases, interest rates, and so forth, that must be entered in the ASSUMPTIONS section. When the data is ready, enter it in the appropriate cells. You will also need to enter some data in the CASH RECEIPTS DETAIL and CASH DISBURSEMENTS DETAIL sections (as discussed earlier). After the data has been entered, the model should be recalculated by typing ! You can save the model by typing `/SSFilename (CR)` and print it by typing `>A8 (CR) /PPR95 (CR)`.

You can also make extensive use of "what if" analysis in this model. Adjust your sales figures, interest rates, minimum cash balance, or any other data, and track the changes through to the BALANCES IN KEY ACCOUNTS section.

Modifications

This model can be modified to fit your business in many ways. Taking the time to customize a cash projection model for your firm can provide you with an extremely valuable financial management tool. Here are some suggestions for modification.

Accounts receivable collection varies significantly from company to company. Some firms do most of their business on a cash basis, whereas others may wait as long as 100 days to receive payment.

You can use the Accounts Receivable Collections Tracker in Chapter 4 to help you determine your own business collection pattern, then substitute your figures for those used in this model.

This model includes only summary data for sales and purchases. You may need a model that shows detailed information for each product you sell. Such a model can be built by adding extra rows to the basic layout to include unit sales, price per unit, unit purchases, cost per unit, and net inventory change for each product. An alternative would be to use a separate spreadsheet to compute totals for this data on all products, then use those totals in the model.

Your company may be in an industry where suppliers do not extend trade credit. The model can reflect this situation if you eliminate the "Total Purchases on Credit" row, and change "Payment for Purchases on Credit" to "Payment for Current Month's Purchases."

Of course, your firm's list of cash disbursements will vary from the one in this model. Any cash outflows you expect in the projection period should be listed under CASH DISBURSEMENTS DETAIL.

CHAPTER 2
Debt Management

Amortizing a Loan
Prepaying a Loan
Tracking a Line of Credit

Amortizing a Loan

Spreadsheet software is often used to compute loan amortization tables. ("Amortization" describes the process of paying off a loan.) Unfortunately, amortizing some loans requires a table that exceeds the memory capacity of most spreadsheets, including VisiCalc's. The usual solution to this problem is to build a mortgage model that computes one portion of the table at a time—for example, 60 months—and then use it repeatedly until the mortgage is completely amortized.

Most financial spreadsheet software cannot repeat the same operation automatically. VisiCalc is no different. Unlike the BASIC programming language, which allows the user to build FOR . . . NEXT loops to repeat processes, VisiCalc can make only one pass through a model at a time. If you want to repeat the process, you must recalculate the model manually. As a result, most VisiCalc loan amortization tables require the manual transfer of data back and forth within the model as the loan is amortized. This is tedious and error-prone work, the kind VisiCalc is supposed to eliminate.

As you may have guessed, VisiCalc can, in fact, perform more of the work than is usually thought possible. The Loan Amortization Calculator includes a trick that lets you calculate a loan amortization table of any length with a minimum amount of keyboard input.

Principles

To build a loan amortization table, you will need three pieces of information: the principal amount borrowed, the annual interest rate charged, and the term of the loan. Using this information, you can compute the monthly payment with the formula:

$$(i/(1-((1+i)^{(-n)})))*P$$

Where: i is the monthly interest rate
n is the term of the loan in months
p is the principal borrowed

Simple relationships govern the computation of month-by-month amortization. The interest paid in any given month is computed by multiplying the monthly interest rate by the outstanding principal balance. The amount of principal paid in a month is determined by subtracting the interest payment from the total monthly payment. The principal balance at the end of the month is derived by subtracting the principal payment for the month from the beginning principal balance.

The model shows how these relationships work. In the example, the principal amount borrowed is $100,000. The annual interest rate is 18%, and the term is 240 months. The monthly payment, computed using the formula above, is $1,543.31. The interest payment for the first month is:

$100,000 X (.18/12) = $1,500

The amount of principal repaid the first month is therefore:

$1,543.31 - $1,500.00 = $43.31

This payment reduces the outstanding principal balance to $99,956.69. For the following month, the interest payment will be:

$99,956.69 X (.18/12) = $1,499.35

The principal repayment in that month has increased by $.65 to $43.96. The same pattern of decreasing interest payments and increasing principal payments continues until the loan is completely repaid after 240 months.

The Model

The Loan Amortization Calculator has two sections: ASSUMPTIONS and the AMORTIZATION TABLE. The ASSUMPTIONS section begins at A10. Cells F14, F15, and F16 are used to input the annual interest rate, the principal borrowed, and the term, in months, of the loan. Cell F17 uses this information to compute the monthly loan payment. The formula in this cell is:

F17 (V) (F14/(100*12))/(1-((1+(F14/(100*12)))^(-F16)))*F15

The AMORTIZATION TABLE, which begins at cell A22, uses the formulas explained above to compute the loan amortization. Cells B28 and C28 contain the looping trick. The formulas in these cells evaluate the status of the amortization and either reset or continue the process each time the model is recalculated. Cell F87 contains the principal that is still outstanding after one pass through the model—in this example, 60 monthly periods.

Notice that the value of this cell will always be zero if the loan has been repaid. If the loan has *not* been repaid after the 60th month, the value of F87 will be greater than zero. Now, look at the formula in cell C28:

C28 (V) @IF(F87<.005,F15,F87)

To clarify the formula: if the value in cell F87 is zero (we use .005 as an approximation of zero to account for minor imperfections in the amortization process), then the loan is fully amortized, and the model should be started over by filling cell C28 with the beginning principal found in cell F15. If F87 is greater than zero, then some portion of the loan has not been repaid, and cell C28 should assume the value of cell F87, so that amortization can continue.

The formula "recycles" the principal remaining at the end of any 60-month period by moving it back up the table and using it as the *beginning* principal balance for the next 60-month period. This procedure is precisely what you would have to do manually in a model without the loop.

Cell B28 is similarly defined:

B28 /FI (V) @IF(F87<.005,1,B87+1)

This conditional formula lets the month labels in the model flow with the mortgage calculations. If F87 is zero, then the loan is fully repaid, and the model should return to the first month; if it is not, then the model has more work to do, and cell B28 will advance by one month.

The first month's interest payment is computed in cell D28:

D28 (V) (F14/(100*12))*C28

The first part of this formula converts the annual interest rate in cell F14 to a monthly rate. This fraction is then applied to the period's beginning principal balance in cell C28 to compute the actual monthly interest payment.

Cell E28 computes the principal payment for the first period, using the formula:

E28 (V) @IF(C28<.005,0,F17-D28)

This cell checks the value of cell C28 (the beginning principal balance) before computing the principal payment. If the principal balance is less than .005 (or approximately zero), then the loan is fully repaid, and the payment should be zero. If the balance is more than .005, then the principal payment should be the difference between the total monthly payment from F17 and the monthly interest payment from cell D28.

Cell F28 computes the ending principal balance for the first month by subtracting the principal payment from the beginning principal balance:

F28 (V) +C28-E28

Finally, the ending principal balance is transferred to cell C29, where it becomes the beginning principal balance for the next month. Cell C29 contains the formula:

C29 (V) +F28

All the cells in rows 28 through 87 use the same formulas. The only exception is cell F87, which contains a formula to clear the model:

F87 (V) @IF(F15=0,0,C87-E87)

Using the Model

To use the model, enter the loan data shown in the example in cells F14, F15, and F16. You can enter the monthly payment in cell F17, or let the model make that computation for you. Be sure to set VisiCalc to perform manual recalculation by row (**/GRM** and **/GOR**).

Now type ! to recalculate the model. It will take a few seconds for the whole table to finish calculating. Scroll the cursor around the table, looking at the "flow" of the amortization through the cells. (You may want to split the screen to view the top and the bottom of the model at the same time.)

Notice that cell F87 contains the value 95832.80. This is the principal balance remaining at the end of 60 months. Before you do anything else, print a copy of this portion of the amortization, using the command:

>A10 (CR) /PPG87 (CR)

Now you are ready to activate the loop. Type ! and watch what happens. If all is well, cell B28 will show the number 61, and cell C28 will assume the value that just appeared in cell F87. The model will then automatically flow through another 60 months. Row 87 will display the 120th amortization period, and cell F87 will contain an ending balance of 85651.40.

Once again, you'll want to print the model. This time, however, begin printing at cell A28, using the command:

>A28 (CR) /PPG87 (CR)

The second 60 months of the table will be printed. If you have not taken out the paper from the first output, your printout will appear as one long table.

To complete the amortization process, you will have to repeat the last steps two more times, because the example has a term of 240 months. Once the loan is completely amortized, type ! to start the amortization over from the beginning.

To clear the model, enter **0** in cell F15 and type ! twice. At the end of that process, the model will be filled with zeros, and you will be ready to begin a new problem.

Modifications

You can use this model even if your computer has less than 64K of RAM memory. By shortening the length of each pass through the table from 60 periods to 30 or 20 periods, you can make the model work on almost any machine. However, it will take more passes to solve a problem completely.

This model illustrates one way to approach a problem creatively while using VisiCalc to the fullest extent. You will find other ways to use this looping technique in your models, altering it to meet your needs.

Prepaying a Loan

If you decide to pay off a loan early, how do you determine what amount to pay? A simple mathematical technique can answer this question. Known as The Rule of 78s, it has been incorporated into this VisiCalc model.

Principles

Many loans are paid off according to a schedule of uniform monthly payments, each consisting of an interest portion and a principal portion. The interest payment is based on the amount of principal owed and the interest rate on the loan. As the payments progress and the amount of principal owed declines, the interest charges are reduced. This reduction changes the composition of the loan payments. At first, each payment consists of a high interest component and a low principal component because interest is being computed based on the full principal amount. Toward the end of the term of the loan, the composition of the loan payment changes to a low interest component and a high principal component.

For example, consider a $1500 loan with an annual interest rate of 12.75% and 24 monthly payments of $71.14. The first payment includes the interest owed on $1500 for one month. This amount is calculated as one twelfth (or one month's worth) of 12.75% of $1500, or $15.94. The rest of the payment, $55.20, is applied to paying off the principal. The interest component for the next monthly payment is computed from the reduced principal of $1444.80 (last month's principal, $1500, minus $55.20). Although the payment is still $71.14, more of that amount is applied to reducing the loan's principal and less toward the interest. Each monthly payment of $71.14 consists of a different interest/principal combination because the principal component increases as the interest component decreases.

When you pay off a loan early, you receive an interest rebate from the bank. The amount of the rebate depends on the amount of interest in the remaining monthly payments. However, because of the changing composition of the monthly payments, it is not easy to determine what part is interest and what part is principal. To solve this problem, use the Rule of 78s formula for calculating the amount of interest in the remaining payments. This amount can then be subtracted from the total of the remaining payments to yield the payment needed to retire the loan early. The Rule of 78s formula for interest rebate is:

$$\frac{(n - k + 1)(n - k)}{n^2 + n} \times \text{total interest cost of loan}$$

where: n = the number of payments in full term
k = the number of payment periods that will have expired when the loan is paid off

The first step in using this formula is to compute the total interest cost of the loan. To do this, multiply the monthly payment amount by the number of original payment periods to determine the total amount that would be paid for the full term of the loan. Then, subtract the principal from the total amount paid to calculate the total interest that would be paid on the loan if all payments were made. For example, in the loan described above, the total amount paid over the term of the loan is $71.14 multiplied by 24 months, or $1707.28. When the $1500 loan is subtracted, the total interest cost of the loan, $207.28, remains.

The next step is to plug this interest cost as well as the other variables into the Rule of 78s equation. Let's assume that 19 payments have been made and that the borrower wants to go ahead and pay off the rest of the loan. Because there is a 24-month payment schedule, "n" in the formula is 24. "K" in the formula is

19 because 19 payments have been made. Plugging in these numbers gives us the equation:

$$\frac{(24 - 19 + 1)(24 - 19)}{24^2 + 24} \times 207.28$$

The solution to this equation is $10.36, which represents the interest rebate due on the loan. This amount must now be subtracted from the amount we would pay if we were to continue making monthly payments, which is calculated as (24 - 19) x $71.14, or $355.68. Subtracting $10.36 from $355.68 yields $345.32 as the amount needed to pay off the loan after 19 monthly payments.

The Model

The Loan Payoff Calculator has two sections: ASSUMPTIONS and SOLUTIONS. The ASSUMPTIONS section, which begins at cell A10, contains information about the loan being evaluated: the principal amount, annual interest rate, term in months, the number of the last payment made, and the monthly payment amount.

The SOLUTIONS section begins at cell A22. Cell F25 contains the calculation for the total amount of interest paid if all payments are made. This amount is computed by multiplying the monthly payment by the term in months:

```
F25 /F$ (V) (F18*F16)-F14
```

Next, cell F27 computes the amount due on the loan by multiplying the number of remaining payments by the monthly payment amount, using the formula:

```
F27 /F$ (V) (F16-F17)*F18
```

Cell F28 uses the Rule of 78s equation to compute the interest component for future payments:

```
F28 /F$ (V) ((F16-F17+1)*(F16-F17))/((F16^2)+F16)*F25
```

Finally, cell F30 displays the amount needed to pay off the loan, which is computed by subtracting the result in cell F28 from the value in cell F27, using the formula:

F30 /F$ (V) +F27-F28

Using the Model

To use this model, enter the ASSUMPTIONS data and recalculate by typing ! The amount required to pay off the loan will appear in cell F30. You can save a completed calculation by typing `/SSFilename (CR)` and print the model by typing `>A10 (CR) /PPH30 (CR)`.

Note that banks in some states use formulas other than the Rule of 78s to compute loan rebates. Be sure to check with your banker to see if this formula applies in your state.

Modifications

This model is designed to work with any loan that has a uniform series of payments. It can be modified to reflect payments made on a quarterly or annual basis. For a quarterly repayment plan, substitute the quarterly payment amount for the monthly payment amount, then state the term of the loan as well as the number of payments made in quarters. For example, if a loan has a five-year term of which two years have elapsed, then the term of the loan is 20 quarters, and the last payment will be number 8 (2 years times 4 quarters per year).

Tracking a Line of Credit

Does your company have a line of credit with a bank? If so, you may have found that following the activity in that line of credit is not an easy task. This VisiCalc model can help you track line-of-credit activity and calculate a total interest expense for each month.

Principles

Knowing how much you use your line of credit and what it costs your company is essential to good financial management. Many short-term credit arrangements require that the borrowing company pay off its loans completely in a specified period of time. Meeting this condition may be difficult for a rapidly growing company. An expanding company must also know when its current line of credit has become inadequate and more funds must be negotiated.

The interest you pay for your line of credit depends on both the amount you borrow and the interest rate on your loan. The amount of your loan can change frequently, depending on the cash inflows and outflows of your operations. Typically, the interest rate on a line of credit is tied to the bank's prime rate; therefore, the rate will vary as the prime goes up or down.

Tracking the activity in your line of credit requires daily monitoring of the interest rate being charged and the amount of the loan outstanding. If you use the line of credit frequently, this monitoring can become a complex task.

The Model

This model is designed to keep a daily record of the outstanding balance of funds borrowed from a line of credit as well as the interest rate applied to that balance. Each day, new extensions or repayments of credit can be added to, or subtracted from, the outstanding balance to yield a new balance. Daily interest charges are also added to the balance. To compute daily interest charges, each day's interest rate is multiplied by the outstanding balance. At the end of the month, the daily interest charges are added to yield the total interest expense for the month. The daily outstanding credit balances are also added and then divided by the number of days in the month to yield the average daily credit balance.

The model has two sections: DAILY ACTIVITY and TOTALS AND AVERAGES. The DAILY ACTIVITY section begins at cell A10. Column B contains the dates for the current month. The first date, in cell B17, is entered as a label:

B17 /FL (L) "9-1

The second date, in cell B18, is entered as the number −2. VisiCalc computes the other dates by subtracting 1 from the date above. For example, cell B19 contains the formula:

B19 /FL (V) +B18-1

This formula is replicated, using relative references, to cells B20 through B47 for a 31-day month. (This technique is similar to the automatic counter used in the Checkbook Balancer model.) The cells in column C contain the balance outstanding at the beginning of each day in the current month. Cell C17 shows the current month's opening credit balance.

Columns D and E are used to post any new borrowing or repayments that occur during the month.

Column F shows the annual interest rate on the line of credit for each day in the current month. Cell F17 contains the rate that is in effect on the first of the month. Notice that cell F18 is defined as equal to F17:

F18 /FG (V) +F17

All the cells in column F are similarly defined. The model assumes that the interest rate in effect on the first of the month will remain in effect, until you change it manually. As the month progresses and interest rates change, you can alter the rate in effect by entering a new number in the appropriate cell in column F. The new rate will be carried forward to the end of the period, or until you change it again.

VisiCalc computes the daily interest expense in column G. First, the annual interest rate is divided by 365 to obtain a daily rate. Then, the daily rate is multiplied by the previous day's balance (column D) plus any new extensions, less repayments. For example, the daily interest expense for September 1, displayed in cell G17, is calculated by the formula:

G17 (V) (F17/365)*(C17+D17-E17)

Column H displays the daily outstanding credit balance. This balance is computed by adding the new extensions of credit to the previous day's balance, subtracting repayments, and adding the day's interest charge. As an example, consider the formula for total outstanding credit on October 1, in cell H17:

H17 (V) +C17+D17-E17+G17

This balance appears again in column C as the following day's "Previous Day's Balance." Each cell in column C refers to a cell in column H on the immediately preceding row. For example, the previous day's balance in cell C25 contains the reference:

C25 (V) +H24

The TOTALS AND AVERAGES section of the model begins at cell A51. The total interest expense for the month, in cell G54, is calculated by adding the daily interest charges. The formula in this cell is:

G54 (V) @SUM(G17...G47)

The average daily outstanding credit, displayed in cell G56, is computed by adding the daily balances in column H and dividing the total by the number of days in the month. This number is calculated by taking the absolute value of the last date in column B. The formula to compute the average credit outstanding is:

G56 (V) @SUM(H17...H47)/@ABS(B47)

Using the Model

Begin each month by entering the outstanding balance and the interest rate for the first day of the month into cells C17 and F17. As the month progresses, post additional borrowings or repayments to the appropriate cells in columns D and E. Be sure to track the rate of interest being charged by your bank and post any changes to the model as they occur. At the end of the day, recalculate by typing !

You should recognize that the Average Daily Outstanding Credit Balance will not be accurate until the entire month's activity has been posted. You can save the model by typing `/SSFilename (CR)`. At the end of the month, print the DAILY ACTIVITY and the TOTALS AND AVERAGES sections by typing `>A10 (CR) /PPH60 (CR)`.

Because some months have less than 31 days, you will need to modify the model at the beginning of these months by using VisiCalc's `/D` command to eliminate one or more rows. When you make this change, be sure you do not delete row 47. Instead, delete a row or rows further up in the model to prevent ERROR messages in cell G56.

Modifications

You may want to consider a few modifications when you build a model to track your firm's line-of-credit activity. If you add a column for the daily prime rate, then you can enter a formula that will compute the interest rate based on the prime rate for you, instead of having to do it manually. For example, your interest rate might be 1 point below the prime if the prime is greater than or equal to 15%, and 14% if the prime is less than or equal to 15%. These conditions can be built into a formula using VisiCalc's @IF function.

With sufficient computer memory and disk space, you can also build several months' credit tracking on one spreadsheet and compute both monthly and quarterly averages on the outstanding principal.

If you have lines of credit with different lenders, you can build a model for each source of funds and then combine the averages of these models into one summary model.

CHAPTER 3
Fixed Asset Management

Calculating ACRS Depreciation
Calculating Internal Rate of Return

Calculating ACRS Depreciation

The Economic Recovery Tax Act of 1981, passed by Congress on August 4, 1981, overhauled the federal income tax system by cutting tax rates, increasing certain deduction amounts, and changing regulations in many areas. One of these changes was the introduction of a new set of depreciation rules called the accelerated cost recovery system (ACRS). ACRS differs from past tax depreciation methods in significant ways. Let's take a look at ACRS and at a VisiCalc model that calculates ACRS depreciation schedules.

Principles

Before ACRS, assets were depreciated using the straight-line, the declining-balance, or the sum-of-the-years'-digits method. All three methods involved assigning a "useful life" to an asset and then computing depreciation expense in relation to the age of the asset. For example, with the straight-line method, a $10,000 asset with a useful life of 10 years would be depreciated at the rate of $1,000 per year, computed as 1/10 times $10,000 (the asset value).

ACRS abandons the concept of useful life. Instead, it assigns assets to one of five recovery-life categories: 3-year property, 5-year property, 10-year property, 15-year utility property, and 15-year real property. The 3-year class includes automobiles, light trucks, and equipment used in research and development.

Most other machinery and equipment fall into the 5-year category. The 10-year property and 15-year utility classes cover public utility property and certain types of real estate, such as theme parks. The 15-year real property category covers all other real estate.

In each range, ACRS specifies the amount of depreciation that may be taken in a year. The tables below show the annual percentages for all five classes of assets. These tables are reproduced in a @LOOKUP table in this VisiCalc model.

ACRS DEPRECIATION TABLES

Property:	Percentage
3-year:	
Year 1	25
Year 2	38
Year 3	37
5-year:	
Year 1	15
Year 2	22
Year 3	21
Year 4	21
Year 5	21
10-year:	
Year 1	8
Year 2	14
Year 3	12
Year 4	10
Year 5	10
Year 6	10
Year 7	9
Year 8	9
Year 9	9
Year 10	9
15-year Public Utility Property	
Year 1	5
Year 2	10
Year 3	9
Year 4	8
Year 5	7
Year 6	7
Year 7	6
Year 8	6
Year 9	6
Year 10	6
Year 11	6
Year 12	6
Year 13	6
Year 14	6
Year 15	6

ACRS COST RECOVERY TABLE FOR REAL ESTATE

If the Recovery Year is:	The percentage is determined by the month in the first year the asset was placed in service:											
	1	2	3	4	5	6	7	8	9	10	11	12
1	12	11	10	9	8	7	6	5	4	3	2	1
2	10	10	11	11	11	11	11	11	11	11	11	12
3	9	9	9	9	10	10	10	10	10	10	10	10
4	8	8	8	8	8	8	9	9	9	9	9	9
5	7	7	7	7	7	7	8	8	8	8	8	8
6	6	6	6	6	7	7	7	7	7	7	7	7
7	6	6	6	6	6	6	6	6	6	6	6	6
8	6	6	6	6	6	6	5	6	6	6	6	6
9	6	6	6	6	5	6	5	5	5	6	6	6
10	5	6	5	6	5	5	5	5	5	5	6	5
11	5	5	5	5	5	5	5	5	5	5	5	5
12	5	5	5	5	5	5	5	5	5	5	5	5
13	5	5	5	5	5	5	5	5	5	5	5	5
14	5	5	5	5	5	5	5	5	5	5	5	5
15	5	5	5	5	5	5	5	5	5	5	5	5
16	0	0	1	1	2	2	3	3	4	4	4	5

"Basis" is another important tax concept. The basis of an asset is the original cost of the asset less depreciation expense. When the asset is purchased, its basis equals its purchase price. After two years, the basis is reduced by two years' depreciation.

Depreciation is not the only expense that affects the basis of an asset. The 1981 Act also allows a business to consider as an expense a portion of its capital investment in the year the expenditure is made. This expense is limited to $5,000 in 1982 and 1983, $7,500 in 1984 and 1985, and $10,000 after 1985. This rule benefits small businesses that make limited capital investments every year. For example, if a company purchases less than $5,000 of assets in 1982, it can fully treat as an expense those assets the same year, lowering income tax by as much as $2,500. Companies that purchase more assets can also benefit under this rule, although the relative benefit declines as the level of investment rises.

The final element in the tax treatment of assets is the investment tax credit (ITC), which was exacted by Congress in the 1960s to encourage businesses to invest in capital goods. The 1981 Act liberalized the ITC rules. Under the new provisions, 3-year assets earn a 6% ITC, and all other assets earn a 10% credit. Unlike depreciation (obtained by deducting tax expense from income to arrive at taxable income), the ITC is a credit that is subtracted directly from the tax owed. For example, if a company invests $25,000 in 5-year class assets in a year, it can claim an ITC of $2,500, which will offset an equal amount of taxes otherwise owed.

The Model

The ACRS Depreciation Calculator has two sections: ASSUMPTIONS and DEPRECIATION TABLE. The ASSUMPTIONS section begins at cell A10. Cells F13 and G13 contain the description of the asset being depreciated. Cell G14 displays the cost (or beginning basis) of the asset. The ACRS life of the asset appears in cell G15, and cells G16 and G17 indicate the year and month that the asset will be placed in service. Cell G18 answers the question: "Is the Asset Real Property?" A *1* is used to signal yes; *2* means no. The amount of available first-year expense is entered in cell G19. If you have not purchased assets in the current year, this number should be 5000; otherwise, enter the amount, if any, that has not been used on other assets.

The DEPRECIATION TABLE begins at cell A22 and continues through row 41. Columns B and C define the term of the table. Cell B27 repeats the date from cell G16. Cell B28 is then defined in terms of cell B26:

B28 /FI (V) +B27+1

Cell C27 contains the number "1," cell C28 contains the number "2," and so on.

In cell D27, the model computes the amount of first-year expense to be taken on this asset by referring to cells G14 and G19. The formula used is:

```
D27 /F$ (V) @IF(G19>G14,G14,G19)
```

If the full $5,000 allowance is available, and the cost of the asset is $4,500, the model will post 4500 to cell D27. If the cost of the asset is $6,000, then 5000 will appear in D27.

Column E computes the ACRS depreciation for each year in the asset's recovery life using the basis of the asset *after* any first-year expense has been taken. In the example, the asset's basis after first-year expense equals $8,900 (its cost) minus $5,000 (first-year depreciation), or $3,900. Using the ACRS table for 5-year assets, you can see that 15% of the cost of the asset should be recovered in the first year. In our example, cell E27 displays 585.00, which is obtained by multiplying .15 by 3,900.

The formula in this cell is:

```
E27 /F$ (V) @LOOKUP(C27,K8...K23)*(G14-D27)/100
```

This formula translates as: in the ACRS table that begins at cell K8, find the depreciation percentage for the year number in cell C27, and multiply that rate by the cost of the asset (from cell G14) minus the first-year expense (from cell D27). All of the cells in column E use this formula. For example, cell E29 is defined as:

```
E29 /F$ (V) @LOOKUP(C29,K8...K23)*(G14-D27)/100
```

The @LOOKUP table in cell J1 holds the ACRS depreciation rates that are used by the model to calculate the values in column E. Thanks to VisiCalc's @IF function, this one table can hold the data for all five ACRS asset classifications. The formulas for each cell in column L are reproduced below.

```
L8 (V)  @IF(G15=3,.25,@IF(G15=5,.15,@IF(G15=10,.08,
        @IF(G18=2,.05,(12-(G17-1))/100))))*100

L9 (V)  @IF(G15=3,.38,@IF(G15=5,.22,@IF(G15=10,.14,
        @IF(G18=2,.1,@IF(G17<3,.1,@IF(G17=12,.12,.11))))))*100

L10 (V)  @IF(G15=3,.37,@IF(G15=5,.21,@IF(G15=10,.12,
         @IF(G18=2,.09,@IF(G17<5,.09,.1)))))*100
```

```
L11 (V) @IF(G15=3,0,@IF(G15=5,.21,@IF(G15=10,.1,
        @IF(G18=2,.08,@IF(G17<7,.08,.09)))))*100

L12 (V) @IF(G15=3,0,@IF(G15=5,.21,@IF(G15=10,.1,
        @IF(G18=2,.07,@IF(G17<7,.07,.08)))))*100

L13 (V) @IF(G15=3,0,@IF(G15=5,0,@IF(G15=10,.1,
        @IF(G18=2,.07,@IF(G17<5,.06,.07)))))*100

L14 (V) @IF(G15=3,0,@IF(G15=5,0,
        @IF(G15=10,.09,.06)))*100

L15 (V) @IF(G15=3,0,@IF(G15=5,0,@IF(G15=10,.09,
        @IF(G18=2,.06,@IF(G17=7,.05,.06)))))*100

L16 (V) @IF(G15=3,0,@IF(G15=5,0,@IF(G15=10,.09,
        @IF(G18=2,.06,@IF(@OR(G17=5,
        @AND(G17<10,G17>6)),.05,.06)))))*100

L17 (V) @IF(G15=3,0,@IF(G15=5,0,@IF(G15=10,.09,
        @IF(G18=2,.06,@IF(@OR(G17=2,
        @OR(G17=4,G17=11)),.06,.05)))))*100

L18 (V) @IF(G15=3,0,@IF(G15=5,0,@IF(G15=10,0,
        @IF(G18=2,.06,.05))))*100

L19 (V) @IF(G15=3,0,@IF(G15=5,0,@IF(G15=10,0,
        @IF(G18=2,.06,.05))))*100

L20 (V) @IF(G15=3,0,@IF(G15=5,0,@IF(G15=10,0,
        @IF(G18=2,.06,.05))))*100

L21 (V) @IF(G15=3,0,@IF(G15=5,0,@IF(G15=10,0,
        @IF(G18=2,.06,.05))))*100

L22 (V) @IF(G15=3,0,@IF(G15=5,0,@IF(G15=10,0,
        @IF(G18=2,.06,.05))))*100

L23 (V) @IF(G18=2,0,@IF(G17=12,.05,@IF(G17>8,.04,
        @IF(G17>6,.03,@IF(G17>4,.02,
        @IF(G17>2,.01,0))))))*100
```

The conditional statements in the @LOOKUP table make the depreciation table adaptable to a variety of situations. Because most microcomputers have memory limitations, a trick like this can be worth its weight in RAM. You'll see the technique used in other ways throughout this book.

Finally, look at cell G26, which calculates the ITC for this asset:

G27 /F$ (V) @IF(G15>3,(G14-D27)*.1,(G14-D27)*.06)

The @IF statement in this cell evaluates the recovery life of the asset to determine the amount of claimable ITC. As discussed earlier, the amount of available ITC varies with the life of the asset, and the base used in the calculation is the cost of the asset less any first-year expense.

Using the Model

To use this model, supply the requested information in cells G13, G14, G15, G16, and G19 and recalculate by typing ! VisiCalc will do the rest. You can save the completed table by typing `/SSFilename (CR)` and print it by typing `>A10 (CR) /PPH42 (CR)`.

Be sure to consult your accountant or other tax professional if you are unsure about the recovery life of a particular asset, its true cost, or the amount of first-year expense that is still available to you. Assuming that the law is not changed, the ACRS rate tables in the model are good for all assets purchased before January 1, 1985.

Modifications

This model can be very useful, particularly if your work involves frequent analyses of fixed assets. Because the model is compact, it can be used also as part of other templates.

Calculating Internal Rate of Return

If you are in the investment or real estate business, you are familiar with the concept of internal rate of return. IRR can be used in any business to evaluate investment decisions and is a useful application for VisiCalc.

Unfortunately, VisiCalc lacks an internal rate of return function, and most techniques that could overcome this deficiency use too much memory. There are ways to overcome this problem, however. The model presented here shows one efficient way to use VisiCalc to compute IRR on an investment.

Principles

The analysis of internal rate of return begins with an investment opportunity. As a rule, investments require that the investor spend a certain amount of money in the present in hopes of future earnings. Investors naturally want to have some idea about the rate of return, or profit, the investment will earn. That question is answered by IRR analysis.

IRR is closely related to the concept of net present value. VisiCalc does have a built-in tool for calculating @NPV. The format of the command is:

@NPV(discount,column/row range)

In this command, the numbers in the "column/row range" represent a stream of cash flows. The "discount" is an interest rate. The result of the @NPV calculation is the discounted value of the stream of cash flows.

Calculating NPV is roughly the opposite of calculating compound interest. Let's use an example to demonstrate the relationship.

Suppose you invested $100 in a savings account today at 5% interest. At the end of one year, you would have $105. At the end of the second year, you would have $110.25. With compound interest, in the second year you earn interest not only on your principal, but also on the interest earned in the first year.

Now, suppose that I offer you a choice: I'll give you $100 today, or $110.25 two years from now. Assuming that 5% is the best return you could earn on an investment, which alternative would you choose?

You would probably be indifferent. If I gave you the $100 today, and you invested it at 5%, at the end of two years you would have $110.25—exactly the amount I offered to give you at that time. We would therefore say that the present value, or discounted value, at 5%, of $110.25 received two years from now, is $100.

To take the example one step further, suppose that I offer you the same deal, but this time you can invest the money at 10%. Which alternative would you choose? You probably would take the $100. If you did, at the end of two years you would have $121—quite a bit more than I was offering. We can then deduce that the net present value, at 10%, of $110.25 received two years from now, is somewhat less than $100. You can use VisiCalc's @NPV function to find out exactly how much less.

Notice that our investment involved only one outflow and one inflow. In many cases, however, the cash inflows from an investment are received in multiple payments across time. Consider a building that you might buy as an investment, for example. The building will cost you $45,000, and you plan to rent it out for $12,000 per year for 10 years. At the end of the lease, the building will be demolished. Your income would be earned across the life of the lease on the building at the rate of $12,000 per year.

Now, suppose that you also had the opportunity to invest your $45,000 in a certificate of deposit at 15% per annum. Which investment should you choose?

Solving this problem requires comparing the rate of return on the building to the interest rate on the CD. IRR analysis is the perfect tool for the job. Unlike NPV, which uses an interest rate and a stream of payments to compute a net present value, IRR uses the stream of payments and the present value of the investment to compute an interest rate that is the rate of return on the project. The internal rate of return on an investment is the rate at which the net present value of the income equals the amount of the outflow required to make the investment. There is another way to say this: at the IRR, the net present value of all inflows and outflows equals zero. In our example, the internal rate of return is the rate at which the net present value of $12,000 per year for 10 years equals $45,000.

Typically, this kind of problem is solved manually using a hit-or-miss approach. First, you would choose an interest rate—for example, 20%—and use that rate to compute the NPV of the income stream. If the NPV generated by that rate was higher than the investment outflow ($45,000), you would select a higher discount rate. If the chosen rate yielded a NPV that was too low, you would increase the rate. This process would be repeated until you found the correct rate.

The Internal Rate of Return Calculator can perform the same computation with just one pass. Let's look at how it works.

The Model

This model solves internal rate of return problems by funneling the estimated IRR into ever-narrower possible ranges until the rate is pinned down precisely. This process calls for a combination of @LOOKUP and @NPV functions.

There are two sections in the model: ASSUMPTIONS and SOLUTION. The ASSUMPTIONS section, beginning at cell A10, contains information about the investment being analyzed. The sample model uses the $45,000 investment. Cell D16 shows the outflow required to make the investment. The cells in the range from E16 to E40 contain the expected annual cash inflows that this investment will generate.

Column C contains the years that define the term of the project.

Cell C16 shows the year in which the original investment was made. Cell C17 is defined as:

C17 /FL (V) +C16+1

The same technique is used in the other cells in column C. The actual IRR computation is performed in the area labeled Internal Rate of Return Table, which begins at cell J1. In row 6 you will see a series of percentages, beginning in cell M6 with 100% (1.00) and ending in cell W6 with 0% (.00). We assume that the rate of return on the project lies somewhere in this range. The cells in row 5 compute the net present value of the stream of income in cells E16 to E40 at each of the rates in cells M6 to W6. For example, cell P5 calculates the NPV of the stream at 70% (.70), using the formula:

P5 (V) @NPV(P6,E16...E40)

Notice that the dollar amounts calculated range from 11988.28 in cell M5 to 73734.81 in cell V5. Although cell W5 contains the amount 120000.00, the display shows only a series of ">" symbols

>>>>>>>>>

because column W is too narrow to display the full 9 digits of the number. These symbols will appear frequently as you use the model.

Cell X6 contains the formula:

X6 /F$ (V) @LOOKUP(D16,M5...W5)

This cell finds the value in the indicated range that comes closest to the value in cell D16—in this case, 30% (.30).

Remember that the IRR is the discount rate that makes the NPV of the income stream equal to the investment outflow. The value returned by this cell is therefore an approximation of the IRR on this investment. To be more precise, this cell shows the upper limit of a range of rates that contains the IRR. The @LOOKUP table indicates that the lower limit of this range is 20% (.20). Cell

M8 contains another NPV computation. This time, however, it uses the discount rate from cell X6:

M8 (V) @NPV(X6,E16...E40)

Cell N8 is then defined as:

N8 (V) @NPV(X6-.01,E16...E40)

The cells in row 8 compute another series of NPVs for the cash flows in the range from E16 to E40. This set of NPVs uses a series of discount rates from 30% (.30) down to 20% (.2). The discount rate used in each cell is 1% (.01) less than the one in the preceding cell.

Cell M9 contains the reference:

M9 (V) +X6

Each cell in the N9 to W9 range is defined by subtracting 1% (.01) from the previous cell. For example, cell N9 contains the formula:

N9 (V) +M9-.01

The result is a new range of possible values for the IRR. This range is used by cell X9 to refine further the IRR for this problem. Cell X9 is defined as:

X9 /F$ (V) @LOOKUP(D16,M8...W8)

The value returned by this @LOOKUP is another approximation of the IRR. Our first approximation (in cell X6) was accurate to only the first decimal place, but this new approximation is accurate to the second decimal place.

The cells in the M11 to W11 range are defined in much the same way as the cells in the range from M8 to W8. This time, however, the discount rate used in each computation is 1/10% (.001) less than the value used in the preceding cell. For example, cell M11 contains the formula:

M11 (V) @NPV(X9,E16...E40)

Cell N11 is defined as:

N11 (V) @NPV(X9-.001,E16...E40)

And cell O11 contains the reference:

O11 (V) @NPV(X9-.002,E16...E40)

The cells in the M12 to W12 range echo the discount rates used in row 11. Cell M12 is defined as:

M12 /FG (V) +9

Cell N12 is then defined as:

N12 /FG (V) +M12-.001

Once again, we have narrowed the range of possible IRRs. Finally, look at cell X12. This cell contains the formula:

X12 /FG (V) @LOOKUP(D16,M11...W11)

By now, this formula should look familiar. The answer to our IRR problem is computed by looking up the value of the investment in the range from M11 to W11. The value displayed in this cell—.235—is our final approximation of the IRR on this project.

The SOLUTION section begins at cell A45. Cell G50, labeled Internal Rate of Return, shows the internal rate of return on this investment. It is defined by referring to cell X12:

G50 /FG (V) +X12*100

The model tells us that the building investment has an IRR of 23.5%. Is this better than buying a CD at 15%? You'd better believe it!

Using the Model

Start by entering the beginning year in cell C16, the required investment amount in cell D16, and the stream of cash flows in column E. When that data is in place, type ! to recalculate the model. You can save the model by typing `/SSFilename (CR)` and print it by typing `>AIO (CR) /PPA50 (CR)`.

Modifications

The IRR Calculator will compute internal rates of return that are accurate within +-.0005. If you need more accuracy, add another pair of rows to the IRR table. Within the limits of VisiCalc's memory, you can make the computation as accurate as you wish. IRR is particularly useful when it is combined with a thorough investment analysis. For example, you may want to add this model to a lease analysis of a real estate purchase projection. The IRR model can help you make most investment decisions.

CHAPTER 4
Working Capital Management

Tracking Accounts Receivable Collections
Calculating Economic Order Quantity

Tracking Accounts Receivable Collections

Because monitoring cash flow is so important to a small business, a simple way of analyzing the monthly accounts receivable collection cycle can be a useful tool. Managers can use this analysis to develop a "feel" for when payments will arrive, which will help in planning cash disbursements and maintaining the required cash balances. One possible result is a reduction in collection time for outstanding bills. Although performing an accounts receivable collections analysis manually is time-consuming and tedious, VisiCalc can make this a quick and easy task.

Principles

Each day of credit that you extend to your customers is equivalent to loaning them the cash generated by one day's sales. If your business has annual sales of $1 million, its average daily sales are nearly $2800. By allowing your customers to wait 30 days before paying, you have "loaned" them the use of 30 days' worth of sales, or over $80,000. If your actual collection cycle increases to 45 days, the loan jumps to nearly $125,000. To look at it yet another way, cutting 10 days from your collection cycle would free close to $30,000—cash that is now being loaned, interest free, to your customers.

Of course, there are also costs associated with *not* offering reasonable credit terms. Some customers may insist on a certain level of credit and shift their business to other vendors if their requirements are not met. Extending credit also makes order-taking more convenient.

The collection cycle begins at the point of sale. Most companies generate both cash and credit sales, although the percentage of each varies widely from business to business. Cash sales have no collection cycle to speak of; the sale is made, and the cash is collected at the same time. Credit sales have a collection cycle that is determined, at least nominally, by the seller. Payment terms specify a time factor (10 days, 30 days, etc.) and sometimes a discount for early payment. The problem occurs when the seller's terms are not honored by customers. The purpose of managing accounts receivable collections is to eliminate, as much as possible, any discrepancy between the terms stated on the invoice—your credit policy—and the actual time the customers take to pay.

Sophisticated accounts receivable systems eliminate the discrepancy by tracking an invoice from the point of sale to the point of collection. However, much of the same information can be acquired by using a model that maintains records on an aggregate basis. The model must provide two pieces of information: data about the percentage of a given period's sales, collected for each period that follows; and the pattern of collections during each month. The percentage of sales collected is a direct result of a company's credit policy. Companies that extend net-30-days terms should have a fairly high collection percentage the following month. A business that offers only net-10-days terms should collect most of its bills within one month. The model illustrates a company that offers 30-days credit to its customers.

The collections pattern for a month is determined by computing the percentage of the month's total collections that are received each day. This computation indicates the flow of payments that can be expected in a given month.

The Model

This model contains two sections: SALES DATA and COLLECTIONS DATA.

The SALES DATA section, beginning at row 10, summarizes all sales and calculates credit sales for the two months that immediately precede the month being monitored. Cells D17 and D18, labeled Total Sales, display gross sales for both months. Cells

E17 and E18, labeled Returns, contain the dollar amount of any returns, discounts, or allowances made during the two-month period. The amount of cash sales for the period is entered in cells F17 and F18. Finally, cells G17 and G18 compute net credit sales by subtracting cash sales and adjustments from total sales. As an example, the formula for cell G17 is:

```
G17 (V) +D17-E17-F17
```

The COLLECTIONS DATA section, beginning at cell A22, lists the dates for the current month in column B. Notice that the automatic dating function, developed in the Checkbook Balancer model, is used again here. Columns C, D, and E list the dollar amount of collections received each day. The total day's collections are split into three groups for posting to the three columns. Collections against invoices written last month are posted to column C, and payments received for bills written the month before that are posted to column D. All other collections are assigned to column E.

For example, on the 8th day of the month, shown in row 37, a total of $3218 was collected, as shown in cell F37 by the formula:

```
F37 (V) @SUM(C37...E37)
```

Of the amount collected, the $1788 related to last month's sales has been posted to cell C37. Collections against two-month-old invoices, $430, have been posted to cell D37. The remaining $1000, posted to cell E37, includes several payments made on even older bills.

Row 62 contains totals for each of the data columns. Cell C62, for example, contains the formula:

```
C62 (V) @SUM(C30...C61)
```

The same relative formula is used in cells D62, E62, F62, and G62.

The model returns its first important information in cells C65 and D65. These cells compute the ratio of the total collected in the current month against prior months' sales to the sales amounts themselves. For example, in cell C65:

C65 /F$ (V) +C62/G17*100

Looking at the numbers in the example, we can see that the total credit sales for the prior month were $94,000 (cell G17). In addition, cell C62 shows that $61,964 was collected against that amount in the current month. When the amount collected is divided as indicated in the formula in C65, it yields 66%.

Move back up the model to cell G30, which contains the formula:

G30 /FI (V) +F30/F62*100

The cells in column G return the second important type of information produced by this model: the percentage of the total month's collections received each day.

Column H takes this analysis one step further by computing the cumulative percentage collected on a day-by-day basis. Each cell in this column adds the cells above it to the cell immediately to its left in column G. For example, cell H38 is defined as:

H38 /FI (V) +H37+G38

Using the Model

At the beginning of every month, set up the model by entering the SALES DATA for the preceding two months. Then, on a daily basis, post your collections to the appropriate cells in the model. You can recalculate the model at any time by typing ! Notice, however, that the collection percentage information in columns G and H and in row 65 will not be correct until the entire month's collections are posted. At the end of the month, you can print the SALES DATA and COLLECTION DATA sections by typing >A10 (CR) /PPH66 (CR).

Interpreting the information provided by this model is fairly simple. When you look at the results in the example, you will see, in row 65, that about 66% of last month's sales and 13% of the previous month's sales were collected in the current month. Assuming that our example company is offering 30-days credit, the collection cycle seems to be fairly close to target. If we extrapolate from the data for this month, we notice that in two months' time, 85% of a month's sales have been collected—not bad at all, but still improvable.

Column G shows a surge of activity between the 16th and the 22nd of the month. Column H indicates that 73% of the total month's collections have already been received by the 22nd, which is just about two-thirds of the way through the month. This slight skewing of the collections flow might have an impact on purchasing or payment decisions.

Modifications

This model can be easily expanded in a number of ways. You may want to add a column to track collections against an additional month. To make that change, insert a column at the current column E and replicate the formulas from columns C or D. This expansion could be particularly useful if you offer unusually long credit terms.

The model can also be condensed for use by companies with shorter collection cycles. If you offer net-10-days terms, each column can represent a two-week period of sales. Because collections would be tracked across a 10-day span, you could delete several rows.

You may use this model to test the effectiveness of different credit policies. For example, suppose that you are currently extending 30-days credit, but your average collection period is 45 days. You wonder whether a 2% discount for early payment would help speed collections. As an experiment, offer the terms for a one-month period, and use the worksheet to track the payments as they come in across the next few months. When completed, the collections worksheet will allow you to compare the results of your experiment to your regular collections pattern.

Calculating Economic Order Quantity

Are you effectively managing your inventory costs? If you stock goods for production or resale, you know the costs associated with carrying inventory. They include the interest cost of financing the inventory until it is resold, as well as the cost of shrinkage, which arises from the inevitable damage, loss, and pilferage that occur over time. The longer you hold your inventory, the greater the interest and shrinkage costs.

The cost of carrying inventory must also be balanced against the cost of ordering it. The ordering cost is usually harder to determine because it is based on the personnel time used to place, track, and receive an order. The more often you order, the higher your ordering costs will be. Yet, at the same time, if you order frequently, you can reduce your inventory carrying costs by keeping less inventory in stock.

There is a way to balance the carrying and ordering costs for inventory. Using a mathematical formula, you can determine the economic order quantity (EOQ), or number of units you should purchase each time you place an order. By ordering the EOQ, you can minimize the total cost of inventory, which is the sum of the ordering and carrying costs.

The Model

This model has two sections: ASSUMPTIONS and SOLUTIONS. To calculate an EOQ, you must first enter several facts about your inventory in the ASSUMPTIONS section of the model, which begins at cell A10.

The number of units sold during a given period of time is entered in cell F13. One week is the period used in this model. If you purchase inventory for production rather than resale, enter the number of units used in production rather than the number of units sold. Enter your per-unit purchase price in cell F14. Cell F15 contains the cost of placing an order, which is assumed to be the same for each order.

The order lead time, entered in cell F16, can help you set a safety stock level. If you know that an order takes two weeks to arrive, then you need at least two weeks of inventory on hand. You would probably want even more on hand in case an order is delayed, but knowing the lead time can help you establish a minimum. The safety stock level is not related to the EOQ.

Cell F17 contains the interest rate for financing the inventory purchase, and cell F18 contains the percentage of your inventory that is lost to shrinkage on an annual basis.

After all assumptions are entered, VisiCalc computes the carrying cost, the EOQ, the required frequency of ordering, and the minimum safety stock level in the SOLUTIONS area, which begins at cell A22. Carrying cost is computed in cell F25 by converting the interest and shrinkage rates to weekly percentages, and then multiplying the result by the per-unit inventory cost. The formula for this computation is:

```
F25 /F$ (V) (((F17+F18)/100)/52)*F14
```

The result, .07 in our example, indicates that the carrying cost for each unit of inventory is seven cents per week. The carrying cost and the demand (or unit) sales are always computed for the same period.

The number of units to order, the EOQ, is displayed in cell F26. It is computed by the formula:

```
F26 /FI (V) @SQRT((2*F15*F13)/F25)
```

Cell F27 displays order frequency, which is determined by dividing the number of units ordered (the EOQ) by the weekly demand, then multiplying by 7 to express the frequency in days rather than weeks. Notice that this formula does not allow for safety stock; the number of units ordered is exactly equal to the demand expected during the time between orders. It is assumed that a safety stock level has already been established. Order frequency is computed by the formula:

F27 /FI (V) (F26/F13)*7

Minimum safety stock can now be computed by multiplying weekly demand by the order lead time, using the formula:

F28 (V) +F13*F16

Using the Model

After you have built the basic model described above, you must gather the required data—about unit sales, purchase prices, ordering costs, and order lead time—to perform the EOQ calculation. Although most of this information should be easily obtained, the ordering cost figure may be tough to pin down. When you try to determine this number, remember to include the time of the person who prepares the order, the cost of any supplies used, the cost of postage or telephone, and any other costs that are relevant to your business.

Once the data is gathered, insert it in the proper places in the model and recalculate by typing ! You can save the completed model by typing `/SSFilename (CR)` and print the ASSUMPTIONS and SOLUTIONS sections by typing `>A10 (CR) /PPH28 (CR)`.

This model, or any EOQ model, is restricted to computing an EOQ for one item at a time, because the cost per item is one of the inputs in the computations. A different EOQ model must be developed for each type of item stocked in inventory. Some items may be ordered from the same supplier; if their demand is similar, it makes sense to order them all on the same P.O. In such a case, you probably will not be able to optimize the EOQ for each item, but by experimenting with your VisiCalc models, you can find a workable compromise.

Modifications

You may want to modify the model by changing the inventory analysis period from weeks to months or days. Assuming that you want to use months, you would first change the demand assumption (Number of Units Sold) to indicate the number of units sold or used in production for one month. Lead time would also be expressed in months. If lead time is less than one month, you can use a fractional number such as .5 to express it. To compute carrying cost per unit, convert the interest and shrinkage rates to monthly rather than weekly percentages, then divide them by 100 and by 12. None of the other formulas will need adjustment when you modify the model in this manner.

CHAPTER 5
Financial Statements

Producing a Comprehensive Financial Statement
Performing Ratio Analysis
Using Interactive Financial Statements

Producing a Comprehensive Financial Statement

Every business produces financial statements at one time or another. For some businesses, this process is reserved for tax time and the infrequent visit to the bank. For others, it is a monthly, or even weekly, procedure. Whatever your situation, this Five-in-One Financial Statement model can make the job easier.

Principles

The most commonly used financial statements and supporting schedules are the Income Statement and its subsidiaries, the Statement of Operating Expenses, the Statement of Cost of Goods Sold, the Balance Sheet, the Statement of Stockholders' Equity, and the Statement of Changes in Financial Position (SCFP). Every business uses the Balance Sheet and the Income Statement. Many businesses use also the other four statements to report the results of operations. This model includes all of these statements, except the Statement of Changes, because its form and content vary too widely from company to company to be useful in a model like this one. If you use the SCFP, you can add it to your version of the model. Let's take a brief look at the other statements.

The Income Statement shows the results of a firm's operations over a period, usually a year, and includes information about sales, cost of goods sold, operating expenses, and interest and tax expenses. The bottom line of the Income Statement is usually labeled net income, which represents the profit earned by the firm during the period covered by the statement.

The Statement of Operating Expenses details the operating expenses line from the income statement. Operating expenses include management salaries, office rent, postage, and telephone expenses, which can be presented in decreasing numerical order, in alphabetical order according to the label assigned to each expense, or in logical groupings (salary-related, office-related, fixed asset-related, etc.). This schedule can help a manager control expenses.

The Statement of Cost of Goods Sold shows the computation of the cost of the products sold by the company in the period. The business in the model illustration is engaged in a simple manufacturing process. If the product sold is purchased for resale, a different set of calculations would be used.

The cost of goods sold has three components: materials cost, labor cost, and overhead. Materials cost is computed by adding inventory purchases in the current period to the inventory balance at the end of the last period. After adjustments for returned goods and any other items are made, the amount remaining, called total goods available for sale, represents the total of all the goods that the firm had to sell during that period.

The materials cost of the goods sold in the period is equal to the total goods available for sale minus the inventory remaining at the end of the month. Think of it this way: if you started the month with 6 widgets, bought 5 more during the month, and had only 4 left at the end of the month, you must have sold 7 widgets. If widgets cost you $2,000 apiece, then the cost of material for the period was $14,000. Cost of goods sold equals the material cost plus any labor and factory costs that went into manufacturing the finished product.

The Statement of Stockholders' Equity shows the changes in equity for the current period. The major activities on this schedule are dividend payments, accumulation of retained earnings, and the sales and purchase of stock by the company.

Finally, the Balance Sheet is a "snapshot" of a company's financial position as of the last date in the reporting period. The Balance Sheet is divided into assets and liabilities (which must always be equal in total). Assets and liabilities are usually subdivided into current and noncurrent (or long-term) portions. The Balance Sheet shows what a company owns (cash, inventory, and equipment) and what it owes (accounts payable and debt). It also shows the firm's retained earnings, which are the accumulated past profits of the business.

The Model

The Five-in-One model uses the financial relationships shown on the chart to build statements. They appear in the spreadsheet at the following locations:

Statement of Operating Expenses	A8
Statement of Cost of Goods Sold	A42
Statement of Income	A72
Statement of Retained Earnings	A108
Balance Sheet - Assets	A132
Balance Sheet - Liabilities	A171

Column A is a margin. When the statements are printed, they will be offset 10 spaces from the left side of the page.

Columns B through D contain the statement labels. The labels in the example are fairly common, but you may have to change them to fit your situation.

Columns G and H contain the actual numbers. Column H shows the balances for the current year (called 19XY in the example), and column G contains the preceding year's balances.

Most of the formulas in this model are simple totals and subtotals that are summarized in the chart at the end of this section. The more complex relationships are discussed below.

FINANCIAL STATEMENT RELATIONSHIPS

Account	**Appears on**
Depreciation	Statement of Operating Expenses Balance Sheet

Depreciation expense in 19XY equals the difference between 19XX and 19XY accumulated depreciation on the balance sheet.

Inventory	Statement of Cost of Goods Sold Balance Sheet

Ending inventory for both years appears on both statements. Beginning inventory in 19XY on the statement of cost of goods sold equals the ending inventory in year 19XX on the same schedule.

Cost of Goods Sold	Statement of Cost of Goods Sold Income Statement

The total from the schedule of cost of goods sold is entered on the income statement.

Operating Expenses	Statement of Operating Expenses Income Statement

The total from the schedule of operating expenses is entered on the income statement.

Net Income	Income Statement Statement of Retained Earnings

Net income for the income statement is entered in the statement of stockholders' equity.

Common Stock Retained Earnings	Statement of Retained Earnings Balance Sheet

Totals for these two items are computed on the statement of stockholders' equity and transferred to the balance sheet.

The STATEMENT OF OPERATING EXPENSES begins at cell A8. Notice that the cells in columns G and H, rows 19 to 35, are input cells. Use them to post your operating expenses to the model. Skip down to the STATEMENT OF COST OF GOODS SOLD, which begins at cell A42. Cells G53 and H53 show each year's beginning inventory.

Although this number must be entered manually for 19XX (column G), in 19XY (column H), the beginning inventory can be computed by drawing on the ending balance in 19XX. This computation is performed by defining cell H53 as:

H53 (V) +G59

Rows 54 and 55 should be used to input purchase data. Enter the ending inventory for the two years in cells G59 and H59. The direct materials expense represents the cost of the materials in the finished goods sold during the period and is determined by subtracting the ending inventory from the total materials available. Cell H61, for example, contains the formula:

H61 (V) +H57-H59

Direct material expense and factory overhead are entered in rows 63 and 65. Row 67 computes the total cost of goods sold by adding the three component costs: materials, labor, and overhead. For example, cell G67 contains the formula:

G67 (V) +G61+G63+G65

The INCOME STATEMENT draws information from the Statement of Operating Expenses and the Statement of Cost of Goods Sold. Gross sales and returns and allowances information, however, must be entered in rows 83 and 85. The cost of goods sold is pulled from that schedule to cells G89 and H89 by a direct cell reference. For example, the formula in cell G89 is:

G89 (V) +G67

Operating expense information is similarly drawn from the operating expense detail schedule. The formula in cell G93 is:

G93 (V) +G37

Interest expense and other income or expense amounts are displayed in rows 95 and 97. Any income tax expense incurred in the two years should be entered in row 101.

The net income for both years is computed in cells G103 and H103, using, for example, the formula:

G103 (V) +G99-G101

The next section of the model, STATEMENT OF RETAINED EARNINGS, begins at cell A108. Notice that this schedule contains data from year 19XW, the year immediately preceding 19XX. This schedule details the activity in the common stock and retained earnings accounts for the two years. Cell H121, which shows the net income earned by the company in 19XX, and cell H125, which shows the same data for 19XY, automatically pull their data from the Income Statement. For example, cell H121 contains the formula:

H121 (V) +G103

Cells F121 and F125 record any sales or purchases of stock made by the company in the two years. In our example, we have assumed that no such activity occurred.

Cells F127 and H127 show the total common stock and retained earnings balances of the company at Any Day, 19XY.

The BALANCE SHEET begins at row 132 and is split into two parts: assets, and liabilities and equity. Notice that the totals computed in row 166 equal those in row 207; in other words, assets equal liabilities. Always check your Balance Sheets to make sure these numbers agree.

Rows 145, 146, 148, and 149 are used to enter the amounts in the current assets accounts. Cells G147 and H147 show the inventory at the end of each year. The data in these cells comes from the Statement of Cost of Goods Sold. Cell G147, for example, contains the formula:

G147 (V) +G59

All other asset accounts must be entered from the keyboard.

Rows 184-188, 193, and 197 are used to enter the amounts for current liabilities, long-term debt, and other liabilities. Cells G202 and G203, and H202 and H203, relate to the firm's stockholders' equity. Because the figures needed for these cells have already been computed on the Schedule of Stockholders' Equity, we can use a simple formula to repeat them here. For example, cell G202 contains the relationship:

G202 (V) +F123

Cell H203 is defined as:

H203 (V) +H127

SUBTOTALS AND TOTALS IN THE MODEL

Row	Label	Range
37	Total Operating Expenses	19...36
57	Total Materials Available	+53+54-55
61	Direct Materials Expense	+57-59
67	Total Cost of Goods Sold	+65+63+61
87	Net Sales	+83-85
91	Gross Margin	+87-89
99	Profit before Taxes	+91-93-95-97
103	Net Income	+99-101
123	Balance at Any Day, 19XX	+119+121
127	Balance at Any Day, 19XY	+123+125
151	Total Current Assets	145...150
158	Total Plant, Property, and Equipment	154...157
162	Net Plant, Property, and Equipment	+158-160
166	Total Assets	+151+162+164
190	Total Current Liabilities	184...189
195	Total Noncurrent Liabilities	193...194
199	Total Liabilities	+197+195+190
205	Total Stockholders' Equity	+202+203
207	Total Liabilities and Equity	+205+199

Using the Model

Begin using this model by entering all of the required data in the financial statements. Notice that you do not have to enter any subtotals or totals—the model computes these for you. You also do not have to enter numbers in any of the cells, like G93 or H121, which contain formulas referring to other cells. Once you have entered the appropriate data, recalculate the model by typing !

Before you print the model, you should save it by typing `/SSFilename (CR)`. You can print the entire model by typing `>A10 (CR) /PPI208 (CR)`, or you can print each section separately by typing:

Operating Expenses	>A10 (CR) /PPI41 (CR)
Cost of Goods Sold	>A44 (CR) /PPI71 (CR)
Income Statement	>A74 (CR) /PPI107 (CR)
Retained Earnings	>A110 (CR) /PPI131 (CR)
Assets	>A134 (CR) /PPI170 (CR)
Liabilities	>A173 (CR) /PPI208 (CR)

Once your statements are printed, take the time to review them carefully for possible errors. For example, compare your total assets to your total liabilities. These numbers should always be equal. Are they? Does the retained earnings line on your balance sheet agree with your statement of retained earnings? A few minutes of review can prevent a great deal of embarrassment.

You will discover another benefit of this model after you start using it. When you update your statements, you can easily set up your Previous Period column by copying the contents of column H in the previous month's model into column G of the new model. To copy the contents, use the DIF format (if you are using a fresh spreadsheet to set up the new month) or the replicate command (if you are building the new model on top of the old one).

Modifications

The advantage of this model is that it provides for financial statements a standard format that can be used again and again. Because your statements are probably different from the samples shown here, you should modify the format to meet your needs. This can be done easily enough by simply adding or deleting rows (or, in some cases, columns) from the the basic format. Be sure to save a master copy of your version for future use.

Performing Ratio Analysis

Ratios are some of the most commonly used financial analysis tools. A few standard ratios computed from a company's balance sheet and income statement can indicate the financial health, stability, and performance of that company. Comparing a company's ratios against a set of budget figures or industry averages can be an important part of measuring its operating success. Ratios do not give a complete picture of a company's financial position, but they do quickly provide information about a firm's significant strengths and weaknesses.

The Ratio Analyzer model is an example of a ratio calculator that can be built into any spreadsheet model of an income statement and balance sheet. The financial statements in this model are only examples—each business will use a different format.

By making ratio analysis an integral part of an Income Statement and Balance Sheet model, or a model of your own, you can add new insight to your analysis of company operations. Keep in mind, however, that the cell references you put in the formulas for ratio calculations must be correct. The references used in the formulas here fit the particular format used in the model's financial statements.

The Model

This model has three sections: INCOME STATEMENT, BALANCE SHEET, and RATIO ANALYSIS.

The INCOME STATEMENT and BALANCE SHEET sections, which begin at cells A10 and A35, hold the assumptions used to calculate the ratios. Columns A-D contain the labels for the accounts shown on the statements, and column E contains the balance in each account.

These two sections, however, are used for entering more than assumptions. Notice the series of percentages in column F next to each account balance. These percentages are the Income Statement and Balance Sheet Ratios.

Income Statement Ratios measure the relationship between sales and each expense item on the income statement. In the example, the ratios are presented in column F, rows 14 through 31. For example, cell F15 measures the ratio between sales and cost of goods sold. This cell is defined as:

F15 /FI (V) +E15/E14*100

Imagine that these percentages are data for a pie chart. The "whole pie" is defined by the amount of sales. Each expense is a slice. Cost of goods sold would be nearly three-quarters of the pie. Earnings after taxes would be only a sliver.

These ratios are useful because they can quickly provide information about business performance; and since they can be added to any income statement easily, they should become a part of all your profit and loss analysis.

In much the same way, *Balance Sheet Ratios* measure the relationship between each asset account and total assets, or between each liability and total liabilities. For example, cell F41 contains the formula:

F41 /FI (V) +E41/E52*100

The result of this calculation, 4%, indicates that cash represents about 1/25th of this company's total assets. The RATIO ANALYSIS section begins at cell A75. Financial ratios can be divided into four major categories:

1. Indicators of Solvency
2. Indicators of Liquidity
3. Funds Management Ratios
4. Profitability Ratios

Each ratio is explained in detail in the following text.

Indicators of Solvency

These ratios measure the long-term financial health of a company by providing information about its capital structure and the management of its current debt burden.

The *Debt/Equity Ratio* is calculated by dividing total debt (both current and long term) by owners' equity (capital stock plus retained earnings). A result greater than one indicates that more long-term financing is being provided by outside creditors than by the owners. This situation is not necessarily cause for alarm, because high levels of debt are common in certain industries, but it does have implications for future financing. A company with a high debt/equity ratio may not be able to obtain more outside debt financing to take advantage of business opportunities or weather a downturn in sales or profits.

Debt/Equity Ratio: F79 /F$ (V) (E59+E61)/E66

Times Interest Earned indicates how well a company's interest obligations are met by its earnings. If a company's interest payments can be covered several times over by its earnings, then there is little risk of defaulting on a loan if earnings drop. If interest payments are barely being met, however, the chance of default is greater.

Times Interest Earned: F80 /F$ (V) +E22/E23

Indicators of Liquidity

These ratios provide signals of a firm's short-term financial health. They show how well a company is able to meet immediate financial obligations, such as bills owed or loan repayments due. *Net Working Capital* is not a ratio, but a dollar amount that is determined by subtracting current liabilities from current assets. To think of it another way, net working capital represents the liquid, unencumbered resources of the company.

To say that an asset is "liquid" is to say that it can be easily converted into cash and spent. Cash is the most liquid asset because it does not need to be converted to be spent. Fixed assets (buildings, machines, and so forth) are not liquid because they cannot be converted to cash quickly.

Similarly, unencumbered assets are not offset by current liabilities. In the example, our company has $51,000 of current assets, $36,000 of current liabilities, and therefore a net working capital of $15,000. This $15,000 is unencumbered, or free to be invested or spent at the discretion of the company's management.

Because current liabilities are those obligations due for payment in a year or less, current assets (cash and items that will soon be converted into cash, such as accounts receivable) should be greater than current liabilities. Net working capital, therefore, should be positive.

Net Working Capital: F83 (V) +E45-E59

Net Working Capital/Assets equals net working capital divided by total assets. This ratio indicates the percentage of a firm's assets that are liquid and unencumbered.

Net Working Capital/Assets: F84 /F$ (V) +F83/E52

The *Current Ratio* is determined by dividing current assets by current liabilities. Like net working capital, current ratio is an indicator of how well a firm can meet its short-term obligations given its current assets. In an ideal situation, where current assets exceed current liabilities, this ratio will have a value greater than one.

Current Ratio: F85 /F$ (V) +E45/E59

The *Quick Ratio,* sometimes called the *Acid Test Ratio,* is calculated by subtracting inventories (the least liquid current asset) from total current assets and dividing the result by current liabilities. The quick ratio is a good indicator of how well current obligations can be met without the difficult task of liquidating inventories.

Quick Ratio: F86 /F$ (V) (E45-E43)/E59

A firm's *Cash Ratio,* figured by dividing cash and near-cash items (marketable securities) by current liabilities, gives an indication of how well the firm can meet its current obligations with the cash and securities it now holds. This ratio shows what percentage of current liabilities could be paid if all short-term creditors demanded *immediate* payment. In the example, cash and marketable securities total $9,000, and current liabilities are $36,000, giving a cash ratio of .25. This ratio indicates that 25% of all current obligations can be met with the cash and marketable securities the firm now holds.

Cash Ratio: F87 /F$ (V) +E41/E59

Funds Management Ratios

Funds Management Ratios measure the amount of cash that is tied up in a business as a result of operations.

Receivables/Sales is calculated by dividing accounts receivable by total sales for the reporting period. The resulting figure shows what percentage of sales has not been paid. For example, if accounts receivable are $24,000, and sales for the year are $100,000, then the receivables/sales ratio is .24, indicating that 24% of the current period's sales have not been collected. This ratio is one indication of how extensively a company is lending money to its customers by extending trade credit.

Receivables/Sales: F90 /F$ (V) +E42/E14

Days Sales Outstanding is another way of expressing the percentage of sales in accounts receivable. This ratio is computed by dividing accounts receivable by sales and multiplying the result by the number of days in the reporting period. Like the receivables/sales example, dividing receivables by sales gives the percentage of sales for which payments have not been collected. In our example, the receivables/sales ratio is .24, and the reporting period is one year; therefore .24 x 365 or 88 days' sales are still unpaid. If customer payments are due in 30 days, this shows a pretty poor collection record!

Day Sales Outstanding: F91 /FI (V) +F90*365

Payables/Cost of Goods Sold is figured by dividing accounts payable by the cost of goods sold for the reporting period. This ratio indicates the percentage of the current period's cost of goods sold that has not been paid. In the example, we assume that all accounts payable represent purchases of items eventually included in cost of goods to be sold.

Payables/Cost of Goods Sold: F92 /F$ (V) +E57/E15

Days Purchases in Payables is calculated by dividing accounts payable by the cost of goods sold for the reporting period and multiplying the result by the number of days in the period. For example, if the accounts payable/cost of goods sold ratio is .15, and the reporting period is one year, 55 days of cost of goods sold have not been paid (.15 x 365 = 55 days). If standard payment terms are 30 days, then the company is delinquent in paying its suppliers.

Days Purchases in Payables: F93 /FI (V) +F92*365

Inventory Turnover measures the average number of times that inventories were replenished during the reporting period. This ratio is calculated by dividing cost of goods sold by inventory currently on hand. High inventory turnover indicates a relatively low level of inventory on hand at any one time. Because stocking inventory ties up funds, most managers prefer to have minimal inventory on hand.

Inventory Turnover: F94 /F$ (V) +E15/E43

Days Sales in Inventory is calculated by dividing inventory by cost of goods sold and multiplying the result by the number of days in the reporting period. In the example, inventory is $18,000, and cost of goods sold for the year is $72,400. Therefore, 91 days of inventory is on hand (calculated as 18,000/72,400 x 365 = 91 days). The target number of days sales in inventory ratio varies widely from industry to industry. Because a low inventory is preferred, 91 days of sales in inventory can be a sign of poor inventory management.

Days Sales in Inventory: F95 /FI (V) (E43/E15)*365

The *Sales/Fixed Assets* ratio is calculated by dividing sales by net fixed assets. Fixed assets can be thought of as the fixed, long-term investment in the business. The sales/fixed assets ratio measures the revenue generated by this investment. A low ratio indicates a capital intensive business, where large amounts of equipment are needed to generate sales. A higher ratio suggests a business with low capital requirements. This ratio, like all of the others, is significant only when compared to a budget, or to the ratios generated by competitors.

Sales/Fixed Assets: F96 /F$ (V) +E14/E50

Profitability Ratios

Profitability ratios measure the dollar return (profit) generated by the resources invested in a business. This return is expressed in relation to sales, assets, and stockholders' equity. These important indicators of business performance provide more useful information than dollar figures alone.

Return on Sales compares a business' profit to the sales required to generate that profit. Return on sales equals earnings after taxes divided by sales. A ratio lower than the industry average may indicate poor expense management or operational inefficiency.

Return on Sales: F99 /F$ (V) +E28/E14*100

The *Return on Total Assets* is calculated by dividing earnings after taxes by total assets. Because assets represent the amount invested in a business, it is important to determine what return is being realized on them. If a business consistently produces returns on assets that are below what could be earned if the assets were employed in a different capacity, management may want to consider shifting to a different product or service.

Return on Total Assets: F100 /F$ (V) +E28/E52*100

Return on Stockholders' Equity equals earnings after taxes divided by total stockholders' equity. This ratio is perhaps the most important profitability ratio because it measures the return the owners of the company are earning on their investment. They may compare this return to other potential investments—real estate, money markets, stock in other companies, etc.—to determine whether their investment in the company is worthwhile.

If the return on equity is below the rate that may be earned on other, similar investments, the stockholders of a publicly traded company may try to bid down the price of the company's stock.

The owners of a small business caught in this situation may consider closing up shop.

Return on Stockholders' Equity: F101 /F$ (V) +E28/E66*100

Using the Model

This model is not only easy to use, but it is also one of the most valuable models in the book. To use it, fill in the INCOME STATEMENT and BALANCE SHEET sections and recalculate by typing ! You can save the model by typing `/SSFilename (CR)` and print it by typing `>A10 (CR) /PPG101 (CR)`.

Interpreting the results of the model is more difficult.

Financial ratios have little meaning until they are compared to the industry's historical data. The importance and acceptable range for some ratios can vary widely among industries. In fact, authorities do not even agree on the definition of some ratios! The moral of this paragraph is to be sure to interpret the results of your model carefully.

Modifications

Although the financial statement formats in this model have been designed to be as widely applicable as possible, you may need to make some changes to meet your particular needs. This can be done easily enough, but be certain to review all of the ratio formulas after you make any changes.

These ratios can be added to your financial statement models. They are a wonderful tool for saving time while improving your analysis. You can also add other ratios to the model. Perhaps you measure your expenses as a percentage of gross margin or dividends as a percentage of earnings after taxes. Feel free to use whatever measures you feel will help you manage your business better.

Using Interactive Financial Statements

Could your planning be improved if you had the time to make detailed financial statement projections? Unfortunately, preparing a financial statement is a tedious, time-consuming, and error-prone chore that overworked small-business managers tend to put off. VisiCalc, however, can help you develop financial statements quickly and easily.

The Interactive Income Statement and Balance Sheet model is useful for both normal reporting and the development of pro forma analyses. This model is called "interactive" because the Balance Sheet and Income Statement share data (interact). Interactive financial statement models reflect the relationships between the numbers reported in the Income Statement and those in the Balance Sheet.

Principles

An Income Statement represents financial events over some period of time. It usually reports revenues and expenses over several months or one year. A Balance Sheet, on the other hand, represents a company's financial situation as of a particular date. It is a "snapshot" of the company's financial condition at that time.

The conditions reported on a Balance Sheet always depend on the events reported in the Income Statement for the previous period. For example, sales made during the year generate cash and accounts receivable, which will be reported on the year-end Balance Sheet. If enough cash is generated, the company may pay off some of its debt, again affecting the year-end Balance Sheet. As earnings boost owners' equity, a company may find that it has greater borrowing capacity, which, if utilized, will increase the amount of debt reported on the Balance Sheet.

A Balance Sheet may also reflect management's expectations about events that will be reported on the next period's Income Statement. For example, the amount of inventory reported is related to the expectation of sales volume for the near future, which will be reported on a future Income Statement as cost of goods sold.

The events reported on the Income Statement are also related to the conditions reported on the Balance Sheet. Depreciation expense is related to a company's fixed assets, and interest expense is based on the amount of debt. If a company has excess cash, it may earn additional revenue from interest.

Any relationship between an Income Statement and a Balance Sheet can be reflected in an interactive spreadsheet model like this one. If you want to build pro forma statements to cover several years, the relationships can be stated once and then replicated to later periods. This feature saves a tremendous amount of setup time. If "what if" analysis is performed at a later date, the model will automatically compute the effect of any change on all the interrelationships.

The relationships built into a pro forma model are usually based on either past performance or future objectives. For example, if the cost of goods sold has always been approximately 55% of sales, then this relationship would be expected to hold true in future periods. If management believes that inventory can be held realistically at two months of cost of goods sold, then this relationship will be built into the pro forma analysis. When a company's results are reported, they can be analyzed by comparing the actual relationships to those expected.

The Model

This model has three sections: ASSUMPTIONS, INCOME STATEMENT, and BALANCE SHEET. The ASSUMPTIONS section begins at cell A10. The first two assumptions compute interest income on excess cash. The interest rate paid on the excess cash invested is entered in cell F13. The cash amount that will *not* be invested to earn interest is entered in cell F14. In the example, 5000 is entered in cell F14. If the balance in the cash account goes over $5000, then 18% annual interest will be earned on the excess amount.

The third assumption, the rate of interest paid on long-term debt, is entered in cell F15. Cell F16 contains the percentage of product sales put towards cost of goods sold. Payroll taxes, in cell F17, are assumed to be a percentage of the salaries and wages expense. Cell F18 displays the percentage of income tax paid on earnings.

Cells F25 and F26 contain assumptions related to fixed assets. The average depreciable life of the company's property, plant, and equipment (PP&E), expressed in months, is entered in cell F25. Cell F26 holds the depreciation accumulated to date on PP&E (that is, the depreciation prior to the periods reported in these financial statements).

In cell F27, enter the number of days' sales represented by accounts receivable. (See the Ratio Analyzer model for a discussion of days' sales in accounts receivable.) Cells F28 and F29, respectively, display the days of cost of goods sold in inventory, and days of cost of goods sold in accounts payable. The final assumption, beginning retained earnings, is entered in cell F30.

The INCOME STATEMENT begins at cell A33. Under the heading Gross Income, you will see a list of revenue categories. For product sales, income from service, and other sales, you should enter the expected quarterly figures. The category Other (Interest Income) is derived from the balance in the cash account. If cash exceeds the amount input in cell F14, then the excess funds are invested at the annual interest rate given in cell F13. If the cash balance is less than or equal to the amount in cell F14, then no interest income will be realized. In calculating interest income, the interest rate, shown in cell F13, is first converted to a percentage by dividing it by 100, then converted to a quarterly rate by dividing it by 4. The formula for this calculation is:

```
E42 (V) @IF(@ISERROR(E86),0,@IF(E86>F14,
        @INT((F13/100/4)*(E86-F14)),0))
```

The integer function (INT) helps to prevent arithmetic errors that arise because of rounding.

Total gross income, displayed in row 44, is computed by totaling all income from the various sources, using the formula:

E44 (V) @SUM(E39. . .E43)

Cost of goods sold is computed by multiplying only product sales revenue by the percentage entered in cell F16, using the formula:

E46 (V) +F16*E39/100

Gross margin is computed by subtracting cost of goods sold from total gross income. In this example, the formula for gross margin is:

E48 (V) +E44-E46

The next category on the Income Statement is operating expenses. Some of these figures must be entered manually, and others are computed for you by VisiCalc. The expenses that must be keyed in are:

Supplies
Dues and Subscriptions
Advertising and Artwork
Maintenance

Payroll taxes are calculated by multiplying salaries and wages by the percentage assumed in cell F17:

E54 (V) +F17*E51/100

Depreciation expense is based on a straight-line schedule and the depreciable life assumed in cell F25. To calculate depreciation expense, divide gross plant, property, and equipment, from cell E99, by the number of months in the life of the assets. Then multiply the result by 3 to obtain the depreciation for one quarter. The formula for computing depreciation expense is:

E64 (V) @INT(E99/F25*3)

Interest expense is based on both the annual interest rate entered in cell F15 and the outstanding long-term debt in cell E120. To compute interest expense, convert the annual interest rate to a percentage by dividing it by 100, then convert it to a quarterly rate by dividing by 4. Multiply the result by the long-term debt balance to obtain the interest expense. The formula for this calculation is:

E66 (V) @INT(F15/100/4*E120)

After all operating expenses have been keyed in or computed, VisiCalc totals them, using the @SUM function, and displays the total in cell E70, using the formula:

E70 (V) @SUM(E51. . .E69)

Profit before tax is computed by subtracting total operating expenses from gross margin, using the formula:

E72 (V) +E48-E70

Next, income taxes are computed, using the tax rate entered in cell F18. Because cell E74 contains a conditional statement, no tax will be paid unless income is earned. Tax expense is computed by the formula:

E74 (V) @IF(E72>0,F18/100*E72,0)

The final figure on the Income Statement, net income, or profit after tax, is computed by subtracting income taxes from profit before taxes, using the formula:

E76 (V) +E72-E74

Column I displays the totals for each Income Statement category. All of these totals are calculated using VisiCalc's @SUM function to add the figures in columns E through H. For example, total product sales for the four quarters is computed by this formula:

I39 (V) @SUM(E39. . .H39)

The BALANCE SHEET begins at cell A81 and continues to row 129. The first account balance, cash, is defined in terms of several other cells in the Balance Sheet. An examination of these cells will help explain the cash formula.

Accounts receivable is based on the assumption made in cell F27. This number is first converted to a fraction (one-fourth) by dividing the number by 90 (the number of days in a quarter), then multiplied by the total gross income for the quarter to obtain an accounts receivable balance. These computations are contained in the formula:

E87 (V) @INT(F27/90*E44)

The balance in the inventory account is based on the assumption made in cell F28 about the number of days of cost of goods sold in inventory. In our example, inventory is equal to 30 days. This figure is converted to one-fourth by dividing it by 90 (days). The inventory balance at the end of the first quarter is similarly computed with the formula:

E88 (V) @INT(F28/90*E46)

Total current assets—equal to the sum of cash, accounts receivable, and inventory—are computed by the formula:

E90 (V) @SUM(E86. . .E89)

The depreciable assets—property, plant, and equipment—are listed under the heading Fixed Assets. The amounts in each fixed asset account appear in rows 94 through 97. Gross PP&E is computed by the formula:

E99 (V) @SUM(E94. . .E98)

Net PP&E equals gross PP&E less accumulated depreciation. Cell E100 computes the new accumulated depreciation balance with the formula:

E100 (V) +F26+E64

This balance is then subtracted from the gross PP&E to arrive at net PP&E.

E102 (V) +E99-E100

There are two other fixed asset accounts in this example: deposits and other. The balances for both of these accounts must be entered manually, then added to net PP&E to obtain total fixed assets, computed by the formula:

E107 (V) +E102+E104+E105

Finally, total assets are figured by adding total current assets and total fixed assets, as follows:

E109 (V) +E90+E107

The first liability account, accounts payable, is determined by the current period's cost of goods sold and the assumption entered in cell F29. The number of days is divided by 90 to convert it to a fraction of one-fourth, then multiplied by the cost of goods sold for the quarter. For example, in cell E114, accounts payable for the first quarter is computed by the formula:

E114 (V) +F29/90*E46

Income taxes payable are assumed to be equal to the income tax expense for the current quarter and are obtained by referring to the taxes computed on the Income Statement in the formula:

E115 (V) +E74

Total current liabilities, which is the sum of all current liabilities, is computed with the formula:

E117 (V) @SUM(E114. . .E116)

In this example, noncurrent liabilities have only one account: long-term debt. This number is entered when the model is built.

Noncurrent and current liabilities are added to obtain total liabilities, using the formula:

E122 (V) +E117+E120

The amount of common stock outstanding should be entered in cell E124. The new retained earnings balance is then computed by adding the prior balance to net income for the period:

E126 (V) +F30+E76

This figure becomes the prior retained earnings balance for the following period.

The last figure on the Balance Sheet, total liabilities and equity, equals the sum of total liabilities, common stock, and retained earnings.

E128 (V) +E122+E124+E126

Now, skip back up to row 86, which is labeled Cash. The cash balance is computed by subtracting accounts receivable, inventory, and total fixed assets from total liabilities and equity. If you study this relationship closely, you will see that cash becomes the "plug" that balances the Balance Sheet. Notice, however, that the plug is an accurate one. The sum of total liabilities and equity can be thought of as all of the cash that has flowed into a company, while accounts receivable, inventory, and total fixed assets represent the cash outflows. Netting these inflows and outflows will yield the cash balance, which is calculated by the formula:

E86 (V) +E128-E107-E88-E87

Using the Model

This model is easy to use. You need only to determine the numerical relationships that exist in your business between the Balance Sheet and the Income Statement and enter the numbers, either actual or pro forma, in the statements for the period you are modeling.

Some relationships in the model are circular references; that is, the contents of one cell determine the formula in another cell, and so on through the model until the first cell is influenced again. For example, in this model, cash balance determines interest income, which affects net income, which affects retained earnings, which determines total liabilities and equity. Because cash is defined, in part, by total liabilities and equity, an increase in cash will lead eventually to an increase in retained earnings, which will lead to another increase in cash, and so on. To overcome the circular reference problem, recalculate the model by typing ! repeatedly. Each recalculation has a decreasing effect on the model until the circular reference is overcome.

After all circular references are cleared, you can save the model by typing /SSFilename (CR) and print it by typing >A10 (CR) /PPI129 (CR).

By using this VisiCalc model to plan your business, you can save a tremendous amount of time that may otherwise be spent tracking the flow of funds. The effects of increases or decreases in sales and expenses, fixed asset purchases and sales, and changes in the collection or payment cycles, will be calculated automatically by the model. Be sure to take advantage of this feature by performing extensive "what if" analysis on your projections.

Modifications

This model was designed to accommodate the financial statements of an "average" company. Most of the concepts included in it probably apply to your business. You can modify the model to fit special needs by changing the labels and inserting or deleting a few rows.

CHAPTER 6
Planning and Budgeting

Performing Statistical Analysis
Calculating Growth Capacity
Managing Queues
Budgeting For A New Venture
Determining Price-Volume Relationships

Performing Statistical Analysis

Managers use statistics regularly to analyze their business situation and to facilitate the decision-making process. For example, in analyzing the past year's sales, a manager may want to know the average sales per month per salesperson, or may want to study the relationship between advertising and sales.

Statistics can also be used to study production processes and to analyze both equipment and employee performance.

VisiCalc has some built-in functions that can help you do basic statistical analysis on a series of numbers. The Statistics Calculator shows you how to perform the analysis.

Principles

Statistics summarize and organize data in a meaningful and useful way. The *mean,* or average, is a commonly used statistic that marks the midpoint, or norm, of a group of data. It is calculated by adding the items in a group and dividing the total by the number of items.

A *moving average* is one of a series of averages calculated for a group of numbers. Moving averages are computed for data that represent observations made over a certain period. For example, many businesses track sales on a monthly basis and construct moving averages from this data. Every month, an average of the last three months' sales is computed, called the three-month moving average. Moving averages can be computed for other periods, such as 2 weeks, 6 months, 12 months, and so on. Statistics can be used to indicate the dispersion of values in a group of numbers, or how much the numbers, as a group, vary from the average. Two of these statistics, the *minimum* and the *maximum,* represent the smallest and largest numbers in a group. Another statistic, the *range,* is the difference between the minimum and the maximum.

The *variance* and the *standard deviation* are related dispersion statistics. To calculate the variance, subtract the mean of the numbers from each number in the group and square each result. Add the squares and divide the total by the number of figures in the group. To compute the standard deviation, take the square root of the variance.

What does the standard deviation tell you? As a general rule, about 68% of the items in a normally distributed population will fall in a range between the mean plus the standard deviation, and the mean minus the standard deviation. That is, 68% of the numbers in the group are no more than one standard deviation from the mean.

Some statistical methods can be used to make predictions. One such method, *linear regression,* is based on the study of the relationship between two variables. For example, suppose a business manager wants to study the relationship between company sales and advertising expenditures. The two variables involved are sales dollars and advertising dollars. In this case, advertising is the "independent" variable, or the variable that can be changed—i.e., more or less can be spent on advertising, as the manager decides. Sales is the "dependent" variable, or the variable that depends on the value of the independent variable.

Let's assume that the manager wants to know what sales for the next quarter will be if advertising expenditures are doubled. This figure can be determined by using linear regression to define the relationship between the sales for the past quarter and the corresponding advertising expenditures. With this relationship, a prediction can be made about next quarter's sales given a certain amount of advertising.

If you are familiar with regression analysis, you know that it is more complex than this brief explanation implies. This example is used to show how VisiCalc can perform a simple linear regression based on one independent variable.

The Model

The Statistics Calculator model has two sections: DATA TABLE AND MOVING AVERAGES and SOLUTIONS. The DATA TABLE, beginning at cell A10, contains the numbers to be analyzed and the moving averages for the series of numbers. Numbers are entered in cells C16 through C39 under the Value heading, then totaled in cell C41 by the formula:

C41 (V) @SUM(C16...C40)

Each cell in column B contains a number for each item in the series. For example, cell B16 contains the number "1," cell B17 contains the number "2," and so on.

The numbers in column B will be used later as the independent variable in the linear regression. After all the data has been entered, moving averages are computed in columns D through F. The first 3-period moving average is displayed in cell D18. It calculates the average of cells C16 through C18 using the formula:

D18 /F$ (V) @AVERAGE(C16...C18)

This formula is replicated with relative references through cell D39.

The first 6-period moving average appears in cell E21, using the formula:

E21 /F$ (V) @AVERAGE(C16...C21)

Cell F27 holds the first 12-period moving average, which is defined as:

F27 /F$ (V) @AVERAGE(C16...C27)

The SOLUTIONS section of the model provides several statistics for the series of numbers being analyzed. The following formulas calculate these statistics:

Number of Items: E46 (V) @COUNT(C16...C39)
Maximum Value: E47 (V) @MAX(C16...C39)

Minimum Value: E48 (V) @MIN(C16...C39)
Range: E49 (V) +E47-E48
Mean: E50 (V) @AVERAGE(C16...C39)

Before the standard deviation or the linear regression can be computed, the model must make some intermediate calculations in the SCRATCH PAD that begins at cell I9.

Under the heading, Difference from Mean, the mean, as calculated in cell E50, is subtracted from each number in column C. For example, the formula in cell J25 is:

J25 /FI (V) +C25-E50

Each figure from column J is squared in column K. This can be done either by raising the number to the power of 2 (e.g., I25△2) or by multiplying each number by itself, the method used in this model. For example:

K25 /FI (V) +J25*J25

Column L contains the result of multiplying the figures in column B by the corresponding ones in column C. For example:

L25 (V) +B25*C25

The results are totaled in cell L41:

L41 (V) @SUM(L16...L40)

The figures from column B are squared in column M. For example, cell M25 contains the formula:

M25 (V) +B25*B25

These results are added, and new totals are displayed in cell M41:

M41 (V) @SUM(M16...M40)

After these calculations have been performed, the model can compute the remaining statistics. The standard deviation is computed by the formula:

E51 (V) (K41/E46)^.5

To perform the linear regression, select a value for the independent variable and enter it in cell E53; 26 was chosen for this example. Then, the value of the dependent variable can be calculated in cell E54 using the rather lengthy formula:

```
E54 /F$ (V) (((((B41*C41)/E46)-L41)/((B41^2/E46)-M41))
    *E53)+((C41/E46)-(((((C41*B41)/E46)-L41)/(((B41^2)
    /E46)-M41))*(B41/E46)))
```

Using the Model

To use this model, enter the data items you want to evaluate in column C. When they are all in place, recalculate by typing ! To perform a regression analysis, enter a target data item in cell E53 and recalculate. You may want to perform this operation several times to evaluate the expected values at a number of different data points.

You can save the model by typing `/SSFilename (CR)` and print it by typing `>A10 (CR) /PPG54 (CR)`.

If you track statistics on a regular basis, a model like this one can be valuable. If you keep monthly sales records for each salesperson, you can use this model to build one that will allow you to enter the latest numbers and adjust the statistical formulas to compute updated statistics.

Modifications

You can evaluate more or less data items than the 24 presented in the example by inserting or deleting rows. Be sure to adjust the cell references in the formulas to reflect your changes.

Calculating Growth Capacity

How fast can your business grow? The growth potential of any business depends on many factors, including the availability of outside financing, profitability, and the percentage of profits paid out in dividends. One way to analyze the growth capacity of your business is to develop financial projections based on realistic assumptions about the factors that constrain growth. This VisiCalc Growth Capacity Calculator model can help you do that.

Principles

A company's sales cannot grow without the necessary financial resources. In other words, "You have to spend money to make money." Before sales can increase, a company must obtain enough working capital (cash) to hire more workers, buy additional raw materials, or invest in new equipment. Higher sales also lead to higher accounts receivable balances that must be financed. In most cases, the increased expenses will be incurred before the first dollar of increased revenue comes through the door. This is true for both service and manufacturing firms.

Building a financial growth model involves making projections about future financing based on the following factors:

1. The debt-to-equity ratio (See the Ratio Analyzer in Chapter 5 for more information.)
2. The interest rate paid on long-term debt
3. The company's profitability
4. The tax rate on the company's earnings
5. The percentage of earnings distributed as dividends

Sales growth financing can come from three sources: selling stock, borrowing from a bank or other outside lender, or reinvesting profits earned by the firm. Each alternative has its strengths and weaknesses. Because you don't have to pay dividends or interest on stock, it is a cheap way to raise money. But selling stock takes some of the control over the business away from the owners. In addition, new stock issues are feasible only if the company can offer real value for each share. Borrowing does not require sacrificing ownership interest, but it can become unsafe or impossible when debt begins to exceed a certain percentage of a firm's total capitalization. Reinvestment of earnings is the least expensive way to raise money, but it requires both profitability *and* investors who are willing to forgo high dividends.

Typically, a firm begins its life with a combination of stock and debt, which, as time passes, is supplemented by retained earnings. Occasionally, a company will be capitalized exclusively with stock. Let's examine why this is not always the best policy. The term "leverage" describes the advantages of careful borrowing. Here's an example of how leverage works. Joe Smith starts Company A by investing $100 of his hard-earned cash. In its first year of operations, Company A makes a profit of $10. Joe Jones, another budding entrepreneur, starts company B at the same time, investing $50 of his own money and borrowing $50 from his bank. Jones' business also makes a profit (in this case, before interest) of $10. After he pays his interest of $4, he is left with $6, or $4 less than Smith. But notice that Smith has $100 invested in Company A, whereas Jones has only $50 in Company B. Smith's $10 profit represents a 10% return on his investment, but Jones' $6 is a 12% return on his smaller investment. Jones has used a lever—the bank loan—to increase the earning power of his investment.

If Jones had invested only $1 and had borrowed $99, his return would have been even higher. But would you lend money to Jones under those circumstances? Probably not. Most lenders want a "cushion" of stock to protect their loan from any losses the borrower may incur. The realities of borrowing can constrain a company from realizing the maximum leverage on its investment.

Debt creates an expense—interest—that affects the third source of financing, the firm's profits. In general, debt is advantageous as long as the company earns a rate of return that is higher than the interest rate it pays on the loan. This is the case in our example. If the loan does not create a positive net return, then the excess interest expense will reduce the amount of earnings that can be plowed back into the firm.

Taxes and dividends also affect the amount of profit that can be retained in the business because they drain cash from the business that could be used to finance growth. As a result, growing firms frequently pay no dividends. Taxes are unavoidable, but every attempt should be made to minimize and defer as much of the tax burden as possible under the law.

The Model

All of the factors discussed above are included in the financial growth model. This model analyzes the growth capacity of a business over a five-year period, given certain assumptions about the company's debt-to-equity ratio, its profitability, the tax rate, and the dividend payout percentage. The model has three sections: CAPITALIZATION, PROFITABILITY, and EARNINGS AND DIVIDENDS.

The CAPITALIZATION section begins at cell A8. Columns A through C contain labels that define the cells in each row. The rows that begin with an asterisk "*" indicate where you should enter your assumptions about each factor.

Cell D12 shows the current amount of equity invested in our sample business, including stock and any profits retained from past years' operations. Cell D13 contains the amount of debt owed by the firm.

VisiCalc uses the inputs in cells D12 and D13 to compute the company's acceptable debt-to-equity ratio in cell D11, using the formula:

```
D11 /F$ (V) +D13/D12
```

Cell D15 contains the formula:

D15 (V) +D12+D13

which represents the total capitalization of the sample firm. The cells in row 18 show the interest rates to be paid on the company's debt in each of the next five years. You must enter a rate for each year. If you have loans at several different rates, these cells should contain a weighted average of all the loan rates.

The next section of the model, PROFITABILITY, begins at cell A22. Cell D25 shows the profit earned for the past year, before interest and taxes.

VisiCalc computes the annual interest expense in row 26 by multiplying total debt by the interest rate. For example, cell D26 contains the formula:

D26 (V) +D18*D13/100

Cell D28 subtracts the interest expense from the profit before interest and taxes using the formula:

D28 (V) +D25-D26

Cell D31 is also an input cell. It displays the amount of income tax paid this year by our sample business. VisiCalc uses this amount to compute the actual tax rate. This calculation is performed in cell D29 by the formula:

D29 /FI (V) +D31/D28*100

Cell D33 shows the profit after both interest and taxes have been deducted, which is computed as:

D33 (V) +D28-D31

The next section of the model, EARNINGS AND DIVIDENDS, begins at cell A37. Cell D41 holds the dividend amount paid out to the firm's stockholders during the current year. VisiCalc computes the target dividend payout percentage in cell D40:

D40 /FI (V) +D41/D33*100

Cell D43 calculates the amount of income reinvested in the firm in the current year. This amount equals net income after interest, dividends, and taxes have been deducted. Cell D43 is defined as:

D43 /FI (V) +D33-D41

The final row in this section, row 46, computes the net return on equity for each of the five years by dividing the profit after tax, but before dividends (row 33), by the company's total equity (row 12). For example, cell D46 contains the formula:

D46 /F$ (V) +D33/D12*100

Row 46 helps measure the effect any changes made to the model will have on the return earned by the stockholders.

Now move back up the worksheet to cell E11. Notice that this cell is defined as:

E11 /F$ (V) +D11

Cell F11 is then defined as:

F11 /F$ (V) +E11

In fact, each cell in row 11 is defined as equal to the ratio calculated in the preceding cell in that row. VisiCalc will assume that the same debt-to-equity ratio will be used for each year in the future, unless you change it.

The same relationship is used in row 25 (profit before interest and taxes). For example, the formula in cell E25 is:

E25 /FI (V) +D25/D15*E15

Cell F25 is defined as:

F25 /FI (V) +E25/E15*F15

This scheme is used to define rows 29 (effective tax rate) and 40 (target dividend payout percentage). The formulas in each cell refer back to the cells immediately to their left, keeping these target relationships constant until you decide to change them. Move the cursor to cell E12, which displays the equity invested in the business at the beginning of the second year. This cell contains the formula:

E12 /FI (V) +D12+D43

In other words, the equity in one year equals the equity from the previous period plus any earnings retained in the business from that year. Therefore, the equity in cell E12 is $717 more than that in cell D12. The $717 represents new capital, which can be used to finance sales growth. It also qualifies the business for additional debt financing. Assuming that the debt-to-equity ratio is maintained at .8, $717 of new equity will allow the company to borrow $574 of new debt. In the real world, this borrowing would not take place all at once, such as on the first day of the new year. But if a company were attempting to "grow" its sales as fast as possible, it would certainly want to consider maintaining its debt at the highest acceptable level by borrowing more money. Cell E13 reflects this assumption with the formula:

E13 /FI (V) +E11*E12

Columns F, G, and H repeat the same relationships.

Using the Model

Take a step back to review what this model does. The model calculates various percentages from a few bits of actual first-year data you enter in column D. These percentages are then used to compute projections for sales, dividends, and taxes in columns E, F, G, and H. Retained earnings from each year carry over to the equity line in the next year, which increases the company's level of indebtedness to the degree specified by the debt-to-equity ratio.

To use the model, enter your data in the following cells:

Current Debt:	D12
Current Equity:	D13
Interest Rates on Debt:	D18 to H18
Current Year Tax Expense:	D31
Current Year Dividend Payout:	D41

As you review the formulas in this model, you will notice that there are several "forward references"—cells that depend on other cells that are either below them or to their right. These cells will not calculate properly on one pass through the model unless recalculation is set to proceed by columns (/GOC).

Recalculate the model by typing ! and review the results. You can save the model by typing `/SSFilename (CR)` and print it by typing `>A8 (CR) /PPH47 (CR)`.

Be sure to "play" with the model to see what effect variations have on your assumptions. For example, look at cell D11. This value should be your present actual debt-to-equity ratio. Is this number as high as you would like? Can you take advantage of leverage by increasing the amount of debt on your books? Or, is the number too high? Do you feel overburdened by the amount of debt you are carrying? If so, make changes in the future periods to adjust this figure.

The projection can be altered either by changing the assumptions computed the first year, or by altering one of the model's "constants"—the debt-to-equity ratio, the tax rate, or the dividend payout percentage. Changing any of these assumptions is easy. Move the cursor to the appropriate cell and enter your new number. For example, suppose that you want to increase your debt-to-equity ratio from .8 to 1 in the fourth year. Move the cursor to cell G11 and enter a 1. Now recalculate the model. Notice that the ratio in cell H11 is now also 1.00. If you want a different ratio in column H, you must make the change manually.

Managing Queues

Every company deals with waiting lines, or queues, at some point in its operations. When you think of a waiting line, you may picture people waiting for a service, such as the line at a bank teller's window, but there are other kinds of queues: machines waiting to be repaired, products waiting to be packaged, programs waiting to be run on a computer, and so on.

As a manager, your goal is to keep waiting time in the queue to a minimum without sacrificing the efficiency of the service system. Queuing theory, as used in VisiCalc models, can help you evaluate your current queuing system and decide when to increase service capacity to meet growing demand. It can answer such questions as: Do my customers wait too long for service? What is the typical backlog of orders waiting to be processed? Should I hire extra workers during the busy season? If so, how many? The *two* models in this section can help you evaluate many different alternatives for queue management to decide which one is best for your business.

Principles

The waiting time in a queue depends on two factors:

(1) Demand—How many people or items require service in a given period

(2) Capacity—How many people or items can be serviced in a given period

To use queuing theory, you will need the demand and capacity information for the system you want to evaluate. For example, if you are the manager of a customer service department that handles telephone calls from people placing orders and asking about products, you will need to know the average number of calls received in an hour, and the average number of calls that can be handled by your department in an hour. You may want to collect separate data for peak service hours and other special times. Some businesses should consider queuing management from a different standpoint. For example, a frame shop may want to find out how many pictures, on average, are brought in each week for framing, and how many can be framed in a week given the current staff and facilities.

After the demand and capacity information has been collected, you can use queuing theory to find the average waiting time for your queue, its average length, the average service time, and what percentage of the service system is being utilized. Using this information, you can vary some of the factors and study the effect on the overall system.

Returning to the customer service example, suppose that you want to cut down the average waiting time for each caller. You may want to consider two possibilities: adding another person to take calls, or streamlining call-handling procedures so that the current number of employees can answer more calls per hour. Either or both of these possibilities can be incorporated into this VisiCalc model to allow you to study their effect on waiting time.

The Models

These models evaluate queue management for two basic types of systems: a single-station service system, and a multistation service system. One example of a single-station service system is a dentist's office where a single dentist handles all patients. A multistation service system may be a fast-food restaurant where several people take orders and collect money. Because the formulas for multiple stations are more complex than those for a single station, the two models will be explained separately.

Each model has two sections: ASSUMPTIONS and SOLUTIONS. The ASSUMPTIONS section begins at cell A10. Cell G14 contains the first assumption, the average number of arrivals per hour, which is equivalent to the demand for service that will be placed on the system in a given period. Although one hour is the period used in these models, it can be changed to minutes, quarter hours, days, weeks, or whatever best fits your queuing situation.

The second assumption, entered in cell G15, is the average service capacity per hour, which is the number of individuals who can receive service during the given period. For the multistation model, this figure should indicate the hourly service capacity of each service station. For example, in a fast-food restaurant, the number of customers handled by each cashier in an hour would be entered here.

The number of stations providing service must be entered in cell G16 in the multistation model. The term "station" in this model refers to an individual service provider. It may be a teller window in a bank or a checkout counter in a grocery store.

Caution: The average number of arrivals in a period must always be less than the average number that can be served in that period. That is, the number input in cell G14 must always be less than the number input in G15 (or, in the multistation model, less than the value in cell G15 times the value in G16). Otherwise, the queue would grow longer and longer as time passed, until it was finally (at least in theory) infinitely long.

Be sure to set both models to recalculate by row, by typing /GR.

Single-Station Facility Model

Let's look at the SOLUTIONS section, cell A22, in the single-station facility model. The first two figures in this section, idle time percentage and utilization percentage, indicate how efficiently the service system is being used. The idle time percentage is the percentage of time that nothing or no one is waiting in the queue or being serviced. It is computed by the formula:

G24 /F$ (V) (1-(G14/G15))*100

Utilization percentage is calculated by subtracting the idle time percentage from 1, using the formula:

G25 /F$ (V) 100-G24

Cell G26 holds the average amount of time required to service each person or item in the queue. It is computed by dividing the 60 minutes in an hour by the hourly service capacity. Therefore, the formula for cell G26 is:

G26 /F$ (V) 60/G15

The next figure, expected number in system, represents the average number of people or items being serviced and waiting for service at any time. It is computed by the formula:

G27 (V) +G14/(G15-G14)

The expected number in the queue, as displayed in cell G28, represents the expected length of the waiting line, and is computed as:

G28 /FI (V) (G14^2)/(G15*(G15-G14))

The average waiting time is computed by dividing the length of the queue by the number of arrivals per hour. The result of this computation was multiplied by 60 to express the waiting time in minutes rather than as a fraction of an hour.

G29 /F$ (V) (G28/G14)*60

The last computation made for a single-station system is the probability of whether the number in the system will be greater than the figure you enter. Remember that the number in the system equals the sum of the number receiving service and the number waiting in the queue. Enter the number that you want to evaluate in cell D31. In this example, we used 5. Cell G28 tells us that the expected number in the system at any time is 5. If we want to know what the chances are of having more than this number, we use the formula:

G31 /FI (V) ((G14/G15)^(D31-1))*100

The result tells us that there is a 48% chance of having more than 5—the expected number—waiting in the queue or being serviced.

Multistation Facility Model

The FACTORIAL TABLE, located at cell K1, contains @LOOKUP tables that allow VisiCalc to solve formulas which contain a factorial expression (like some of the multistation queuing formulas).

A factorial, denoted by an exclamation point (!) after a number, is interpreted as the product of the number multiplied by each positive integer less than that number. For example, 5 factorial would be denoted by 5! and interpreted as 5*4*3*2*1 = 120.

Because VisiCalc has no built-in factorial function, a table of factorial values was created for the numbers 1 through 25. This table is very easy to construct. In one column, list the numbers for which you want factorial values. In this example, the numbers 1 through 25 are listed in cells L6 through L30.

Each factorial value can be based on the factorial for the number that immediately precedes it. For example, four factorial (4!) is equal to 4 x 3! We can begin computing the factorial values by entering a 1 in cell M6. Then, in cell M7, we use the formula:

M7 (V) +M6*L7

This formula makes the value for 2! appear in cell M7. Using relative values, you can replicate the formula down through cell M30. Because the factorial values become large quickly, many of them will appear in scientific notation.

The numbers in cells N6 through N30 of the table compute the formula for idle time percentage, on which some of the other formulas for multistation queues are based. The formula contains the expression:

$$\frac{(A/C)^1}{1!} + \frac{(A/C)^2}{2!} + \ldots + \frac{(A/C)^{S-1}}{(S-1)!}$$

where:

A = Average Number of Arrivals per Hour
C = Average Service Capacity per Hour
S = Number of Service Stations

Clearly, this expression cannot be handled by VisiCalc's built-in functions. Column N of the table computes a sum based on the expression and the number of service stations as given in cell G16. To build this part of the table, the following formula is entered in cell L6:

N6 (V) @IF((G16-1)>=L6,((G14/G15)^L6)/M6,0)

The same formula is replicated through cell N30. Cells L6 and M6 are adjusted for each replication, but cells G14, G15, and G16 remain unchanged. Cell N32 displays the total of cells N6 through N30, using the formula:

```
N32 (V) @SUM(N6...N31)
```

The first calculation in the SOLUTIONS section of the model, which begins at cell A30, is the idle time percentage, in cell G34. It is computed by the formula:

```
G34 /F$ (V) (((G14/G15)^G16)/(@LOOKUP(G16,L6...L30)
            *(1-((G14/G15)/G16)))+1+N32)^(-1)*100
```

The result is subtracted from 1 to obtain the utilization percentage. This percentage is displayed in cell G35, which contains the formula:

```
G35 /F$ (V) 100-G34
```

The formula for computing average service time is the same for both the multi- and the single-station models. It is entered in cell G36 as:

```
G36 /F$ (V) 60/G15
```

The expected number in the queue is displayed in cell G37 and computed by the formula:

```
G37 /FI (V) ((G14/G15)^(G16+1))
            /((G16*(@LOOKUP(G16,L6...L30))
            *(1-((G14 /G15)/G16)^2)))*G34 /100
```

The result of this calculation is used to compute the average waiting time in the queue. This figure appears in cell G38, which contains the formula:

```
G38 /FI (V) (G37/G14)*60
```

Using the Model

The instructions for the single-station and the multistation models are similar. To start, enter the ASSUMPTIONS in the appropriate cells and recalculate by typing ! Next, save the model by typing `/SSFilename (CR)`.

The commands for printing the two models are slightly different. Type >`A10 (CR) /PPH31 (CR)` to print the single-station model and >`A10 (CR) /PPH38 (CCR)` to print the multistation one.

You can use both of these models to determine the effects of increasing your service capacity. For example, if you now have one person handling phone-in orders, the single-station model will evaluate the service being provided by this one person. You can then use the multistation model to see what would happen to callers' waiting time if two people were receiving phone-in orders.

Modifications

This model can be modified to evaluate queue information using a basis other than one hour. To do the modification, change the assumptions at the top of the models to reflect the new basis. For example, to analyze the number of machines brought in for repair each day, your assumptions should read: Average Number of Arrivals per Day and Average Service Capacity per Day. Then, change the average service time and average waiting time to an hourly or daily basis.

The commands for printing the two reports are slightly different. [illegible]

You can use both of these models to determine the effects of [illegible] one person [illegible] will evaluate the service [illegible]

Modifications

This model can be modified to [illegible] other [illegible] models [illegible] the number of [illegible] each day [illegible] average service time [illegible]

Budgeting for a New Venture

New venture budgets are used frequently by product managers, sales managers, and entrepreneurs to analyze the potential of a new product or business. New venture budgets are also used by venture capitalists to determine investment potential.

Unfortunately, developing such a budget can be a complex process. The budget must include all revenues and expenses associated with the new venture and calculate expected profits and retained earnings over a certain period. Because expectations about these factors can vary widely and change rapidly, start-up budgets are usually changed many times before they are finalized. With VisiCalc and this budget model, however, you can build and modify budget projections quickly and easily.

Principles

The profit potential of any new product or business depends on two factors: how much money is expected to flow in, and how much is expected to flow out. The level of inflows and outflows depends on the number of units sold of a product or service, unit price, unit cost, selling costs, the overhead level that must be maintained to support the sales effort, and so on. Let's take a look at some important relationships that affect the profitability of a new product.

The gross margin of a product equals its sale price minus its cost and direct selling expenses. If the product is purchased and resold, both the cost and sales price are easily measured.

Estimating the true cost for manufactured goods, however, is more difficult. Gross margin equals the real income (the value added, so to speak) that is gained by selling a product. All expenses must be paid out of this amount. Anything left over after expenses is profit.

The direct selling cost of a product, which may include sales commissions and shipping and handling costs, varies from product to product. In general, direct selling cost is estimated as a percentage or a fixed dollar amount per unit sold.

Overhead expenses can also be linked to sales. Selling more units requires more support staff, more space to house that staff, and so on. These relationships are not as closely linked to the level of sales as gross margin, but an accurate model will find the "stepping points" where these expenses increase, and include them.

The goal of this model is to determine the profit level a product will generate. Profit is the net income (sales minus expenses) generated in a period. Retained earnings equals the accumulated profit earned by a product across many periods. Naturally, both numbers vary with revenues and expenses.

To build a start-up budget, you must analyze the relationships between cash inflows and outflows. In an ideal world, all interrelationships would be incorporated into the model. Unfortunately, not even VisiCalc can include every relationship, although the following model does include all the ones discussed above.

The Model

This model makes projections for a product that consists of two components sold together as a single package. You might think of it as a specialized computer system where the two components are hardware and software. Where unit sales are projected, each unit is composed of these two separate components.

The model has three sections: PRODUCT PRICE AND COST DATA, EXPENSE DATA, and PROJECTIONS. The PRODUCT PRICE section, which begins at cell A10, contains data about the variable costs and sales price for the product being analyzed. The unit costs of components 1 and 2 equal either the total variable manufacturing costs, or the purchase costs of the components. These figures are entered in cells E15 and E16 respectively. Cells D15 and D16 contain the individual selling prices for the components, even though they will be sold together as a single package. The package price is calculated in cell D18 by the formula:

D18 (V) +D15+D16

Cell E18 shows the total cost of the product:

E18 (V) +E15+E16

Cells F15 and F16 compute the gross margin earned on each component by subtracting the cost of the part from its sale price. For example, cell F16 contains the formula:

F16 (V) +D16-E16

Cells G15 and G16 convert these dollar margins into percentages by dividing them by the components' price. For example, cell G16 is defined as:

G16 /FI (V) +F16/D16*100

The second section of the model, EXPENSE DATA, begins at cell A22. It shows the assumptions about payroll, office, and advertising expenses that will be used later in the model. The first expense, sales commissions, is expressed as a percentage of the total unit price. In this example, an 8% commission will be paid for each unit sold, so 8 is entered in cell D24.

Assumptions about salary and wage overhead expenses are located in cells D25, D26, D27, and F26. Cell D25 contains the base quarterly salary expense. Cell D26 shows the increase in salary that is anticipated after the sale of a certain number of units, which is displayed in cell F25. Finally, cell D27 contains the assumed wage overhead rate. Wage overhead includes such items as payroll taxes and employee benefits.

Office expense assumptions are entered in a similar way in cells D29, D30, and F30. Cell D29 holds the base office expense number, and cell D30 shows the expected increase in this expense. The number of units that must be sold before this increase can take effect is shown in cell F30.

Implicit in our estimates for salaries and office expenses is the assumption that expenses will increase once our new product begins to sell. The increased salary may be used to hire a customer service representative or more order entry clerks; the increased office expenses reflect the extra rent and supplies needed to support these people.

The last expense item, advertising, is defined as a percentage of sales. The assumed percentage should be entered in cell D32. We have also included a first-year lump sum advertising expense in cell G32.

The PROJECTIONS section of the model, beginning at cell A35, uses the assumptions to build a sales and expense projection for the new product. The first year's projections assume that no units are sold, and that no variable costs are incurred. Significant overhead costs, however, are incurred. This year is the development and start-up year. After the first year, projections of revenues and expenses are made on a quarterly basis for two more years.

The first step in making projections is to estimate unit sales for each quarter. These amounts are entered in row 42, Unit Sales. For the second and third years, VisiCalc totals the quarterly unit sales to obtain annual unit sales. Total unit sales for the second year appears in cell I42, which contains the formula:

```
I42 (V) @SUM(E42...H42)
```

A similar formula is used in cell N42 to total unit sales for the third year.

In row 43, unit sales are converted to dollar sales by multiplying the unit sales projections by the sales price per unit, as given in cell D18. For example, dollar sales for the second quarter of the second year, which appear in cell F43, are calculated by the formula:

```
F43 (V) +F42*D18
```

Row 45 displays the cost of goods sold. These figures are calculated by multiplying unit sales by the total cost per unit from cell E18. For example, the cost of goods sold for the first quarter of the second year is displayed in cell E44 by the formula:

```
E45 (V) +E42*E18
```

Direct sales expenses, as displayed in row 46, are calculated by multiplying the sales commission percentage from cell D24 by the dollar sales figure in row 43. For the second year, second quarter, these expenses are calculated by the formula:

F46 (V) (F43*D24)/100

Next, VisiCalc computes the gross margin, in row 48, by subtracting direct sales expense and cost of goods sold from dollar sales. For example, for the first quarter of the year, gross margin is calculated by the formula:

E48 (V) +E43-E45-E46

Operating expenses, listed in rows 51 through 54, are based on the estimates entered in the EXPENSE DATA section. For example, cell D51, which displays total salary expenses for the first year, contains the formula:

D51 (V) (D25+@IF(@SUM(D42...D42)>F26,D26,0))*4

(Multiplying by four converts the number from a quarterly to an annual amount.)

Salary expenses for the first quarter of the second year are computed by the formula:

E51 (V) (D25+@IF(@SUM(D42...E42)>F26,D26,0))

These formulas mean: the salary expense for the period equals the base salary shown in cell D25, plus the amount shown in cell D26 if the total number of units sold to date exceeds the number in cell F26. Whenever the cumulative number of units sold exceeds the number in cell F26, the additional salary will be posted automatically to the cells in row 51.

The total salary expense for the first year is shown in cell I51:

I51 (V) @SUM(E51...H51)

Cells I52, I53, and I54 use the same formula to compute annual totals for wage overhead, office expenses, and advertising costs. Wage overhead is computed by multiplying the total salary expense in each period by the wage overhead percentage shown in cell D26.

For example, cell E52 is defined as:

E52 (V) (D27/100*E51)

The office expenses in row 53 are also related to our expense assumptions. For example, in the first quarter of the second year, the formula for computing office expenses is:

E53 (V) (D29+@IF(@SUM(D42...E42)>F30,D30,0))

This formula is almost identical to the one used to compute salary expense and works the same way.

Advertising expense for the first year equals the first-year lump sum specified in cell G32. The formula in cell D54 is:

D54 (V) +G32

Quarterly advertising expense in each of the following periods is based on the sales volume for that period and the percentage found in cell D32. For example, cell E54 contains the formula:

E54 (V) +E43*D32/100

Total operating expenses, shown in row 56, are computed as the sum of the individual operating expenses. For example, the formula for total operating expenses for the first quarter of the second year is:

E56 (V) @SUM(E51...E55)

Net income is calculated by subtracting total operating expenses from gross margin. The formula for calculating net income for the first quarter of the second year is:

E58 (V) +E48-E56

The retained earnings figure in row 60 represents the cumulative net income generated by the product being analyzed. In the first year, retained earnings equal net income. For the following periods, retained earnings are computed by adding the net income for the current period to the previous period's retained earnings. For example, retained earnings for the first quarter of the second year are calculated by the formula:

E60 (V) +E58+D60

Column O shows the three-year total for each income and expense item. For example, cell O42 is defined as:

O42 (V) +N42+I42+D42

Cell O58 computes the total net income for the three-year period with the formula:

O58 (V) +N58+I58+D58

Using the Model

To use this model, you must first develop assumptions for sales and expenses, then enter them in the appropriate cells in the PRODUCT DATA and EXPENSE DATA sections. Your projected quarterly unit sales figures should be entered in row 41.

After the data is entered, recalculate the model by typing ! You can save the model by typing `/SSFilename CR)` and print it by typing `>A10 (CR) /PPH60 (CR)`.

Be sure to take advantage of VisiCalc's "what if" powers when using this model. Change your price, cost, and expense assumptions, then examine the changes in net income and retained earnings. Some of the "what if" questions you may want to consider are:

1. What if unit sales are not as high as I expect?
2. What if I raise the price and sell fewer units? What if I lower the price?
3. What if fixed and variable costs increase by 10% each year?
4. What if start-up and development costs in the first year are much higher than I expect?
5. What if it takes more than one year to get the product to market?

Analyzing these and other scenarios will make this model a more effective and valuable planning tool for your business.

Modifications

This model can be modified to provide more information on product profitability. For example, the net present value of the net income figures can be calculated using VisiCalc's @NPV function.

In our example, no tax effects are considered. Because of loss carry-forward, taxes would not be paid until the fourth quarter of the third year, when they would begin to reduce the amount of the retained earnings account shown in the example. You may want to include a tax table in your version of the model.

Determining Price-Volume Relationships

What price should I charge for my product? Almost every businessperson faces that tough decision at some point.

Generally, there is a trade-off between charging a high price, with the risk of losing sales volume, and charging a low price to gain market volume, with the chance that you will not be able to cover costs. When a new product is introduced, the pricing decision can be particularly difficult because of the uncertainty about how well the product will sell, and what price the market will bear.

Sometimes the price-volume relationship for a particular product can be determined by test marketing. In most cases, however, assumptions must be made about what the relationship will be.

Examining numerous assumptions to come up with the "most likely" price-volume scenario can be accomplished quickly and easily with VisiCalc.

Principles

The ideal price for a product, one that maximizes profits, will be different under different market conditions and cost structures. Unfortunately, the relationship between price and profit is not linear. Raising the price of a product will sometimes increase profit, but at other times reduce it. Even if price and volume move up and down together, they rarely move in direct proportion to each other.

A demand curve represents the price-volume relationship. In most markets, as the price increases, fewer people buy the product. Of course, each market has characteristics that help shape the price-volume relationship, including the amount and intensity of competition, the financial resources of the customers, the relative importance of the product to them, and their ability to perceive significant differences between competitive products. The classic demand curve demonstrates this price-volume relationship:

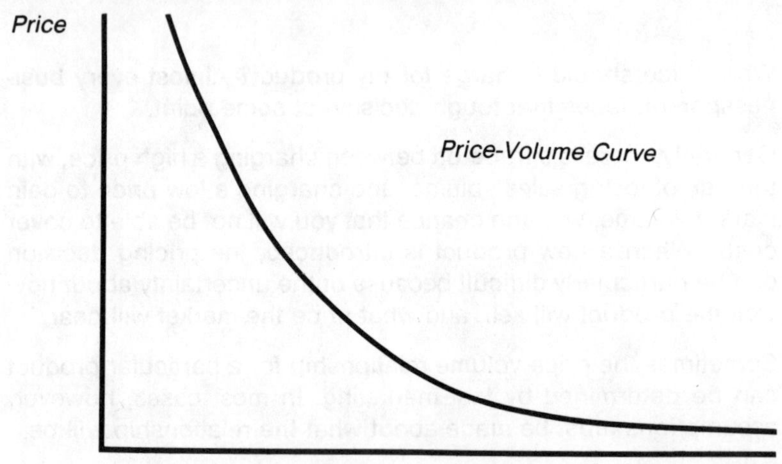

As unit price increases, the number of units sold decreases, and vice versa. The two end points of the curve illustrate the "lowest volume" and "highest volume" cases. In most cases, however, these extreme points can be dismissed as lying outside the "relevant range" of realistic opportunities available to the seller. For example, a car dealer could sell all the cars in his inventory if he charged only $10 per car, but he would lose his shirt in the process. On the other hand, the dealer could have a tremendous profit margin if he charged $50,000 per car, but it is doubtful that he would sell even one.

Most businesses want to find the price-volume relationship that will maximize profits. That relationship usually lies within a narrow range on the demand curve. The trick is to pin down the point with a careful analysis of prices, costs, and sales volumes.

The Model

This model has two sections: ASSUMPTIONS and SOLUTIONS. The ASSUMPTIONS section begins at cell A10. Cell D13 is used to enter the estimated fixed costs associated with a product. Because fixed costs do not vary with changes in sales volume, only one figure for fixed costs is needed. The variable costs per unit are entered in cell D15. This number should be expressed as a dollar amount. The sample model shows a product with per-unit variable costs of $.35.

Rows 17 and 19 are used to enter the five price-volume combinations you select for testing. Notice that in the example, the expected sales volume decreases as the price increases.

In the SOLUTIONS section, which begins at cell A22, VisiCalc computes the total dollar sales, variable costs, net income, and return on sales for each price selected. In row 24, dollar sales for each price-volume pair are computed by multiplying the sales price by the expected volume. For example, cell D24 contains the formula:

D24 (V) +D17*D19

The same formula is repeated in cells E24, F24, G24, and H24 with relative references. Total variable costs are computed in cells D25 through H25. This calculation is made by multiplying the expected sales volume in row 19 by the variable cost factor in cell D15. For example, the formula for cell D25 is:

D25 (V) +D15*D19

Similarly, the formula in cell G25 is:

G25 (V) +D15*G19

Now look at row 26. Each cell in this row is defined in terms of the fixed cost assumption made in cell D13. For example, cell F26 is defined as:

F26 (V) +D13

The variable and fixed costs are subtracted from the dollar sales figures to obtain a net income for each price point. These computations appear in cells D28 through H28. For example, the formula in cell D28 is:

D28 (V) +D24-D25-D26

In row 31, the model calculates the return on sales for each price-point combination. Return on sales is an expression of net income as a percentage of sales, and it is calculated by dividing net income (row 28) by dollar sales (row 24) and multiplying by 100. For example, the formula in cell D31 is:

D31 /FI (V) (D28/D24)*100

This formula is repeated, using relative references, in cells E31, F31, G31, and H31.

Using the Model

Before sitting down with this model, you will need to accumulate data about fixed and variable costs and select several different sets of price-volume combinations for testing. After the data has been assembled, enter it in the appropriate locations and recalculate by typing ! You can save the model by typing `/SSFilename (CR)` and print the ASSUMPTIONS and SOLUTIONS sections by typing `>A10 (CR) /PPH32 (CR)`.

The key to success with this model is the extensive use of "what if" analysis. By raising and lowering your expectations for sales volume at each price, you can measure the effects of changes in your sales volume on your return on sales.

If you are lucky enough to have a graphics program, consider plotting several sets of price-volume pairs, using a line chart.

Conclusion

In this book we have examined 20 ways that VisiCalc can be used to help you run your business. We have learned a great deal about the powers and capabilities of VisiCalc. We have also learned about some of its limitations.

The most important thing we have learned is that spreadsheet software is a tool not merely for building projections and budgets, but also for *managing* nearly every part of a business, from cash to fixed assets. We hope you now have a different impression of VisiCalc and are already thinking of innovative applications of your own.

More and more companies are using spreadsheets to meet their accounting and business management needs. Many companies use VisiCalc to spread their checkbook every month, to track the collections of their accounts receivable, to prepare invoices and purchase orders, and to perform a multitude of other accounting functions. Although none of the current crop of spreadsheet software is powerful enough to automate fully an accounting system, there are literally hundreds of accounting-related functions that can be done on VisiCalc or SuperCalc.

Because of its flexibility, ease of use, and power, spreadsheet software is probably the most widely used application for microcomputers. Most exciting of all, it is likely that the limits of spreadsheet software are still nowhere in sight. The signs are that a new generation of superspreadsheets will expand the use of spreadsheets into many new areas. As newer programs like Multiplan™, ProCalc™, 1-2-3™, and advanced versions of VisiCalc become available, the use of spreadsheets in all aspects of business management is bound to increase. These new programs overcome many of the current limitations of VisiCalc and other first generation spreadsheets. The new programs also have enough power and flexibility to be used for extremely sophisticated applications, such as payroll and general ledger accounting, but retain the attractive features of VisiCalc: visual orientation, ease of use, and low price.

As spreadsheeting develops in importance, you can look to Que Corporation for two sources of information for spreadsheet users: books about spreadsheeting; and preconfigured spreadsheet models, such as Que's *CalcSheets*™ *for Business. CalcSheets* present on diskette VisiCalc Models discussed in this book, and other models. *CalcSheets* come with extensive documentation and are ready to run on your computer so that you can put the power of VisiCalc to work quickly for your particular spreadsheeting needs. Future models will provide applications in the areas of personal financial planning, tax planning, accounting, banking, and insurance.

Whether your interest is information about spreadsheeting or actual applications—or both, it is certain that prospects for the emerging field are exciting. Becoming a proficient spreadsheet user should help you to gain and maintain control over your business opportunities in ways that have never been possible before.

INDEX

The formulas used to calculate each number are listed below. They are read from bottom to top and right to left and are referenced by their location in the model.

```
>D115:"NTS >A107
>C115:"6.1 CONTE
>E114:"A93
>D114:"UCTIONS >
>C114:"5.1 INSTR
>E113:" >A73
>D113:"CILIATION
>C113:"4.1 RECON6
>G112:"9
>F112:"ITEMS >A5
>E112:"STANDING
>D112:"OUSLY OUT
>C112:"3.1 PREVI
>E111:"8
>D111:"G DATA >I
>C111:"2.1 CODIN
>D110:" DATA >A8
>C110:"1.1 CHECK
>H108:/-=
>G108:/-=
>F108:/-=
>E108:/-=
>D108:/-=
>C108:/-=
>B108:/-=
>A108:/-=
>H107:"Sheet 6.1
>A107:"CONTENTS
>H103:"85 (CR)
>G103:"(CR) /PPH
>F103:"ng: >A73
>E103:"N by typi
>D103:"NCILIATIO
>C103:"only RECO
>B103:"7) PRINT
>G102:"L85 (CR)
>F102:" (CR) /PP
>E102:"ping: >A8
>D102:"del by ty
>C102:"entire mo
>B102:"6) PRINT e
>E101:"ame (CR)
>D101:" /SSFilen
>C101:"y typing:
>B101:"5) SAVE b
>D100:"typing: l
>C100:"ULATE by
>B100:"4) RECALC
>H99:"ts
>G99:"nd Deposi
>F99:" Checks a
>E99:"tstanding
>D99:", CODE Ou
>C99:" of month
>B99:"3) At end
>D98:"A (>A8)
>C98:"CHECK DAT
>B98:"2) Enter
>F97:" (CR)
>E97:") /PPH115
>D97:" >A93 (CR
>C97:"y typing:
>B97:"         b
>E96:"ONTENTS
>D96:"ONS and C
>C96:"INSTRUCTI
>B96:"1) PRINT
>H94:/-=
>G94:/-=
>F94:/-=
>E94:/-=
>D94:/-=
>C94:/-=
>B94:/-=
>A94:/-=
>H93:"Sheet 5.1
>B93:"ONS
>A93:"INSTRUCTI
>G85:"  =======
>G84:+G78+G80-G81-G82
>C84:"nce:
>B84:"Bank Bala
>G83:"  -------
>G82:/F$0
>D82:"k Balance
>C82:"ts to Ban
>B82:"Adjustmen
>G81:/F$@SUM(L15...L72)
>D81:"t
>C81:"in Transi6
>B81:"Deposits
>G80:/F$@SUM(K15...K72)
>C80:"ng Checks
>B80:"Outstandi
>G78:+G75-G76
>D78:"nce
>C78:"Book Bala
>B78:"Adjusted
>G77:"  -------
>G76:/F$5
>D76:"r Credits
>C76:"ges and/o
>B76:"Bank Char
>G75:/F$+H57
>D75:"e:
>C75:"ok Balanc
>B75:"Ending Bo
>H74:/-=
>G74:/-=
>F74:/-=
>E74:/-=
>D74:/-=
>C74:/-=
>B74:/-=
>A74:/-=
>H73:"Sheet 4.1
>B73:"ATION
>A73:"RECONCILI
>L68:/F$@IF(J68=1,G68,0)
>K68:/F$@IF(I68=1,F68,0)
>F68:/F$112
>D68:"arage
>C68:"Parking G
>B68:/FL1002
>A68:"7-15
>L67:/F$@IF(J67=1,G67,0)
>K67:/F$@IF(I67=1,F67,0)
>F67:/F$200
>D67:"t
>C67:"Accountan
>B67:/FL990
>A67:"7-17
>L66:/F$@IF(J66=1,G66,0)
>K66:/F$@IF(I66=1,F66,0)
>F66:/F$345.67
>C66:"Landlord
>B66:/FL967
>A66:"7-12
>L65:/F$@IF(J65=1,G65,0)
>K65:/F$@IF(I65=1,F65,0)
>I65:1
>F65:/F$100
>D65:"pply Co.
>C65:"Office Su
>B65:/FL955
>A65:"6-5
>L64:" --------
>K64:" --------
>J64:" --------
>I64:" --------
>G64:" --------
>F64:" --------
>E64:"----------
>D64:"----------
>C64:"----------
>B64:"------
>A64:"----
>L63:" Transit
>K63:"  Checks
>J63:" Deposits
>I63:"  Checks
>G63:"  Amount
>F63:"  Amount
>D63:"scription
>C63:"        De
>B63:"Number
>A63:"Date
>L62:"   in
>K62:"   OS
>J62:"anding
>I62:"    Outst
>G62:"  Deposit
>F62:"  Check
>B62:"Check
>H60:/-=
>G60:/-=
>F60:/-=
>E60:/-=
>D60:/-=
>C60:/-=
>B60:/-=
>A60:/-=
>H59:"Sheet 2.1
>D59:"S
>C59:"DING ITEM
>B59:"Y OUTSTAN
>A59:"PREVIOUSL
>H57:+H56
>E57:" Balance:
>D57:"riod Book
>C57:"End of Pe
>L56:/F$@IF(J56=1,G56,0)
>K56:/F$@IF(I56=1,F56,0)
>H56:/F$+H55-F56+G56
>G56:/F$
>F56:/F$
>B56:/FL+B55+1
>A56:/FL
>L55:/F$@IF(J55=1,G55,0)
>K55:/F$@IF(I55=1,F55,0)
>H55:/F$+H54-F55+G55
>G55:/F$
>F55:/F$
>B55:/FL+B54+1
>L54:/F$@IF(J54=1,G54,0)
>K54:/F$@IF(I54=1,F54,0)
>H54:/F$+H53-F54+G54
>G54:/F$
>F54:/F$
>B54:/FL+B53+1
>L53:/F$@IF(J53=1,G53,0)
>K53:/F$@IF(I53=1,F53,0)
>H53:/F$+H52-F53+G53
>G53:/F$
>F53:/F$
>B53:/FL+B52+1
>L52:/F$@IF(J52=1,G52,0)
>K52:/F$@IF(I52=1,F52,0)
>H52:/F$+H51-F52+G52
>G52:/F$
>F52:/F$
>B52:/FL+B51+1
>L51:/F$@IF(J51=1,G51,0)
>K51:/F$@IF(I51=1,F51,0)
>H51:/F$+H50-F51+G51
>G51:/F$
>F51:/F$
>B51:/FL+B50+1
>L50:/F$@IF(J50=1,G50,0)
>K50:/F$@IF(I50=1,F50,0)
>H50:/F$+H49-F50+G50
>G50:/F$
>F50:/F$
>B50:/FL+B49+1
>L49:/F$@IF(J49=1,G49,0)
>K49:/F$@IF(I49=1,F49,0)
>H49:/F$+H48-F49+G49
>G49:/F$
>F49:/F$
>B49:/FL+B48+1
>L48:/F$@IF(J48=1,G48,0)
>K48:/F$@IF(I48=1,F48,0)
>H48:/F$+H47-F48+G48
>G48:/F$
>F48:/F$
>B48:/FL+B47+1
>L47:/F$@IF(J47=1,G47,0)
>K47:/F$@IF(I47=1,F47,0)
>H47:/F$+H46-F47+G47
>G47:/F$
>F47:/F$
>B47:/FL+B46+1
>L46:/F$@IF(J46=1,G46,0)
>K46:/F$@IF(I46=1,F46,0)
>H46:/F$+H45-F46+G46
>G46:/F$
>F46:/F$
>B46:/FL+B45+1
>L45:/F$@IF(J45=1,G45,0)
>K45:/F$@IF(I45=1,F45,0)
>H45:/F$+H44-F45+G45
>G45:/F$
>F45:/F$
>B45:/FL+B44+1
>L44:/F$@IF(J44=1,G44,0)
>K44:/F$@IF(I44=1,F44,0)
>H44:/F$+H43-F44+G44
>G44:/F$
>F44:/F$
>B44:/FL+B43+1
>L43:/F$@IF(J43=1,G43,0)
>K43:/F$@IF(I43=1,F43,0)
>H43:/F$+H42-F43+G43
>G43:/F$
>F43:/F$
>B43:/FL+B42+1
>L42:/F$@IF(J42=1,G42,0)
>K42:/F$@IF(I42=1,F42,0)
>H42:/F$+H41-F42+G42
>G42:/F$
>F42:/F$
>B42:/FL+B41+1
>L41:/F$@IF(J41=1,G41,0)
>K41:/F$@IF(I41=1,F41,0)
>H41:/F$+H40-F41+G41
>G41:/F$
>F41:/F$
>B41:/FL+B40+1
>L40:/F$@IF(J40=1,G40,0)
>K40:/F$@IF(I40=1,F40,0)
>H40:/F$+H39-F40+G40
>G40:/F$
>F40:/F$
>B40:/FL+B39+1
>L39:/F$@IF(J39=1,G39,0)
>K39:/F$@IF(I39=1,F39,0)
>H39:/F$+H38-F39+G39
>G39:/F$
>F39:/F$
>B39:/FL+B38+1
>L38:/F$@IF(J38=1,G38,0)
>K38:/F$@IF(I38=1,F38,0)
>H38:/F$+H37-F38+G38
>G38:/F$
>F38:/F$
>B38:/FL+B37+1
>L37:/F$@IF(J37=1,G37,0)
>K37:/F$@IF(I37=1,F37,0)
>H37:/F$+H36-F37+G37
>G37:/F$
>F37:/F$
>B37:/FL+B36+1
>L36:/F$@IF(J36=1,G36,0)
>K36:/F$@IF(I36=1,F36,0)
>H36:/F$+H35-F36+G36
>G36:/F$
>F36:/F$2164
>D36:"#5
>C36:"Supplier
>B36:/FL+B35+1
>A36:"8-30
>L35:/F$@IF(J35=1,G35,0)
>K35:/F$@IF(I35=1,F35,0)
>H35:/F$+H34-F35+G35
>G35:/F$
>F35:/F$150
>D35:"t
>C35:"Consultant
>B35:/FL+B34+1
>A35:"8-28
>L34:/F$@IF(J34=1,G34,0)
>K34:/F$@IF(I34=1,F34,0)
>H34:/F$+H33-F34+G34
>G34:/F$
>F34:/F$13.07
>C34:"Landlord
>B34:/FL+B33+1
>A34:"8-27
>L33:/F$@IF(J33=1,G33,0)
>K33:/F$@IF(I33=1,F33,0)
>J33:1
>H33:/F$+H32-F33+G33
>G33:/F$110
>F33:/F$288.75
>D33:"#4
>C33:"Supplier
>B33:/FL+B32+1
>A33:"8-25
>L32:/F$@IF(J32=1,G32,0)
>K32:/F$@IF(I32=1,F32,0)
>H32:/F$+H31-F32+G32
>G32:/F$3000
>F32:/F$2335
>D32:"#1
>C32:"Supplier
>B32:/FL+B31+1
>A32:"8-25
>L31:/F$@IF(J31=1,G31,0)
>K31:/F$@IF(I31=1,F31,0)
>H31:/F$+H30-F31+G31
>G31:/F$
>F31:/F$40
>C31:"Postage
>B31:/FL+B30+1
>A31:"8-24
>L30:/F$@IF(J30=1,G30,0)
>K30:/F$@IF(I30=1,F30,0)
>H30:/F$+H29-F30+G30
>G30:/F$
>F30:/F$10
>E30:"e
>D30:"pply Store
>C30:"Office Su
>B30:/FL+B29+1
>A30:"8-22
>L29:/F$@IF(J29=1,G29,0)
>K29:/F$@IF(I29=1,F29,0)
>H29:/F$+H28-F29+G29
>G29:/F$
>F29:/F$311.67
>C29:"Landlord
>B29:/FL+B28+1
>A29:"8-21
>L28:/F$@IF(J28=1,G28,0)
>K28:/F$@IF(I28=1,F28,0)
>H28:/F$+H27-F28+G28
>G28:/F$
>F28:/F$975
>D28:"t
>C28:"Accountan
>B28:/FL+B27+1
>A28:"8-20
>L27:/F$@IF(J27=1,G27,0)
>K27:/F$@IF(I27=1,F27,0)
>H27:/F$+H26-F27+G27
>G27:/F$
>F27:/FR"VOID
>B27:/FL+B26+1
>A27:"8-17
>L26:/F$@IF(J26=1,G26,0)
>K26:/F$@IF(I26=1,F26,0)
>H26:/F$+H25-F26+G26
>G26:/F$
>F26:/F$1303.33
>D26:"y
>C26:"FAB Salar
>B26:/FL+B25+1
>A26:"8-17
>L25:/F$@IF(J25=1,G25,0)
>K25:/F$@IF(I25=1,F25,0)
>H25:/F$+H24-F25+G25
>G25:/F$
>F25:/F$2556
>D25:"#3
>C25:"Supplier
>B25:/FL+B24+1
>A25:"8-17
>L24:/F$@IF(J24=1,G24,0)
>K24:/F$@IF(I24=1,F24,0)
>H24:/F$+H23-F24+G24
>G24:/F$
>F24:/F$2550
>D24:"#2
>C24:"Supplier
>B24:/FL+B23+1
>A24:"8-14
>L23:/F$@IF(J23=1,G23,0)
>K23:/F$@IF(I23=1,F23,0)
>H23:/F$+H22-F23+G23
>G23:/F$
>F23:/F$30.35
>C23:"Postage
>B23:/FL+B22+1
>A23:"8-14
>L22:/F$@IF(J22=1,G22,0)
>K22:/F$@IF(I22=1,F22,0)
>H22:/F$+H21-F22+G22
>G22:/F$
>F22:/F$55
>C22:"Lawyer
>B22:/FL+B21+1
>A22:"8-11
>L21:/F$@IF(J21=1,G21,0)
>K21:/F$@IF(I21=1,F21,0)
>H21:/F$+H20-F21+G21
>G21:/F$
>F21:/FR"VOID
>B21:/FL+B20+1
>A21:"8-10
>L20:/F$@IF(J20=1,G20,0)
>K20:/F$@IF(I20=1,F20,0)
>H20:/F$+H19-F20+G20
>G20:/F$
>F20:/F$55.87
>D20:"surance
>C20:"Health In
>B20:/FL+B19+1
>A20:"8-8
>L19:/F$@IF(J19=1,G19,0)
>K19:/F$@IF(I19=1,F19,0)
>I19:1
>H19:/F$+H18-F19+G19
>G19:/F$
>F19:/F$40
>E19:"ription
>D19:"e - Subsc
>C19:"A Magazin
>B19:/FL+B18+1
>A19:"8-5
>L18:/F$@IF(J18=1,G18,0)
>K18:/F$@IF(I18=1,F18,0)
>H18:/F$+H17-F18+G18
>G18:/F$
>F18:/F$25
>E18:"cription
>D18:"er - Subs
>C18:"A Newspap
>B18:/FL+B17+1
>A18:"8-3
>L17:/F$@IF(J17=1,G17,0)
>K17:/F$@IF(I17=1,F17,0)
>H17:/F$+H16-F17+G17
>G17:/F$
>F17:/F$1200
>D17:"y
>C17:"CEB Salar
>B17:/FL+B16+1
>A17:"8-2
>L16:/F$@IF(J16=1,G16,0)
>K16:/F$@IF(I16=1,F16,0)
>H16:/F$+H15-F16+G16
>G16:/F$
>F16:/F$234.15
>D16:"ravel
>C16:"CEB for T
>B16:/FL+B15+1
>A16:"8-2
>L15:/F$@IF(J15=1,G15,0)
>K15:/F$@IF(I15=1,F15,0)
>H15:/F$+H14-F15+G15
>G15:/F$12500
>F15:/F$440
>C15:"Dividend
>B15:/FL1005
>A15:/FL"8-1
>L14:/F$@IF(J14=1,G14,0)
>K14:/F$@IF(I14=1,F14,0)
>H14:443.01
>D14:"alance
>C14:"Opening B
>L13:" --------
>K13:" --------
>J13:" --------
>I13:" --------
>H13:" --------
>G13:" --------
>F13:" --------
>E13:"----------
>D13:"----------
>C13:"----------
>B13:"------
>A13:"----
>L12:" Transit
>K12:"  Checks
>J12:" Deposits
>I12:"  Checks
>H12:"  Balance
>G12:"  Amount
>F12:"  Amount
>D12:"scription
>C12:"        De
>B12:"Number
>A12:"Date
>L11:"   in
>K11:"   OS
>J11:"anding
>I11:"    Outst
>H11:"  Running
>G11:"  Deposit
>F11:"  Check
>B11:"Check
>L10:" Deposits
>L9:/-=
>K9:/-=
>J9:/-=
>I9:/-=
>H9:/-=
>G9:/-=
>F9:/-=
>E9:/-=
>D9:/-=
>C9:/-=
>B9:/-=
>A9:/-=
>J8:"ATA
>I8:" CODING D
>H8:"Sheet 1.1
>D8:"w 57)
>C8:"ues to ro
>B8:"A (Contin
>A8:"CHECK DAT
>L7:/-=
>K7:/-=
>J7:/-=
>I7:/-=
>H7:/-=
>G7:/-=
>F7:/-=
>E7:/-=
>D7:/-=
>C7:/-=
>B7:/-=
>A7:/-=
>G5:">A107
>F5:"CONTENTS
>C5:"ONS >A93
>B5:"INSTRUCTI
>L3:/-=
>K3:/-=
>J3:/-=
>I3:/-=
>H3:/-=
>G3:/-=
>F3:/-=
>E3:/-=
>D3:/-=
>C3:/-=
>B3:/-=
>A3:/-=
>H2:"orp. 1983
>G2:"(C) Que C
>F2:"opyright
>E2:"          C
>B2:" MANAGER
>A2:"CHECKBOOK
>L1:/-=
>K1:/-=
>J1:/-=
>I1:/-=
>H1:/-=
>G1:/-=
>F1:/-=
>E1:/-=
>D1:/-=
>C1:/-=
>B1:/-=
>A1:/-=
/W1
/GOC
/GRM
/GC9
/X>A1:>A7:/TH
/X>A86:>A93:
```

CHECKBOOK MANAGER

CHECKBOOK MANAGER Copyright (C) Que Corp. 1983

INSTRUCTIONS >A93 CONTENTS >A107

CHECK DATA (Continues to row 57) Sheet 1.1 CODING DATA

Date	Check Number	Description	Check Amount	Deposit Amount	Running Balance	Outstanding Checks	Outstanding Deposits	OS Checks	Deposits in Transit
		Opening Balance			443.01			0.00	0.00
8-1	1005	Dividend	440.00	12500.00	12503.01			0.00	0.00
8-2	1006	CEB for Travel	234.15		12268.86			0.00	0.00
8-2	1007	CEB Salary	1200.00		11068.86			0.00	0.00
8-3	1008	A Newspaper - Subscription	25.00		11043.86			0.00	0.00
8-5	1009	A Magazine - Subscription	40.00		11003.86	1		40.00	0.00
8-8	1010	Health Insurance	55.87		10947.99			0.00	0.00
8-10	1011		VOID		10947.99			0.00	0.00
8-11	1012	Lawyer	55.00		10892.99			0.00	0.00
8-14	1013	Postage	30.35		10862.64			0.00	0.00
8-14	1014	Supplier #2	2550.00		8312.64			0.00	0.00
8-17	1015	Supplier #3	2556.00		5756.64			0.00	0.00
8-17	1016	FAB Salary	1303.33		4453.31			0.00	0.00
8-17	1017		VOID		4453.31			0.00	0.00
8-20	1018	Accountant	975.00		3478.31			0.00	0.00
8-21	1019	Landlord	311.67		3166.64			0.00	0.00
8-22	1020	Office Supply Store	10.00		3156.64			0.00	0.00
8-24	1021	Postage	40.00		3116.64			0.00	0.00
8-25	1022	Supplier #1	2335.00	3000.00	3781.64			0.00	0.00
8-25	1023	Supplier #4	288.75	110.00	3602.89		1	0.00	110.00
8-27	1024	Landlord	13.07		3589.82			0.00	0.00
8-28	1025	Consultant	150.00		3439.82			0.00	0.00
8-30	1026	Supplier #5	2164.00		1275.82			0.00	0.00
	1027				1275.82			0.00	0.00
	1028				1275.82			0.00	0.00
	1029				1275.82			0.00	0.00
	1030				1275.82			0.00	0.00
	1031				1275.82			0.00	0.00
	1032				1275.82			0.00	0.00
	1033				1275.82			0.00	0.00
	1034				1275.82			0.00	0.00
	1035				1275.82			0.00	0.00
	1036				1275.82			0.00	0.00
	1037				1275.82			0.00	0.00
	1038				1275.82			0.00	0.00
	1039				1275.82			0.00	0.00
	1040				1275.82			0.00	0.00
	1041				1275.82			0.00	0.00
	1042				1275.82			0.00	0.00
	1043				1275.82			0.00	0.00
	1044				1275.82			0.00	0.00
	1045				1275.82			0.00	0.00
	1046				1275.82			0.00	0.00
		End of Period Book Balance:			1275.82				

PREVIOUSLY OUTSTANDING ITEMS Sheet 2.1

Date	Check Number	Description	Check Amount	Deposit Amount	Outstanding Checks	Outstanding Deposits	OS Checks	in Transit
6-5	955	Office Supply Co.	100.00		1		100.00	0.00
7-12	967	Landlord	345.67				0.00	0.00
7-17	990	Accountant	200.00				0.00	0.00
7-15	1002	Parking Garage	112.00				0.00	0.00

RECONCILIATION Sheet 4.1

Ending Book Balance:	1275.82
Bank Charges and/or Credits	5.00
Adjusted Book Balance	1270.82
Outstanding Checks	140.00
Deposits in Transit	110.00
Adjustments to Bank Balance	0.00
Bank Balance:	1300.82

INSTRUCTIONS Sheet 5.1

1) PRINT INSTRUCTIONS and CONTENTS
   by typing: >A93 (CR) /PPH115 (CR)
2) Enter CHECK DATA (>A8)
3) At end of month, CODE Outstanding Checks and Deposits
4) RECALCULATE by typing: !
5) SAVE by typing: /SSFilename (CR)
6) PRINT entire model by typing: >A8 (CR) /PPL85 (CR)
7) PRINT only RECONCILIATION by typing: >A73 (CR) /PPH85 (CR)

CONTENTS Sheet 6.1

```
>Q39:/F$@IF(G39=Q13,F39,0)
>P39:/F$@IF(G39=P13,F39,0)
>O39:/F$@IF(G39=O13,F39,0)
>N39:/F$@IF(G39=N13,F39,0)
>M39:/F$@IF(G39=M13,F39,0)
>L39:/F$@IF(G39=L13,F39,0)
>K39:/F$@IF(G39=K13,F39,0)
>J39:/F$@IF(G39=J13,F39,0)
>I39:/F$@IF(G39=I13,F39,0)
>G39:1
>F39:/F$100
>D39:"on
>C39:"Contributi
>B39:/FL+B38+1
>A39:"8-30
>V38:/F$@SUM(I38...U38)
>U38:/F$@IF(G38=U13,F38,0)
>T38:/F$@IF(G38=T13,F38,0)
>S38:/F$@IF(G38=S13,F38,0)
>R38:/F$@IF(G38=R13,F38,0)
>Q38:/F$@IF(G38=Q13,F38,0)
>P38:/F$@IF(G38=P13,F38,0)
>O38:/F$@IF(G38=O13,F38,0)
>N38:/F$@IF(G38=N13,F38,0)
>M38:/F$@IF(G38=M13,F38,0)
>L38:/F$@IF(G38=L13,F38,0)
>K38:/F$@IF(G38=K13,F38,0)
>J38:/F$@IF(G38=J13,F38,0)
>I38:/F$@IF(G38=I13,F38,0)
>G38:10
>F38:/F$155.9
>C38:"Accountant
>B38:/FL+B37+1
>A38:"8-30
>V37:/F$@SUM(I37...U37)
>U37:/F$@IF(G37=U13,F37,0)
>T37:/F$@IF(G37=T13,F37,0)
>S37:/F$@IF(G37=S13,F37,0)
>R37:/F$@IF(G37=R13,F37,0)
>Q37:/F$@IF(G37=Q13,F37,0)
>P37:/F$@IF(G37=P13,F37,0)
>O37:/F$@IF(G37=O13,F37,0)
>N37:/F$@IF(G37=N13,F37,0)
>M37:/F$@IF(G37=M13,F37,0)
>L37:/F$@IF(G37=L13,F37,0)
>K37:/F$@IF(G37=K13,F37,0)
>J37:/F$@IF(G37=J13,F37,0)
>I37:/F$@IF(G37=I13,F37,0)
>G37:11
>F37:/F$544.77
>C37:"Consultant
>B37:/FL+B36+1
>A37:"8-28
>V36:/F$@SUM(I36...U36)
>U36:/F$@IF(G36=U13,F36,0)
>T36:/F$@IF(G36=T13,F36,0)
>S36:/F$@IF(G36=S13,F36,0)
>R36:/F$@IF(G36=R13,F36,0)
>Q36:/F$@IF(G36=Q13,F36,0)
>P36:/F$@IF(G36=P13,F36,0)
>O36:/F$@IF(G36=O13,F36,0)
>N36:/F$@IF(G36=N13,F36,0)
>M36:/F$@IF(G36=M13,F36,0)
>L36:/F$@IF(G36=L13,F36,0)
>K36:/F$@IF(G36=K13,F36,0)
>J36:/F$@IF(G36=J13,F36,0)
>I36:/F$@IF(G36=I13,F36,0)
>G36:4
>F36:/F$779.45
>E36:"e Co.
>D36:"nce Servic
>C36:"Long Dista
>B36:/FL+B35+1
>A36:"8-27
>V35:/F$@SUM(I35...U35)
>U35:/F$@IF(G35=U13,F35,0)
>T35:/F$@IF(G35=T13,F35,0)
>S35:/F$@IF(G35=S13,F35,0)
>R35:/F$@IF(G35=R13,F35,0)
>Q35:/F$@IF(G35=Q13,F35,0)
>P35:/F$@IF(G35=P13,F35,0)
>O35:/F$@IF(G35=O13,F35,0)
>N35:/F$@IF(G35=N13,F35,0)
>M35:/F$@IF(G35=M13,F35,0)
>L35:/F$@IF(G35=L13,F35,0)
>K35:/F$@IF(G35=K13,F35,0)
>J35:/F$@IF(G35=J13,F35,0)
>I35:/F$@IF(G35=I13,F35,0)
>G35:5
>F35:/F$55.55
>D35:"ply Store
>C35:"Office Sup
>B35:/FL+B34+1
>A35:"8-25
>V34:/F$@SUM(I34...U34)
>U34:/F$@IF(G34=U13,F34,0)
>T34:/F$@IF(G34=T13,F34,0)
>S34:/F$@IF(G34=S13,F34,0)
>R34:/F$@IF(G34=R13,F34,0)
>Q34:/F$@IF(G34=Q13,F34,0)
>P34:/F$@IF(G34=P13,F34,0)
>O34:/F$@IF(G34=O13,F34,0)
>N34:/F$@IF(G34=N13,F34,0)
>M34:/F$@IF(G34=M13,F34,0)
>L34:/F$@IF(G34=L13,F34,0)
>K34:/F$@IF(G34=K13,F34,0)
>J34:/F$@IF(G34=J13,F34,0)
>I34:/F$@IF(G34=I13,F34,0)
>G34:8
>F34:/F$367.82
>E34:"o.
>D34:"Delivery C
>C34:"Overnight
>B34:/FL+B33+1
>A34:"8-25
>V33:/F$@SUM(I33...U33)
>R29:/F$@IF(G29=R13,F29,0)
>Q29:/F$@IF(G29=Q13,F29,0)
>P29:/F$@IF(G29=P13,F29,0)
>O29:/F$@IF(G29=O13,F29,0)
>N29:/F$@IF(G29=N13,F29,0)
>M29:/F$@IF(G29=M13,F29,0)
>L29:/F$@IF(G29=L13,F29,0)
>K29:/F$@IF(G29=K13,F29,0)
>J29:/F$@IF(G29=J13,F29,0)
>I29:/F$@IF(G29=I13,F29,0)
>G29:6
>F29:/F$183.77
>D29:"Co.
>C29:"Insurance
>B29:/FL+B28+1
>A29:"8-17
>V28:/F$@SUM(I28...U28)
>U28:/F$@IF(G28=U13,F28,0)
>T28:/F$@IF(G28=T13,F28,0)
>S28:/F$@IF(G28=S13,F28,0)
>R28:/F$@IF(G28=R13,F28,0)
>Q28:/F$@IF(G28=Q13,F28,0)
>P28:/F$@IF(G28=P13,F28,0)
>O28:/F$@IF(G28=O13,F28,0)
>N28:/F$@IF(G28=N13,F28,0)
>M28:/F$@IF(G28=M13,F28,0)
>L28:/F$@IF(G28=L13,F28,0)
>K28:/F$@IF(G28=K13,F28,0)
>J28:/F$@IF(G28=J13,F28,0)
>I28:/F$@IF(G28=I13,F28,0)
>G28:8
>F28:/F$12.31
>D28:"Service
>C28:"US Postal
>B28:/FL+B27+1
>A28:"8-17
>V27:/F$@SUM(I27...U27)
>U27:/F$@IF(G27=U13,F27,0)
>T27:/F$@IF(G27=T13,F27,0)
>S27:/F$@IF(G27=S13,F27,0)
>R27:/F$@IF(G27=R13,F27,0)
>Q27:/F$@IF(G27=Q13,F27,0)
>P27:/F$@IF(G27=P13,F27,0)
>O27:/F$@IF(G27=O13,F27,0)
>N27:/F$@IF(G27=N13,F27,0)
>M27:/F$@IF(G27=M13,F27,0)
>L27:/F$@IF(G27=L13,F27,0)
>K27:/F$@IF(G27=K13,F27,0)
>J27:/F$@IF(G27=J13,F27,0)
>I27:/F$@IF(G27=I13,F27,0)
>G27:9
>F27:/F$33.19
>E27:"n
>D27:"ubscriptio
>C27:"Magazine S
>B27:/FL+B26+1
>A27:"8-17
>V26:/F$@SUM(I26...U26)
>U26:/F$@IF(G26=U13,F26,0)
>T26:/F$@IF(G26=T13,F26,0)
>S26:/F$@IF(G26=S13,F26,0)
>R26:/F$@IF(G26=R13,F26,0)
>Q26:/F$@IF(G26=Q13,F26,0)
>P26:/F$@IF(G26=P13,F26,0)
>O26:/F$@IF(G26=O13,F26,0)
>N26:/F$@IF(G26=N13,F26,0)
>M26:/F$@IF(G26=M13,F26,0)
>L26:/F$@IF(G26=L13,F26,0)
>K26:/F$@IF(G26=K13,F26,0)
>J26:/F$@IF(G26=J13,F26,0)
>I26:/F$@IF(G26=I13,F26,0)
>G26:5
>F26:/F$89.45
>D26:"ply Store
>C26:"Office Sup
>B26:/FL+B25+1
>A26:"8-14
>V25:/F$@SUM(I25...U25)
>U25:/F$@IF(G25=U13,F25,0)
>T25:/F$@IF(G25=T13,F25,0)
>S25:/F$@IF(G25=S13,F25,0)
>R25:/F$@IF(G25=R13,F25,0)
>Q25:/F$@IF(G25=Q13,F25,0)
>P25:/F$@IF(G25=P13,F25,0)
>O25:/F$@IF(G25=O13,F25,0)
>N25:/F$@IF(G25=N13,F25,0)
>M25:/F$@IF(G25=M13,F25,0)
>L25:/F$@IF(G25=L13,F25,0)
>K25:/F$@IF(G25=K13,F25,0)
>J25:/F$@IF(G25=J13,F25,0)
>I25:/F$@IF(G25=I13,F25,0)
>G25:2
>F25:/F$2555.67
>C25:"IRS
>B25:/FL+B24+1
>A25:"8-14
>V24:/F$@SUM(I24...U24)
>U24:/F$@IF(G24=U13,F24,0)
>T24:/F$@IF(G24=T13,F24,0)
>S24:/F$@IF(G24=S13,F24,0)
>R24:/F$@IF(G24=R13,F24,0)
>Q24:/F$@IF(G24=Q13,F24,0)
>P24:/F$@IF(G24=P13,F24,0)
>O24:/F$@IF(G24=O13,F24,0)
>N24:/F$@IF(G24=N13,F24,0)
>M24:/F$@IF(G24=M13,F24,0)
>L24:/F$@IF(G24=L13,F24,0)
>K24:/F$@IF(G24=K13,F24,0)
>J24:/F$@IF(G24=J13,F24,0)
>I24:/F$@IF(G24=I13,F24,0)
>G24:7
>F24:/F$188.9
>D24:"vice
>C24:"Typing Ser
>B24:/FL+B23+1
>A24:'8-11
>R19:/F$@IF(G19=R13,F19,0)
>Q19:/F$@IF(G19=Q13,F19,0)
>P19:/F$@IF(G19=P13,F19,0)
>O19:/F$@IF(G19=O13,F19,0)
>N19:/F$@IF(G19=N13,F19,0)
>M19:/F$@IF(G19=M13,F19,0)
>L19:/F$@IF(G19=L13,F19,0)
>K19:/F$@IF(G19=K13,F19,0)
>J19:/F$@IF(G19=J13,F19,0)
>I19:/F$@IF(G19=I13,F19,0)
>G19:3
>F19:/F$545
>C19:"Landlord
>B19:/FL+B18+1
>A19:"8-2
>V18:/F$@SUM(I18...U18)
>U18:/F$@IF(G18=U13,F18,0)
>T18:/F$@IF(G18=T13,F18,0)
>S18:/F$@IF(G18=S13,F18,0)
>R18:/F$@IF(G18=R13,F18,0)
>Q18:/F$@IF(G18=Q13,F18,0)
>P18:/F$@IF(G18=P13,F18,0)
>O18:/F$@IF(G18=O13,F18,0)
>N18:/F$@IF(G18=N13,F18,0)
>M18:/F$@IF(G18=M13,F18,0)
>L18:/F$@IF(G18=L13,F18,0)
>K18:/F$@IF(G18=K13,F18,0)
>J18:/F$@IF(G18=J13,F18,0)
>I18:/F$@IF(G18=I13,F18,0)
>G18:1
>F18:/F$3500
>C18:"ASC Salary
>B18:/FL+B17+1
>A18:"8-2
>V17:/F$@SUM(I17...U17)
>U17:/F$@IF(G17=U13,F17,0)
>T17:/F$@IF(G17=T13,F17,0)
>S17:/F$@IF(G17=S13,F17,0)
>R17:/F$@IF(G17=R13,F17,0)
>Q17:/F$@IF(G17=Q13,F17,0)
>P17:/F$@IF(G17=P13,F17,0)
>O17:/F$@IF(G17=O13,F17,0)
>N17:/F$@IF(G17=N13,F17,0)
>M17:/F$@IF(G17=M13,F17,0)
>L17:/F$@IF(G17=L13,F17,0)
>K17:/F$@IF(G17=K13,F17,0)
>J17:/F$@IF(G17=J13,F17,0)
>I17:/F$@IF(G17=I13,F17,0)
>G17:7
>F17:/F$100
>D17:"vice
>C17:"Typing Ser
>B17:/FL1001
>A17:"8-1
>V16:" ---------
>U16:" ---------
>T16:" ---------
>S16:" ---------
>R16:" ---------
>Q16:" ---------
>P16:" ---------
>O16:" ---------
>N16:" ---------
>M16:" ---------
>L16:" ---------
>K16:" ---------
>J16:" ---------
>I16:" ---------
>G16:"      ----
>F16:"  --------
>E16:/--
>D16:/--
>C16:"----------
>B16:"------
>A16:"----
>V15:"   Total
>U15:"  Other
>T15:" Interest
>S15:"  Rental
>R15:" Services
>Q15:" Subscrip
>P15:"  Postage
>O15:" Services
>N15:"Insurance
>M15:" Supplies
>L15:"   Phone
>K15:"   Rent
>J15:"   Taxes
>I15:" Salaries
>G15:"      Code
>F15:"   Amount
>D15:"escription
>C15:"         D
>B15:"Number
>A15:"Date
>S14:"Equipment
>R14:"   Prof
>Q14:" Dues and
>O14:"  Office
>K14:"  Office
>J14:"  Payroll
>F14:"   Check
>B14:"Check
>U13:13
>T13:12
>S13:11
>R13:10
>Q13:9
>P13:8
>O13:7
>N13:6
>M13:5
>L13:4
>K13:3
>J13:2
>I13:1
>D7:" >P10
>C7:"LE, PAGE 2
>B7:"EADING TAB
>A7:"   2.2 SPR
>X6:"E >I10
>V6:">I10
>U6:"ING TABLE
>T6:"2.1 SPREAD
>R6:"10
>Q6:"CK DATA >A
>P6:"   1.1 CHE
>O6:">I10
>N6:"ING TABLE
>M6:"2.1 SPREAD
>K6:"10
>J6:"CK DATA >A
>I6:"   1.1 CHE
>G6:">I10
>F6:"ING TABLE
>E6:"2.1 SPREAD
>C6:"10
>B6:"CK DATA >A
>A6:"   1.1 CHE
>U4:"ENTS
>S4:" CONTENTS
>L4:" CONTENTS
>D4:" CONTENTS
>V3:/-=
>U3:/-=
>T3:/-=
>S3:/-=
>R3:/-=
>Q3:/-=
>P3:/-=
>O3:/-=
>N3:/-=
>M3:/-=
>L3:/-=
>K3:/-=
>J3:/-=
>I3:/-=
>H3:/-=
>G3:/-=
>F3:/-=
>E3:/-=
>D3:/-=
>C3:/-=
>B3:/-=
>A3:/-=
>X2:"orp. 1983
>V2:"Corp. 1983
>U2:"t (C) QUE
>T2:"  Copyrigh
>R2:"PREADSHEET
>Q2:"RSEMENTS S
>P2:"CASH DISBU
>O2:"Corp. 1983
>N2:"t (C) QUE
>M2:"  Copyrigh
>K2:"PREADSHEET
>J2:"RSEMENTS S
>I2:"CASH DISBU
>G2:"Corp. 1983
>F2:"t (C) QUE
>E2:"  Copyrigh
>C2:"PREADSHEET
>B2:"RSEMENTS S
>A2:"CASH DISBU
>V1:/-=
>U1:/-=
>T1:/-=
>S1:/-=
>R1:/-=
>Q1:/-=
>P1:/-=
>O1:/-=
>N1:/-=
>M1:/-=
>L1:/-=
>K1:/-=
>J1:/-=
>I1:/-=
>H1:/-=
>G1:/-=
>F1:/-=
>E1:/-=
>D1:/-=
>C1:/-=
>B1:/-=
>A1:/-=
/W1
/GOC
/GRM
/GC10
/X>A1:>A9:/TH
/X>L1:>M1:
```

CASH DISBURSEMENTS SPREADSHEET

The formulas used to calculate each number are listed below. They are read from bottom to top and right to left and are referenced by their location in the model.

CASH DISBURSEMENTS SPREADSHEET Copyright (C) QUE Corp. 1983

CONTENTS

CASH DISBURSEMENTS SPREADSHEET Copyright (C) QUE Corp. 1983

CONTENTS

1.1 CHECK DATA >A10
2.2 SPREADING TABLE, PAGE 2 >P10
2.1 SPREADING TABLE >I10
3.1 INSTRUCTIONS >A51

CASH DISBURSEMENTS SPREADSHEET Copyright (C) QUE Corp. 1983

CONTENTS ENTS

1.1 CHECK DATA >A10
2.2 SPREADING TABLE, PAGE 2 >P10
2.1 SPREADING TABLE >I10
3.1 INSTRUCTIONS >A51

CHECK DATA (Continues to row 43) Sheet 1.1

SPREADING TABLE (Continues to row 43) Sheet 2.1

SPREADING TABLE (Continues to row 43) Sheet 2.1

Disbursements for Month of: August 83

Date	Check Number	Description	Check Amount	Code	1 Salaries	2 Payroll Taxes	3 Office Rent	4 Phone	5 Supplies	6 Insurance	7 Office Services	8 Postage	9 Dues and Subscrip	10 Prof Services	11 Equipment Rental	12 Interest	13 Other	Total
8-1	1001	Typing Service	100.00	7	0.00	0.00	0.00	0.00	0.00	0.00	100.00	0.00	0.00	0.00	0.00	0.00	0.00	100.00
8-2	1002	ASC Salary	3500.00	1	3500.00	0.00	0.00	0.00	0.00	0.00	0.00	0.00	0.00	0.00	0.00	0.00	0.00	3500.00
8-2	1003	Landlord	545.00	3	0.00	0.00	545.00	0.00	0.00	0.00	0.00	0.00	0.00	0.00	0.00	0.00	0.00	545.00
8-3	1004	Phone Company	244.00	4	0.00	0.00	0.00	244.00	0.00	0.00	0.00	0.00	0.00	0.00	0.00	0.00	0.00	244.00
8-5	1005	Office Supply Store	567.99	5	0.00	0.00	0.00	0.00	567.99	0.00	0.00	0.00	0.00	0.00	0.00	0.00	0.00	567.99
8-8	1006	WSC Salary	4478.90	1	4478.90	0.00	0.00	0.00	0.00	0.00	0.00	0.00	0.00	0.00	0.00	0.00	0.00	4478.90
8-10	1007	Landlord	35.88	3	0.00	0.00	35.88	0.00	0.00	0.00	0.00	0.00	0.00	0.00	0.00	0.00	0.00	35.88
8-11	1008	Typing Service	188.90	7	0.00	0.00	0.00	0.00	0.00	0.00	188.90	0.00	0.00	0.00	0.00	0.00	0.00	188.90
8-14	1009	IRS	2555.67	2	0.00	2555.67	0.00	0.00	0.00	0.00	0.00	0.00	0.00	0.00	0.00	0.00	0.00	2555.67
8-14	1010	Office Supply Store	89.45	5	0.00	0.00	0.00	0.00	89.45	0.00	0.00	0.00	0.00	0.00	0.00	0.00	0.00	89.45
8-17	1011	Magazine Subscription	33.19	9	0.00	0.00	0.00	0.00	0.00	0.00	0.00	0.00	33.19	0.00	0.00	0.00	0.00	33.19
8-17	1012	US Postal Service	12.31	8	0.00	0.00	0.00	0.00	0.00	0.00	0.00	12.31	0.00	0.00	0.00	0.00	0.00	12.31
8-17	1013	Insurance Co.	183.77	6	0.00	0.00	0.00	0.00	0.00	183.77	0.00	0.00	0.00	0.00	0.00	0.00	0.00	183.77
8-20	1014	IRS	122.89	13	0.00	0.00	0.00	0.00	0.00	0.00	0.00	0.00	0.00	0.00	0.00	0.00	122.89	122.89
8-21	1015	Insurance Co.	2258.23	6	0.00	0.00	0.00	0.00	0.00	2258.23	0.00	0.00	0.00	0.00	0.00	0.00	0.00	2258.23
8-22	1016	State Government	447.99	2	0.00	447.99	0.00	0.00	0.00	0.00	0.00	0.00	0.00	0.00	0.00	0.00	0.00	447.99
8-24	1017	Trade Show Company	111.55	9	0.00	0.00	0.00	0.00	0.00	0.00	0.00	0.00	111.55	0.00	0.00	0.00	0.00	111.55
8-25	1018	Overnight Delivery Co.	367.82	8	0.00	0.00	0.00	0.00	0.00	0.00	0.00	367.82	0.00	0.00	0.00	0.00	0.00	367.82
8-25	1019	Office Supply Store	55.55	5	0.00	0.00	0.00	0.00	55.55	0.00	0.00	0.00	0.00	0.00	0.00	0.00	0.00	55.55
8-27	1020	Long Distance Service Co.	779.45	4	0.00	0.00	0.00	779.45	0.00	0.00	0.00	0.00	0.00	0.00	0.00	0.00	0.00	779.45
8-28	1021	Consultant	544.77	11	0.00	0.00	0.00	0.00	0.00	0.00	0.00	0.00	0.00	0.00	544.77	0.00	0.00	544.77
8-30	1022	Accountant	155.90	10	0.00	0.00	0.00	0.00	0.00	0.00	0.00	0.00	0.00	155.90	0.00	0.00	0.00	155.90
8-30	1023	Contribution	100.00	1	100.00	0.00	0.00	0.00	0.00	0.00	0.00	0.00	0.00	0.00	0.00	0.00	0.00	100.00
			17479.21		8078.90	3003.66	580.88	1023.45	712.99	2442.00	288.90	380.13	144.74	155.90	544.77	0.00	122.89	17479.21

INSTRUCTIONS Sheet 3.1

1) Daily, Enter CHECK DATA (>A10)
2) RECALCULATE by typing: !
3) SAVE by typing: /SSFilename (CR)
4) PRINT by typing: >A10 (CR) /PPV43 (CR)

CASH FLOW MANAGER

The formulas used to calculate each number are listed below. They are read from bottom to top and right to left and are referenced by their location in the model.

```
>G93:"(CR)
>F93:") /PPH84
>E93:": >A9 (CR
>D93:"by typing
>C93:"4) PRINT
>F92:"ame (CR)
>E92:" /SSFilen
>D92:"y typing:
>C92:"3) SAVE b
>E91:"typing: !
>D91:"ULATE by
>C91:"2) RECALC
>F90:"9)
>E90:"IVITY (>A
>D90:"DAILY ACT
>C90:"1) Enter
>H88:/-=
>G88:/-=
>F88:/-=
>E88:/-=
>D88:/-=
>C88:/-=
>B88:/-=
>A88:/-=
>H87:"Sheet 2.1
>B87:"ONS
>A87:"INSTRUCTI
>H83:+H82+D83-G83
>G83:7500
>F83:"Purchase
>E83:" Machine
>D83:6500
>C83:"Jobs
>B83:" Various
>A83:" MONTH
>H82:+H80+D82-G82
>A82:" NEXT
>H81:/--
>G81:/--
>F81:/--
>E81:/--
>D81:/--
>C81:/--
>B81:/--
>A81:/--
>H80:+H79+D80-G80
>A80:/FI
>H79:+H78+D79-G79
>A79:/FI+A77-1
>H78:+H77+D78-G78
>A78:/FI
>H77:+H76+D77-G77
>A77:/FI+A75-1
>H76:+H75+D76-G76
>A76:/FI
>H75:+H74+D75-G75
>A75:/FI+A73-1
>H74:+H73+D74-G74
>A74:/FI
>H73:+H72+D73-G73
>G73:2500
>F73:"ice
>E73:"Debt Serv
>A73:/FI+A71-1
>H72:+H71+D72-G72
>A72:/FI
>H71:+H70+D71-G71
>G71:1000
>E71:"Payroll
>A71:/FI+A69-1
>H70:+H69+D70-G70
>A70:/FI
>H69:+H68+D69-G69
>A69:/FI+A67-1
>H68:+H67+D68-G68
>A68:/FI
>H67:+H66+D67-G67
>D67:2400
>C67:" Job 1019
>B67:" Payment,
>A67:/FI+A65-1
>H66:+H65+D66-G66
>A66:/FI
>H65:+H64+D65-G65
>A65:/FI+A63-1
>H64:+H63+D64-G64
>A64:/FI
>H63:+H62+D63-G63
>A63:/FI+A61-1
>H62:+H61+D62-G62
>A62:/FI
>H61:+H60+D61-G61
>G61:2987.2
>F61:"005
>E61:"Invoice 1
>A61:/FI+A59-1
>H60:+H59+D60-G60
>A60:/FI
>H59:+H58+D59-G59
>D59:3577
>C59:" Job 1017
>B59:" Payment,
>A59:/FI+A57-1
>H58:+H57+D58-G58
>A58:/FI
>H57:+H56+D57-G57
>G57:1000
>E57:"Payroll
>A57:/FI+A55-1
>H56:+H55+D56-G56
>A56:/FI
>H55:+H54+D55-G55
>A55:/FI+A53-1
>H54:+H53+D54-G54
>A54:/FI
>H53:+H52+D53-G53
>A53:/FI+A51-1
>H52:+H51+D52-G52
>A52:/FI
>H51:+H50+D51-G51
>A51:/FI+A49-1
>H50:+H49+D50-G50
>A50:/FI
>H49:+H48+D49-G49
>G49:450
>E49:"Telephone
>A49:/FI+A47-1
>H48:+H47+D48-G48
>A48:/FI
>H47:+H46+D47-G47
>A47:/FI+A45-1
>H46:+H45+D46-G46
>A46:/FI
>H45:+H44+D45-G45
>A45:/FI+A43-1
>H44:+H43+D44-G44
>G44:250
>F44:"surance
>E44:"Health In
>A44:/FI
>H43:+H42+D43-G43
>G43:1000
>E43:"Payroll
>A43:/FI+A41-1
>H42:+H41+D42-G42
>A42:/FI
>H41:+H40+D41-G41
>A41:/FI+A39-1
>H40:+H39+D40-G40
>A40:/FI
>H39:+H38+D39-G39
>D39:2499
>C39:" Job 1010
>B39:" Payment,
>A39:/FI+A37-1
>H38:+H37+D38-G38
>A38:/FI
>H37:+H36+D37-G37
>A37:/FI+A35-1
>H36:+H35+D36-G36
>A36:/FI
>H35:+H33+D35-G35
>G35:2389
>F35:"5-234
>E35:"Invoice 3
>A35:/FI+A32-1
>H34:/--
>G34:/--
>F34:/--
>E34:/--
>D34:/--
>C34:/--
>B34:/--
>A34:/--
>H33:+H32+D33-G33
>A33:/FI
>H32:+H31+D32-G32
>A32:/FI+A30-1
>H31:+H30+D31-G31
>A31:/FI
>H30:+H29+D30-G30
>D30:3575
>C30:" Job 1003
>B30:" Payment,
>A30:/FI+A28-1
>H29:+H28+D29-G29
>A29:/FI
>H28:+H27+D28-G28
>A28:/FI+A26-1
>H27:+H26+D27-G27
>A27:/FI
>H26:+H25+D26-G26
>G26:1000
>E26:"Payroll
>A26:/FI+A24-1
>H25:+H24+D25-G25
>A25:/FI
>H24:+H23+D24-G24
>A24:/FI+A22-1
>H23:+H22+D23-G23
>A23:/FI
>H22:+H21+D22-G22
>D22:1255
>C22:" Job 1004
>B22:" Payment,
>A22:/FI+A20-1
>H21:+H20+D21-G21
>H20:+H19+D20-G20
>A20:/FI-2
>H19:+H18+D19-G19
>G19:309
>F19:" Lease
>E19:"Equipment
>H18:+H17+D18-G18
>G18:312
>E18:"Rent
>A18:/FR" 4-1
>H17:+D17
>D17:3156
>C17:"alance
>B17:"Opening B
>H16:" --------
>G16:" --------
>F16:/--
>E16:" --------
>D16:" --------
>C16:/--
>B16:" --------
>A16:"   ------
>H15:" Balance
>G15:"  Amount
>F15:"ption
>E15:"   Descri
>D15:"  Amount
>C15:"ption
>B15:"   Descri
>A15:"    Date
>G14:/--
>F14:/--
>E14:" --------
>D14:/--
>C14:/--
>B14:" --------
>G13:"nts
>F13:"isburseme
>E13:"        D
>D13:"s
>C13:"  Receipts
>B11:" April 83
>A11:"Month of:
>H10:/-=
>G10:/-=
>F10:/-=
>E10:/-=
>D10:/-=
>C10:/-=
>B10:/-=
>A10:/-=
>H9:"Sheet 1.1
>B9:"IVITY
>A9:"DAILY ACT
>H8:/-=
>G8:/-=
>F8:/-=
>E8:/-=
>D8:/-=
>C8:/-=
>B8:/-=
>A8:/-=
>H6:"A87
>G6:"UCTIONS >
>F6:"2.1 INSTR
>D6:" >A9
>C6:" ACTIVITY
>B6:"1.1 DAILY
>E4:"ENTS
>D4:"      CONT
>H3:/-=
>G3:/-=
>F3:/-=
>E3:/-=
>D3:/-=
>C3:/-=
>B3:/-=
>A3:/-=
>H2:"orp. 1983
>G2:"(C) Que C
>F2:"opyright
>E2:"         C
>B2:" MANAGER
>A2:"CASH FLOW
>H1:/-=
>G1:/-=
>F1:/-=
>E1:/-=
>D1:/-=
>C1:/-=
>B1:/-=
>A1:/-=
/W1
/GOC
/GRM
/GF$
/GC9
/X>A1:>A8:/TH
/X>A1:>A1:
```

```
=========================================================================
CASH FLOW MANAGER                               Copyright (C) Que Corp. 1983
=========================================================================
                               CONTENTS

      1.1 DAILY ACTIVITY >A9               2.1 INSTRUCTIONS >A87

=========================================================================
DAILY ACTIVITY                                                 Sheet 1.1
=========================================================================
Month of: April 83

                   Receipts                  Disbursements
          -------------------------- --------------------------
   Date   Description         Amount  Description        Amount  Balance
  ------ ----------------- -------- ----------------- -------- --------
      Opening Balance      3156.00                              3156.00
    4-1                               Rent               312.00  2844.00
                                      Equipment Lease    309.00  2535.00
     -2                                                          2535.00
                                                                 2535.00
     -3 Payment, Job 1004  1255.00                              3790.00
                                                                 3790.00
     -4                                                          3790.00
                                                                 3790.00
     -5                               Payroll           1000.00  2790.00
                                                                 2790.00
     -6                                                          2790.00
                                                                 2790.00
     -7 Payment, Job 1003  3575.00                              6365.00
                                                                 6365.00
     -8                                                          6365.00
                                                                 6365.00
-------------------------------------------------------------------------
     -9                               Invoice 35-234    2389.00  3976.00
                                                                 3976.00
    -10                                                          3976.00
                                                                 3976.00
    -11 Payment, Job 1010  2499.00                              6475.00
                                                                 6475.00
    -12                                                          6475.00
                                                                 6475.00
    -13                               Payroll           1000.00  5475.00
                                      Health Insurance   250.00  5225.00
    -14                                                          5225.00
                                                                 5225.00
    -15                                                          5225.00
                                                                 5225.00
    -16                               Telephone          450.00  4775.00
                                                                 4775.00
    -17                                                          4775.00
                                                                 4775.00
    -18                                                          4775.00
                                                                 4775.00
    -19                                                          4775.00
                                                                 4775.00
    -20                               Payroll           1000.00  3775.00
                                                                 3775.00
    -21 Payment, Job 1017  3577.00                              7352.00
                                                                 7352.00
    -22                               Invoice 1005      2987.20  4364.80
                                                                 4364.80
    -23                                                          4364.80
                                                                 4364.80
    -24                                                          4364.80
                                                                 4364.80
    -25 Payment, Job 1019  2400.00                              6764.80
                                                                 6764.80
    -26                                                          6764.80
                                                                 6764.80
    -27                               Payroll           1000.00  5764.80
                                                                 5764.80
    -28                               Debt Service      2500.00  3264.80
                                                                 3264.80
    -29                                                          3264.80
                                                                 3264.80
    -30                                                          3264.80
                                                                 3264.80
    -31                                                          3264.80
                                                                 3264.80
-------------------------------------------------------------------------
 NEXT                                                            3264.80
 MONTH     Various Jobs        6500.00 Machine Purchase  7500.00  2264.80


INSTRUCTIONS                                                   Sheet 2.1
=========================================================================

                  1) Enter DAILY ACTIVITY (>A9)
                  2) RECALCULATE by typing: !
                  3) SAVE by typing: /SSFilename (CR)
                  4) PRINT by typing: >A9 (CR) /PPH84 (CR)
```

[illegible]

[illegible]

INSTRUCTIONS

[illegible]

```
>R94:/FI+R87+R88+R89-R91-R92
>Q94:/FI+Q87+Q88+Q89-Q91-Q92
>P94:/FI+P87+P88+P89-P91-P92
>O94:/FI+O87+O88+O89-O91-O92
>N94:/FI+N87+N88+N89-N91-N92
>M94:/FI+M87+M88+M89-M91-M92
>L94:/FI+L87+L88+L89-L91-L92
>K94:/FI+K87+K88+K89-K91-K92
>J94:/FI+J87+J88+J89-J91-J92
>I94:/FI+I87+I88+I89-I91-I92
>H94:/FI+H87+H88+H89-H91-H92
>G94:/FI+G87+G88+G89-G91-G92
>F94:/FI
>R93:"  ------
>Q93:"  ------
>P93:"  ------
>O93:"  ------
>N93:"  ------
>M93:"  ------
>L93:"  ------
>K93:"  ------
>J93:"  ------
>I93:"  ------
>H93:"  ------
>G93:"  ------
>R92:/FI+R78
>Q92:/FI+Q78
>P92:/FI+P78
>O92:/FI+O78
>N92:/FI+N78
>M92:/FI+M78
>L92:/FI+L78
>K92:/FI+K78
>J92:/FI+J78
>I92:/FI+I78
>H92:/FI+H78
>G92:/FI+G78
>F92:/FI+F28
>B92:"Credit
>A92:"Line of
>R91:/FI+R25
>Q91:/FI+Q25
>P91:/FI+P25
>O91:/FI+O25
>N91:/FI+N25
>M91:/FI+M25
>L91:/FI+L25
>K91:/FI+K25
>J91:/FI+J25
>I91:/FI+I25
>H91:/FI+H25
>G91:/FI+G25
>F91:/FI
>B91:" Payable
>A91:"Accounts
>R89:/FI(R25-((R19/100)*R11))+Q89
>Q89:/FI(Q25-((Q19/100)*Q11))+P89
>P89:/FI(P25-((P19/100)*P11))+O89
>O89:/FI(O25-((O19/100)*O11))+N89
>N89:/FI(N25-((N19/100)*N11))+M89
>M89:/FI(M25-((M19/100)*M11))+L89
>L89:/FI(L25-((L19/100)*L11))+K89
>K89:/FI(K25-((K19/100)*K11))+J89
>J89:/FI(J25-((J19/100)*J11))+I89
>I89:/FI(I25-((I19/100)*I11))+H89
>H89:/FI(H25-((H19/100)*H11))+G89
>G89:/FI(G25-((G19/100)*G11))+F89
>F89:/FI(F25-((F19/100)*F11))+E89
>B89:"y
>A89:"Inventor
>R88:/FI((Q11*Q14)+((R14+R15)*R11))/100
>Q88:/FI((P11*P14)+((Q14+Q15)*Q11))/100
>P88:/FI((O11*O14)+((P14+P15)*P11))/100
>O88:/FI((N11*N14)+((O14+O15)*O11))/100
>N88:/FI((M11*M14)+((N14+N15)*N11))/100
>M88:/FI((L11*L14)+((M14+M15)*M11))/100
>L88:/FI((K11*K14)+((L14+L15)*L11))/100
>K88:/FI((J11*J14)+((K14+K15)*K11))/100
>J88:/FI((I11*I14)+((J14+J15)*J11))/100
>I88:/FI((H11*H14)+((I14+I15)*I11))/100
>H88:/FI((G11*G14)+((H14+H15)*H11))/100
>G88:/FI((F11*F14)+((G14+G15)*G11))/100
>F88:/FI(G17+((F14+F15)*F11))/100
>C88:"ble
>B88:" Receiva
>A88:"Accounts
>R87:/FI+R80
>Q87:/FI+Q80
>P87:/FI+P80
>O87:/FI+O80
>N87:/FI+N80
>M87:/FI+M80
>L87:/FI+L80
>K87:/FI+K80
>J87:/FI+J80
>I87:/FI+I80
>H87:/FI+H80
>G87:/FI+G80
>F87:/FI35000
>A87:"Cash
>R85:" =======
>Q85:" =======
>P85:" =======
>O85:" =======
>N85:" =======
>M85:" =======
>L85:" =======
>K85:" =======
>J85:" =======
>I85:" =======
>H85:" =======
>G85:" =======
>F85:" =======
>E85:/-=
>D85:/-=
>C85:/-=
>B85:/-=
>A85:/-=
>R84:"    Dec
>Q84:"    Nov
>P84:"    Oct
>O84:"    Sep
>N84:"    Aug
>M84:"    Jul
>L84:"    Jun
>K84:"    May
>J84:"    Apr
>I84:"    Mar
>H84:"    Feb
>G84:"    Jan
>F84:"    Dec
>E84:"heet 5.1
>D84:"        S
>C84:"ACCOUNTS
>B84:" IN KEY
>A84:"BALANCES
>R81:" =======
>Q81:" =======
>P81:" =======
>O81:" =======
>N81:" =======
>M81:" =======
>L81:" =======
>K81:" =======
>J81:" =======
>I81:" =======
>H81:" =======
>G81:" =======
>R80:/FI+R77+R74
>Q80:/FI+Q77+Q74

>M72:+L87
>L72:+K87
>K72:+J87
>J72:+I87
>I72:+H87
>H72:+G87
>G72:+F87
>C72:"alance
>B72:"g Cash B
>A72:"Beginnin
>R71:/FI+R45-R64
>Q71:/FI+Q45-Q64
>P71:/FI+P45-P64
>O71:/FI+O45-O64
>N71:/FI+N45-N64
>M71:/FI+M45-M64
>L71:/FI+L45-L64
>K71:/FI+K45-K64
>J71:/FI+J45-J64
>I71:/FI+I45-I64
>H71:/FI+H45-H64
>G71:/FI+G45-G64
>D71:"Period
>C71:"ed this
>B71:" Generate
>A71:"Net Cash
>R70:" =======
>Q70:" =======
>P70:" =======
>O70:" =======
>N70:" =======
>M70:" =======
>L70:" =======
>K70:" =======
>J70:" =======
>I70:" =======
>H70:" =======
>G70:" =======
>E70:/-=
>D70:/-=
>C70:/-=
>B70:/-=
>A70:/-=
>R69:"    Dec
>Q69:"    Nov
>P69:"    Oct
>O69:"    Sep
>N69:"    Aug
>M69:"    Jul
>L69:"    Jun
>K69:"    May
>J69:"    Apr
>I69:"    Mar
>H69:"    Feb
>G69:"    Jan
>E69:"heet 4.1
>D69:"MENTS  S
>C69:" REQUIRE
>B69:" OF CASH
>A69:"ANALYSIS
>R65:"  ======
>Q65:"  ======
>P65:"  ======
>O65:"  ======
>N65:"  ======
>M65:"  ======
>L65:"  ======
>K65:"  ======
>J65:"  ======
>I65:"  ======
>H65:"  ======
>G65:"  ======
>R64:/FI@SUM(R56...R63)
>Q64:/FI@SUM(Q56...Q63)
>P64:/FI@SUM(P56...P63)
>O64:/FI@SUM(O56...O63)
>N64:/FI@SUM(N56...N63)
>M64:/FI@SUM(M56...M63)
>L64:/FI@SUM(L56...L63)
>K64:/FI@SUM(K56...K63)
>J64:/FI@SUM(J56...J63)
>I64:/FI@SUM(I56...I63)
>H64:/FI@SUM(H56...H63)
>G64:/FI@SUM(G56...G63)
>D64:"ts
>C64:"bursemen
>B64:"Cash Dis
>A64:"  Total
>R63:"  ------
>Q63:"  ------
>P63:"  ------
>O63:"  ------
>N63:"  ------
>M63:"  ------
>L63:"  ------
>K63:"  ------
>J63:"  ------
>I63:"  ------
>H63:"  ------
>G63:"  ------
>R62:0
>Q62:50000
>P62:100000
>O62:0
>N62:0
>M62:0
>L62:0
>K62:0
>J62:0
>I62:0
>H62:0
>G62:0
>A62:"Other
>R61:0
>Q61:10000
>P61:10000
>O61:0
>N61:0
>M61:10000
>L61:0
>K61:0
>J61:10000
>I61:0
>H61:0
>G61:10000
>B61:"axes
>A61:"Income T
>R60:/FI+R27/12/100*Q92
>Q60:/FI+Q27/12/100*P92
>P60:/FI+P27/12/100*O92
>O60:/FI+O27/12/100*N92
>N60:/FI+N27/12/100*M92
>M60:/FI+M27/12/100*L92
>L60:/FI+L27/12/100*K92
>K60:/FI+K27/12/100*J92
>J60:/FI+J27/12/100*I92
>I60:/FI+I27/12/100*H92
>H60:/FI+H27/12/100*G92
>G60:+G27/12/100*F92
>E60:"it
>D60:" of Cred
>C60:" on Line
>B60:" Payment
>A60:"Interest
>R59:/FI+R32-R58
>Q59:/FI+Q32-Q58
>P59:/FI+P32-P58
>O59:/FI+O32-O58
>N59:/FI+N32-N58
>M59:/FI+M32-M58

>J45:@SUM(J41...J44)
>I45:@SUM(I41...I44)
>H45:@SUM(H41...H44)
>G45:@SUM(G41...G44)
>C45:"eipts
>B45:"Cash Rec
>A45:"  Total
>R44:"  ------
>Q44:"  ------
>P44:"  ------
>O44:"  ------
>N44:"  ------
>M44:"  ------
>L44:"  ------
>K44:"  ------
>J44:"  ------
>I44:"  ------
>H44:"  ------
>G44:"  ------
>R43:0
>Q43:0
>P43:0
>O43:0
>N43:0
>M43:0
>L43:0
>K43:0
>J43:0
>I43:0
>H43:0
>G43:0
>A43:"Other
>R42:((P11*P15)+(Q11*Q14))/100
>Q42:((O11*O15)+(P11*P14))/100
>P42:((N11*N15)+(O11*O14))/100
>O42:((M11*M15)+(N11*N14))/100
>N42:((L11*L15)+(M11*M14))/100
>M42:((K11*K15)+(L11*L14))/100
>L42:((J11*J15)+(K11*K14))/100
>K42:((I11*I15)+(J11*J14))/100
>J42:((H11*H15)+(I11*I14))/100
>I42:((G11*G15)+(H11*H14))/100
>H42:((F11*F15)+(G11*G14))/100
>G42:(G17+(F11*F14))/100
>D42:"s
>C42:"ceivable
>B42:"on of Re
>A42:"Collecti
>R41:(R11*R13)/100
>Q41:(Q11*Q13)/100
>P41:(P11*P13)/100
>O41:(O11*O13)/100
>N41:(N11*N13)/100
>M41:(M11*M13)/100
>L41:(L11*L13)/100
>K41:(K11*K13)/100
>J41:(J11*J13)/100
>I41:(I11*I13)/100
>H41:(H11*H13)/100
>G41:(G11*G13)/100
>B41:"es
>A41:"Cash Sal
>R39:" =======
>Q39:" =======
>P39:" =======
>O39:" =======
>N39:" =======
>M39:" =======
>L39:" =======
>K39:" =======
>J39:" =======
>I39:" =======
>H39:" =======
>G39:" =======
>E39:/-=
>D39:/-=
>C39:/-=
>B39:/-=
>A39:/-=
>R38:"    Dec
>Q38:"    Nov
>P38:"    Oct
>O38:"    Sep
>N38:"    Aug
>M38:"    Jul
>L38:"    Jun
>K38:"    May
>J38:"    Apr
>I38:"    Mar
>H38:"    Feb
>G38:"    Jan
>E38:"heet 2.1
>D38:"        S
>C38:"TAIL
>B38:"EIPTS DE
>A38:"CASH REC
>R34:20000
>Q34:20000
>P34:20000
>O34:20000
>N34:20000
>M34:20000
>L34:20000
>K34:20000
>J34:20000
>I34:20000
>H34:20000
>G34:20000
>F34:20000
>D34:"Balance:
>C34:"le Cash
>B34:"Acceptab
>A34:"Minimum
>R32:2500
>Q32:2500
>P32:2500
>O32:2500
>N32:2500
>M32:2500
>L32:2500
>K32:2500
>J32:2500
>I32:2500
>H32:2500
>G32:2500
>F32:2500
>D32:"chedule:
>C32:"ayment S
>B32:"m Debt P
>A32:"Long-Ter
>F31:100000
>E31:"er:
>D31:"n Decemb
>C31:"alance i
>B31:"m Debt B
>A31:"Long-Ter
>G30:" %
>F30:14
>D30:"Rate:
>C30:"nterest
>B30:"m Debt I
>A30:"Long-Ter
>F28:0
>E28:"er:
>D28:"n Decemb
>C28:"alance i
>B28:"Credit B
>A28:"Line-of-
>R27:12
>Q27:14

>P14:40
>O14:40
>N14:40
>M14:40
>L14:40
>K14:40
>J14:40
>I14:40
>H14:40
>G14:40
>F14:40
>E14:"ys
>D14:"in 30 Da
>C14:"Collect
>B14:"nt
>A14:"es Perce
>R13:10
>Q13:10
>P13:10
>O13:10
>N13:10
>M13:10
>L13:10
>K13:10
>J13:10
>I13:10
>H13:10
>G13:10
>F13:10
>D13:"es
>C13:"Cash Sal
>B13:"ons
>A13:"Collecti
>R11:121000
>Q11:110000
>P11:110000
>O11:110000
>N11:121000
>M11:154000
>L11:187000
>K11:242000
>J11:240000
>I11:180000
>H11:140000
>G11:120000
>F11:110000
>C11:"es
>B11:"llar Sal
>A11:"Total Do
>R9:" =======
>Q9:" =======
>P9:" =======
>O9:" =======
>N9:" =======
>M9:" =======
>L9:" =======
>K9:" =======
>J9:" =======
>I9:" =======
>H9:" =======
>G9:" =======
>F9:" =======
>D9:"=
>C9:/-=
>B9:/-=
>A9:/-=
>R8:"    Dec
>Q8:"    Nov
>P8:"    Oct
>O8:"    Sep
>N8:"    Aug
>M8:"    Jul
>L8:"    Jun
>K8:"    May
>J8:"    Apr
>I8:"    Mar
>H8:"    Feb
>G8:"    Jan
>F8:"    Dec
>D8:"1
>C8:"Sheet 1.
>B8:"ONS
>A8:"ASSUMPTI
>J7:/-=
>I7:/-=
>H7:/-=
>G7:/-=
>F7:/-=
>E7:/-=
>D7:/-=
>C7:/-=
>B7:/-=
>A7:/-=
>G5:" >A114
>F5:"CONTENTS
>D5:"9
>C5:"IONS >A9
>B5:"INSTRUCT
>J3:/-=
>I3:/-=
>H3:/-=
>G3:/-=
>F3:/-=
>E3:/-=
>D3:/-=
>C3:/-=
>B3:/-=
>A3:/-=
>I2:"rp. 1983
>H2:"] QUE Co
>G2:"right (C
>F2:"    Copy
>C2:"TION
>B2:"W PROJEC
>A2:"CASH FLO
>J1:/-=
>I1:/-=
>H1:/-=
>G1:/-=
>F1:/-=
>E1:/-=
>D1:/-=
>C1:/-=
>B1:/-=
>A1:/-=
/W1
/GOC
/GRM
/GCB
/X>A1:>A7:/TH
/X>A1:>A1:

>R77:/FI@IF(R75<0,@ABS(R75),@IF(@AND(R75>=0,Q92>0),@IF(Q92>@ABS(R75),-R75,-Q78),0))
>Q77:/FI@IF(Q75<0,@ABS(Q75),@IF(@AND(Q75>=0,P92>0),@IF(P92>@ABS(Q75),-Q75,-P78),0))
>P77:/FI@IF(P75<0,@ABS(P75),@IF(@AND(P75>=0,O92>0),@IF(O92>@ABS(P75),-P75,-O78),0))
>O77:/FI@IF(O75<0,@ABS(O75),@IF(@AND(O75>=0,N92>0),@IF(N92>@ABS(O75),-O75,-N78),0))
>N77:/FI@IF(N75<0,@ABS(N75),@IF(@AND(N75>=0,M92>0),@IF(M92>@ABS(N75),-N75,-M78),0))
>M77:/FI@IF(M75<0,@ABS(M75),@IF(@AND(M75>=0,L92>0),@IF(L92>@ABS(M75),-M75,-L78),0))
>L77:/FI@IF(L75<0,@ABS(L75),@IF(@AND(L75>=0,K92>0),@IF(K92>@ABS(L75),-L75,-K78),0))
>K77:/FI@IF(K75<0,@ABS(K75),@IF(@AND(K75>=0,J92>0),@IF(J92>@ABS(K75),-K75,-J78),0))
>J77:/FI@IF(J75<0,@ABS(J75),@IF(@AND(J75>=0,I92>0),@IF(I92>@ABS(J75),-J75,-I78),0))
>I77:/FI@IF(I75<0,@ABS(I75),@IF(@AND(I75>=0,H92>0),@IF(H92>@ABS(I75),-I75,-H78),0))
>H77:/FI@IF(H75<0,@ABS(H75),@IF(@AND(H75>=0,G92>0),@IF(G92>@ABS(H75),-H75,-G78),0))
>G77:/FI@IF(G75<0,@ABS(G75),@IF(@AND(G75>=0,F92>0),@IF(F92>@ABS(G75),G75,-F92),0))
```

CASH FLOW PROJECTION

The formulas used to calculate each number are listed below. They are read from bottom to top and right to left and are referenced by their location in the model.

```
>E124:"14
>D124:"ENTS >A1
>C124:"7.1 CONT
>E123:" >A99
>D123:"RUCTIONS
>C123:"6.1 INST
>G122:"4
>F122:"UNTS >A8
>E122:"KEY ACCO
>D122:"NCES IN
>C122:"5.1 BALA
>G121:"S >A69
>F121:"UIREMENT6
>E121:"CASH REQ
>D121:"YSIS OF
>C121:"4.1 ANAL
>G120:"53
>F120:"ETAIL >A
>E120:"EMENTS D
>D120:" DISBURS
>C120:"3.1 CASH
>F119:" >A38
>E119:"S DETAIL
>D119:" RECEIPT
>C119:"2.1 CASH
>F118:">A23
>E118:" PAGE 2
>D118:"MPTIONS,
>C118:"2.2 ASSU
>E117:">A8
>D117:"MPTIONS
>C117:"1.1 ASSU
>I115:/-=
>H115:/-=
>G115:/-=
>F115:/-=
>E115:/-=
>D115:/-=
>C115:/-=
>B115:/-=
>A115:/-=
>I114:"heet 7.1
>H114:"        S
>A114:"CONTENTS
>G109:"R95 (CR)
>F109:"(CR) /PP
>E109:"ng: >A8
>D109:" by typi
>C109:"7) PRINT
>G108:"CR)
>F108:"lename (
>E108:"g: /SSFi
>D108:"by typin
>C108:"6) SAVE
>F107:": !
>E107:"y typing
>D107:"CULATE b
>C107:"5) RECAL
>H106:")
>G106:"IL (>A53
>F106:"NTS DETA
>E106:"SBURSEME
>D106:" CASH DI
>C106:"4) Enter/r
>G105:"A38)
>F105:"ETAIL (>
>E105:"CEIPTS D
>D105:" CASH RE
>C105:"3) Enter/r
>F104:"8)
>E104:"IONS (>A
>D104:" ASSUMPT
>C104:"2) Enter/r
>F103:"R)
>E103:"PI124 (C
>D103:" (CR) /P
>C103:"     >A99
>H102:"ping:
>G102:"TS by ty
>F102:"d CONTEN
>E102:"TIONS an
>D102:" INSTRUC
>C102:"1) PRINT
>I100:/-=
>H100:/-=
>G100:/-=
>F100:/-=
>E100:/-=
>D100:/-=
>C100:/-=
>B100:/-=
>A100:/-=
>I99:"heet 6.1
>H99:"        S
>B99:"IONS
>A99:"INSTRUCT
>R95:"  ======
>Q95:"  ======
>P95:"  ======
>O95:"  ======
>N95:"  ======
>M95:"  ======
>L95:"  ======
>K95:"  ======
>J95:"  ======
>I95:"  ======
>H95:"  ======
>G95:"  ======
```

```
>P80:/FI+P77+P74
>O80:/FI+O77+O74
>N80:/FI+N77+N74
>M80:/FI+M77+M74
>L80:/FI+L77+L74
>K80:/FI+K77+K74
>J80:/FI+J77+J74
>I80:/FI+I77+I74
>H80:/FI+H77+H74
>G80:/FI+G77+G74
>C80:"nce
>B80:"ash Balance
>A80:"Ending C
>R79:"  ------
>Q79:"  ------
>P79:"  ------
>O79:"  ------
>N79:"  ------
>M79:"  ------
>L79:"  ------
>K79:"  ------
>J79:"  ------
>I79:"  ------
>H79:"  ------
>G79:"  ------
>R78:/FI+Q78+R77
>Q78:/FI+P78+Q77
>P78:/FI+O78+P77
>O78:/FI+N78+O77
>N78:/FI+M78+N77
>M78:/FI+L78+M77
>L78:/FI+K78+L77
>K78:/FI+J78+K77
>J78:/FI+I78+J77
>I78:/FI+H78+I77
>H78:/FI+G78+H77
>G78:/FI+F92+G77
>D78:"ngs
>C78:" Borrowi
>B78:"ort Term
>A78:"Total Sh
```

see formula below

```
>E77:"ings
>D77:"m Borrow
>C77:"hort Ter
>B77:"Period S
>A77:"Current
>R75:/FI+R74-R34
>Q75:/FI+Q74-Q34
>P75:/FI+P74-P34
>O75:/FI+O74-O34
>N75:/FI+N74-N34
>M75:/FI+M74-M34
>L75:/FI+L74-L34
>K75:/FI+K74-K34
>J75:/FI+J74-J34
>I75:/FI+I74-I34
>H75:/FI+H74-H34
>G75:/FI+G74-G34
>E75:"Balance
>D75:"eptable
>C75:"imum Acc
>B75:"elow Min
>A75:"Amount B
>R74:/FI+R71+R72
>Q74:/FI+Q71+Q72
>P74:/FI+P71+P72
>O74:/FI+O71+O72
>N74:/FI+N71+N72
>M74:/FI+M71+M72
>L74:/FI+L71+L72
>K74:/FI+K71+K72
>J74:/FI+J71+J72
>I74:/FI+I71+I72
>H74:/FI+H71+H72
>G74:/FI+G71+G72
>D74:"owings
>C74:"ore Borr
>B74:"ance bef
>A74:"Cash Bal
>R73:"  ------
>Q73:"  ------
>P73:"  ------
>O73:"  ------
>N73:"  ------
>M73:"  ------
>L73:"  ------
>K73:"  ------
>J73:"  ------
>I73:"  ------
>H73:"  ------
>G73:"  ------
>R72:+Q87
>Q72:+P87
>P72:+O87
>O72:+N87
>N72:+M87
```

```
>L59:/FI+L32-L58
>K59:/FI+K32-K58
>J59:/FI+J32-J58
>I59:/FI+I32-I58
>H59:/FI+H32-H58
>G59:/FI+G32-G58
>D59:"l
>C59:"Principa
>R58:/FI+F30/100/12*(F31-@SUM(G59...Q59))
>Q58:/FI+F30/100/12*(F31-@SUM(G59...P59))
>P58:/FI+F30/100/12*(F31-@SUM(G59...O59))
>O58:/FI+F30/100/12*(F31-@SUM(G59...N59))
>N58:/FI+F30/100/12*(F31-@SUM(G59...M59))
>M58:/FI+F30/100/12*(F31-@SUM(G59...L59))
>L58:/FI+F30/100/12*(F31-@SUM(G59...K59))
>K58:/FI+F30/100/12*(F31-@SUM(G59...J59))
>J58:/FI+F30/100/12*(F31-@SUM(G59...I59))
>I58:/FI+F30/100/12*(F31-@SUM(G59...H59))
>H58:/FI+F30/100/12*(F31-@SUM(G59...G59))
>G58:/FI+F30/100/12*F31
>C58:"Interest
>B58:"m Debt
>A58:"Long-Ter
>R57:12250
>Q57:12250
>P57:12250
>O57:12250
>N57:12250
>M57:12250
>L57:12250
>K57:12250
>J57:12250
>I57:12250
>H57:12250
>G57:12250
>C57:"es
>B57:"g Expens
>A57:"Operatin
>R56:+Q25
>Q56:+P25
>P56:+O25
>O56:+N25
>N56:+M25
>M56:+L25
>L56:+K25
>K56:+J25
>J56:+I25
>I56:+H25
>H56:+G25
>G56:+F25
>D56:" Credit
>C56:"hases on
>B56:"for Purc
>A56:"Payment
>R54:" =======
>Q54:" =======
>P54:" =======
>O54:" =======
>N54:" =======
>M54:" =======
>L54:" =======
>K54:" =======
>J54:" =======
>I54:" =======
>H54:" =======
>G54:" =======
>E54:/-=
>D54:/-=
>C54:/-=
>B54:/-=
>A54:/-=
>R53:"    Dec
>Q53:"    Nov
>P53:"    Oct
>O53:"    Sep
>N53:"    Aug
>M53:"    Jul
>L53:"    Jun
>K53:"    May
>J53:"    Apr
>I53:"    Mar
>H53:"    Feb
>G53:"    Jan
>E53:"heet 3.1
>D53:"L       S
>C53:"TS DETAI
>B53:"BURSEMEN
>A53:"CASH DIS
>R46:"  ======
>Q46:"  ======
>P46:"  ======
>O46:"  ======
>N46:"  ======
>M46:"  ======
>L46:"  ======
>K46:"  ======
>J46:"  ======
>I46:"  ======
>H46:"  ======
>G46:"  ======
>R45:@SUM(R41...R44)
>Q45:@SUM(Q41...Q44)
>P45:@SUM(P41...P44)
>O45:@SUM(O41...O44)
>N45:@SUM(N41...N44)
>M45:@SUM(M41...M44)
>L45:@SUM(L41...L44)
>K45:@SUM(K41...K44)
```

```
>P27:15
>O27:16
>N27:16
>M27:16
>L27:16
>K27:16
>J27:18
>I27:17
>H27:15
>G27:14
>F27:14
>D27:"Rate:
>C27:"nterest
>B27:"Credit I
>A27:"Line-of-
>R25:117000
>Q25:90000
>P25:90000
>O25:90000
>N25:81000
>M25:90000
>L25:99000
>K25:126000
>J25:153000
>I25:198000
>H25:192000
>G25:144000
>F25:112000
>D25:"t:
>C25:"on Credi
>B25:"rchases
>A25:"Total Pu
>R24:" =======
>Q24:" =======
>P24:" =======
>O24:" =======
>N24:" =======
>M24:" =======
>L24:" =======
>K24:" =======
>J24:" =======
>I24:" =======
>H24:" =======
>G24:" =======
>F24:" =======
>D24:"=
>C24:/-=
>B24:/-=
>A24:/-=
>R23:"    Dec
>Q23:"    Nov
>P23:"    Oct
>O23:"    Sep
>N23:"    Aug
>M23:"    Jul
>L23:"    Jun
>K23:"    May
>J23:"    Apr
>I23:"    Mar
>H23:"    Feb
>G23:"    Jan
>F23:"    Dec
>D23:"2
>C23:"Sheet 1.
>B23:"ONS
>A23:"ASSUMPTI
>R19:70
>Q19:70
>P19:70
>O19:70
>N19:70
>M19:70
>L19:70
>K19:70
>J19:70
>I19:70
>H19:70
>G19:70
>F19:70
>D19:"centage
>C19:"rgin Per
>B19:"Gross Ma
>A19:"Average
>G17:50000
>F17:40000
>D17:"Sales
>C17:"ovember
>B17:"ons on N
>A17:"Collecti
>R15:100-R13-R14
>Q15:100-Q13-Q14
>P15:100-P13-P14
>O15:100-O13-O14
>N15:100-N13-N14
>M15:100-M13-M14
>L15:100-L13-L14
>K15:100-K13-K14
>J15:100-J13-J14
>I15:100-I13-I14
>H15:100-H13-H14
>G15:100-G13-G14
>F15:100-F13-F14
>E15:"ys
>D15:"in 60 Da
>C15:"Collect
>A15:"of Sales
>R14:40
>Q14:40
```

CASH FLOW PROJECTION

Copyright (C) QUE Corp. 1983

INSTRUCTIONS >A99 CONTENTS >A114

ASSUMPTIONS Sheet 1.1

	Dec	Jan	Feb	Mar	Apr	May	Jun	Jul	Aug	Sep	Oct	Nov	Dec
Total Dollar Sales	110000	120000	140000	180000	240000	242000	187000	154000	121000	110000	110000	110000	121000
Collections as Percent of Sales: Cash Sales	10	10	10	10	10	10	10	10	10	10	10	10	10
Collect in 30 Days	40	40	40	40	40	40	40	40	40	40	40	40	40
Collect in 60 Days	50	50	50	50	50	50	50	50	50	50	50	50	50
Collections on November Sales	40000	50000											
Average Gross Margin Percentage	70	70	70	70	70	70	70	70	70	70	70	70	70

ASSUMPTIONS Sheet 1.2

	Dec	Jan	Feb	Mar	Apr	May	Jun	Jul	Aug	Sep	Oct	Nov	Dec
Total Purchases on Credit:	112000	144000	192000	198000	153000	126000	99000	90000	81000	90000	90000	90000	117000
Line-of-Credit Interest Rate:	14	14	15	17	18	16	16	16	16	16	15	14	12
Line-of-Credit Balance in December:	0												
Long-Term Debt Interest Rate:	14 %												
Long-Term Debt Balance in December:	100000												
Long-Term Debt Payment Schedule:	2500	2500	2500	2500	2500	2500	2500	2500	2500	2500	2500	2500	2500
Minimum Acceptable Cash Balance:	20000	20000	20000	20000	20000	20000	20000	20000	20000	20000	20000	20000	20000

CASH RECEIPTS DETAIL Sheet 3.1

	Jan	Feb	Mar	Apr	May	Jun	Jul	Aug	Sep	Oct	Nov	Dec
Cash Sales	12000	14000	18000	24000	24200	18700	15400	12100	11000	11000	11000	12100
Collection of Receivables	44500	103000	116000	142000	186000	216800	195800	155100	125400	104500	99000	99000
Other	0	0	0	0	0	0	0	0	0	0	0	0
Total Cash Receipts	56500	117000	134000	166000	210200	235500	211200	167200	136400	115500	110000	111100

CASH DISBURSEMENTS DETAIL Sheet 4.1

	Jan	Feb	Mar	Apr	May	Jun	Jul	Aug	Sep	Oct	Nov	Dec
Payment for Purchases on Credit	112000	144000	192000	198000	153000	126000	99000	90000	81000	90000	90000	90000
Operating Expenses	12250	12250	12250	12250	12250	12250	12250	12250	12250	12250	12250	12250
Long-Term Debt Interest	1167	1151	1135	1119	1103	1087	1071	1054	1037	1020	1003	985
Principal	1333	1349	1365	1381	1397	1413	1429	1446	1463	1480	1497	1515
Interest Payment on Line of Credit	0	816	1527	2731	3221	2698	1471	324	0	0	243	758
Income Taxes	10000	0	0	10000	0	0	10000	0	0	10000	10000	0
Other	0	0	0	0	0	0	0	0	0	100000	50000	0
Total Cash Disbursements	136750	159566	208277	225481	170971	143448	125221	105074	95750	214750	164993	105508

ANALYSIS OF CASH REQUIREMENTS Sheet 4.1

	Jan	Feb	Mar	Apr	May	Jun	Jul	Aug	Sep	Oct	Nov	Dec
Net Cash Generated this Period	-80250	-42566	-74277	-59481	39229	92052	85979	62126	40650	-99250	-54993	5592
Beginning Cash Balance	35000	20000	20000	20000	20000	20000	20000	20000	57811.9	98461.9	20000	20000
Cash Balance before Borrowings	-45250	-22566	-54277	-39481	59229	112052	105979	82126	98462	-788	-34993	25592
Amount Below Minimum Acceptable Balance	-65250	-42566	-74277	-59481	39229	92052	85979	62126	78462	-20788	-54993	5592
Current Period Short Term Borrowings	65250	42566	74277	59481	-39229	-92052	-85979	-24314	0	20788	54993	-5592
Total Short Term Borrowings	65250	107816	182093	241574	202345	110293	24314	0	0	20788	75781	70188
Ending Cash Balance	20000	20000	20000	20000	20000	20000	20000	57812	98462	20000	20000	20000

BALANCES IN KEY ACCOUNTS Sheet 5.1

	Dec	Jan	Feb	Mar	Apr	May	Jun	Jul	Aug	Sep	Oct	Nov	Dec
Cash	35000	20000	20000	20000	20000	20000	20000	20000	57812	98462	20000	20000	20000
Accounts Receivable	99500	152000	174000	218000	288000	313800	265100	213400	170500	147400	143000	143000	152900
Inventory	35000	95000	189000	261000	246000	202600	170700	152900	149200	162200	175200	188200	220500
Accounts Payable		144000	192000	198000	153000	126000	99000	90000	81000	90000	90000	90000	117000
Line of Credit	0	65250	107816	182093	241574	202345	110293	24314	0	0	20788	75781	70188
		57750	83184	118907	159426	208055	246507	271986	296512	318062	227412	185419	206212

INSTRUCTIONS Sheet 6.1

1) PRINT INSTRUCTIONS and CONTENTS by typing:
   >A99 (CR) /PPI124 (CR)
2) Enter ASSUMPTIONS (>A8)
3) Enter CASH RECEIPTS DETAIL (>A38)
4) Enter CASH DISBURSEMENTS DETAIL (>A53)
5) RECALCULATE by typing: !
6) SAVE by typing: /SSFilename (CR)
7) PRINT by typing: >A8 (CR) /PPR95 (CR)

CONTENTS Sheet 7.1

1.1 ASSUMPTIONS >A8
2.2 ASSUMPTIONS, PAGE 2 >A23
2.1 CASH RECEIPTS DETAIL >A38
3.1 CASH DISBURSEMENTS DETAIL >A53
4.1 ANALYSIS OF CASH REQUIREMENTS >A69
5.1 BALANCES IN KEY ACCOUNTS >A84
6.1 INSTRUCTIONS >A99
7.1 CONTENTS >A114

A LOAN AMORTIZATION CALCULATOR

The formulas used to calculate each number are listed below. They are read from bottom to top and right to left and are referenced by their location in the model.

```
>F101:"t cell F15
>E101:"nter "0" a
>D101:"R model, e
>C101:"5) To CLEA
>F100:"inished
>E100:"b) until f
>D100:"at a) and
>C100:"    c) Repe
>G99:"(CR)
>F99:"R) /PPG87
>E99:"g: >A28 (C
>D99:"T by typin
>C99:"    b) PRIN
>F98:"ing: !
>E98:"ain by typ
>D98:"LCULATE ag
>C98:"    a) RECA
>F97:"iods:
>E97:"eds 60 per
>D97:" term exce
>C97:"4) If loan
>G96:")
>F96:"/PPG87 (CR
>E96:">A10 (CR)
>D96:"y typing:
>C96:"3) PRINT b
>E95:"ping: !
>D95:"LATE by ty
>C95:"2) RECALCU
>E94:" (>A10)
>D94:"SSUMPTIONS
>C94:"1) Enter A
>G92:/-=
>F92:/-=
>E92:/-=
>D92:/-=
>C92:/-=
>B92:/-=
>A92:/-=
>G91:" Sheet 3.1
>B91:"NS
>A91:"INSTRUCTIO
>F87:@IF(F15=0,0,C87-E87)
>E87:@IF(C87<.005,0,F17-D87)
>D87:(F14/(100*12))*C87
>C87:+F86
>B87:/FI+B86+1
>F86:+C86-E86
>E86:@IF(C86<.005,0,F17-D86)
>D86:(F14/(100*12))*C86
>C86:+F85
>B86:/FI+B85+1
>F85:+C85-E85
>E85:@IF(C85<.005,0,F17-D85)
>D85:(F14/(100*12))*C85
>C85:+F84
>B85:/FI+B84+1
>F84:+C84-E84
>E84:@IF(C84<.005,0,F17-D84)
>D84:(F14/(100*12))*C84
>C84:+F83
>B84:/FI+B83+1
>F83:+C83-E83
>E83:@IF(C83<.005,0,F17-D83)
>D83:(F14/(100*12))*C83
>C83:+F82
>B83:/FI+B82+1
>F82:+C82-E82
>E82:@IF(C82<.005,0,F17-D82)
>D82:(F14/(100*12))*C82
>C82:+F81
>B82:/FI+B81+1
>F81:+C81-E81
>E81:@IF(C81<.005,0,F17-D81)
>D81:(F14/(100*12))*C81
>C81:+F80
>B81:/FI+B80+1
>F80:+C80-E80
>E80:@IF(C80<.005,0,F17-D80)
>D80:(F14/(100*12))*C80
>C80:+F79
>B80:/FI+B79+1
>F79:+C79-E79
>E79:@IF(C79<.005,0,F17-D79)
>D79:(F14/(100*12))*C79
>C79:+F78
>B79:/FI+B78+1
>F78:+C78-E78
>E78:@IF(C78<.005,0,F17-D78)
>D78:(F14/(100*12))*C78
>C78:+F77
>B78:/FI+B77+1
>F77:+C77-E77
>E77:@IF(C77<.005,0,F17-D77)
>D77:(F14/(100*12))*C77
>C77:+F76
>B77:/FI+B76+1
>F76:+C76-E76
>E76:@IF(C76<.005,0,F17-D76)
>D76:(F14/(100*12))*C76
>C76:+F75
>B76:/FI+B75+1
>F75:+C75-E75
>E75:@IF(C75<.005,0,F17-D75)
>D75:(F14/(100*12))*C75
>C75:+F74
>B75:/FI+B74+1
>F74:+C74-E74
>E74:@IF(C74<.005,0,F17-D74)
>D74:(F14/(100*12))*C74
>C74:+F73
>B74:/FI+B73+1
>F73:+C73-E73
>E73:@IF(C73<.005,0,F17-D73)
>D73:(F14/(100*12))*C73
>C73:+F72
>B73:/FI+B72+1
>F72:+C72-E72
>E72:@IF(C72<.005,0,F17-D72)
>D72:(F14/(100*12))*C72
>C72:+F71
>B72:/FI+B71+1
>F71:+C71-E71
>E71:@IF(C71<.005,0,F17-D71)
>D71:(F14/(100*12))*C71
>C71:+F70
>B71:/FI+B70+1
>F70:+C70-E70
>E70:@IF(C70<.005,0,F17-D70)
>D70:(F14/(100*12))*C70
>C70:+F69
>B70:/FI+B69+1
>F69:+C69-E69
>E69:@IF(C69<.005,0,F17-D69)
>D69:(F14/(100*12))*C69
>C69:+F68
>B69:/FI+B68+1
>F68:+C68-E68
>E68:@IF(C68<.005,0,F17-D68)
>D68:(F14/(100*12))*C68
>C68:+F67
>B68:/FI+B67+1
>F67:+C67-E67
>E67:@IF(C67<.005,0,F17-D67)
>D67:(F14/(100*12))*C67
>C67:+F66
>B67:/FI+B66+1
>F66:+C66-E66
>E66:@IF(C66<.005,0,F17-D66)
>D66:(F14/(100*12))*C66
>C66:+F65
>B66:/FI+B65+1
>F65:+C65-E65
>E65:@IF(C65<.005,0,F17-D65)
>D65:(F14/(100*12))*C65
>C65:+F64
>B65:/FI+B64+1
>F64:+C64-E64
>E64:@IF(C64<.005,0,F17-D64)
>D64:(F14/(100*12))*C64
>C64:+F63
>B64:/FI+B63+1
>F63:+C63-E63
>E63:@IF(C63<.005,0,F17-D63)
>D63:(F14/(100*12))*C63
>C63:+F62
>B63:/FI+B62+1
>F62:+C62-E62
>E62:@IF(C62<.005,0,F17-D62)
>D62:(F14/(100*12))*C62
>C62:+F61
>B62:/FI+B61+1
>F61:+C61-E61
>E61:@IF(C61<.005,0,F17-D61)
>D61:(F14/(100*12))*C61
>C61:+F60
>B61:/FI+B60+1
>F60:+C60-E60
>E60:@IF(C60<.005,0,F17-D60)
->D60:(F14/(100*12))*C60
>C60:+F59
>B60:/FI+B59+1
>F59:+C59-E59
>E59:@IF(C59<.005,0,F17-D59)
>D59:(F14/(100*12))*C59
>C59:+F58
>B59:/FI+B58+1
>F58:+C58-E58
>E58:@IF(C58<.005,0,F17-D58)
>D58:(F14/(100*12))*C58
>C58:+F57
>B58:/FI+B57+1
>F57:+C57-E57
>E57:@IF(C57<.005,0,F17-D57)
>D57:(F14/(100*12))*C57
>C57:+F56
>B57:/FI+B56+1
>F56:+C56-E56
>E56:@IF(C56<.005,0,F17-D56)
>D56:(F14/(100*12))*C56
>C56:+F55
>B56:/FI+B55+1
>F55:+C55-E55
>E55:@IF(C55<.005,0,F17-D55)
>D55:(F14/(100*12))*C55
>C55:+F54
>B55:/FI+B54+1
>F54:+C54-E54
>E54:@IF(C54<.005,0,F17-D54)
>D54:(F14/(100*12))*C54
>C54:+F53
>B54:/FI+B53+1
>F53:+C53-E53
>E53:@IF(C53<.005,0,F17-D53)
>D53:(F14/(100*12))*C53
>C53:+F52
>B53:/FI+B52+1
>F52:+C52-E52
>E52:@IF(C52<.005,0,F17-D52)
>D52:(F14/(100*12))*C52
>C52:+F51
>B52:/FI+B51+1
>F51:+C51-E51
>E51:@IF(C51<.005,0,F17-D51)
>D51:(F14/(100*12))*C51
>C51:+F50
>B51:/FI+B50+1
>F50:+C50-E50
>E50:@IF(C50<.005,0,F17-D50)
>D50:(F14/(100*12))*C50
>C50:+F49
>B50:/FI+B49+1
>F49:+C49-E49
>E49:@IF(C49<.005,0,F17-D49)
>D49:(F14/(100*12))*C49
>C49:+F48
>B49:/FI+B48+1
>F48:+C48-E48
>E48:@IF(C48<.005,0,F17-D48)
>D48:(F14/(100*12))*C48
>C48:+F47
>B48:/FI+B47+1
>F47:+C47-E47
>E47:@IF(C47<.005,0,F17-D47)
>D47:(F14/(100*12))*C47
>C47:+F46
>B47:/FI+B46+1
>F46:+C46-E46
>E46:@IF(C46<.005,0,F17-D46)
>D46:(F14/(100*12))*C46
>C46:+F45
>B46:/FI+B45+1
>F45:+C45-E45
>E45:@IF(C45<.005,0,F17-D45)
>D45:(F14/(100*12))*C45
>C45:+F44
>B45:/FI+B44+1
>F44:+C44-E44
>E44:@IF(C44<.005,0,F17-D44)
>D44:(F14/(100*12))*C44
>C44:+F43
>B44:/FI+B43+1
>F43:+C43-E43
>E43:@IF(C43<.005,0,F17-D43)
>D43:(F14/(100*12))*C43
>C43:+F42
>B43:/FI+B42+1
>F42:+C42-E42
>E42:@IF(C42<.005,0,F17-D42)
>D42:(F14/(100*12))*C42
>C42:+F41
>B42:/FI+B41+1
>F41:+C41-E41
>E41:@IF(C41<.005,0,F17-D41)
>D41:(F14/(100*12))*C41
>C41:+F40
>B41:/FI+B40+1
>F40:+C40-E40
>E40:@IF(C40<.005,0,F17-D40)
>D40:(F14/(100*12))*C40
>C40:+F39
>B40:/FI+B39+1
>F39:+C39-E39
>E39:@IF(C39<.005,0,F17-D39)
>D39:(F14/(100*12))*C39
>C39:+F38
>B39:/FI+B38+1
>F38:+C38-E38
>E38:@IF(C38<.005,0,F17-D38)
>D38:(F14/(100*12))*C38
>C38:+F37
>B38:/FI+B37+1
>F37:+C37-E37
>E37:@IF(C37<.005,0,F17-D37)
>D37:(F14/(100*12))*C37
>C37:+F36
>B37:/FI+B36+1
>F36:+C36-E36
>E36:@IF(C36<.005,0,F17-D36)
>D36:(F14/(100*12))*C36
>C36:+F35
>B36:/FI+B35+1
>F35:+C35-E35
>E35:@IF(C35<.005,0,F17-D35)
>D35:(F14/(100*12))*C35
>C35:+F34
>B35:/FI+B34+1
>F34:+C34-E34
>E34:@IF(C34<.005,0,F17-D34)
>D34:(F14/(100*12))*C34
>C34:+F33
>B34:/FI+B33+1
>F33:+C33-E33
>E33:@IF(C33<.005,0,F17-D33)
>D33:(F14/(100*12))*C33
>C33:+F32
>B33:/FI+B32+1
>F32:+C32-E32
>E32:@IF(C32<.005,0,F17-D32)
>D32:(F14/(100*12))*C32
>C32:+F31
>B32:/FI+B31+1
>F31:+C31-E31
>E31:@IF(C31<.005,0,F17-D31)
>D31:(F14/(100*12))*C31
>C31:+F30
>B31:/FI+B30+1
>F30:+C30-E30
>E30:@IF(C30<.005,0,F17-D30)
>D30:(F14/(100*12))*C30
>C30:+F29
>B30:/FI+B29+1
>F29:+C29-E29
>E29:@IF(C29<.005,0,F17-D29)
>D29:(F14/(100*12))*C29
>C29:+F28
>B29:/FI+B28+1
>F28:+C28-E28
>E28:@IF(C28<.005,0,F17-D28)
>D28:(F14/(100*12))*C28
>C28:@IF(F87<.005,F15,F87)
>B28:/FI@IF(F87<.005,1,B87+1)
>F27:" ---------
>E27:" ---------
>D27:" ---------
>C27:" ---------
>B27:"      -----
>F26:"  Balance
>E26:"    Paid
>D26:"     Paid
>C26:"  Balance
>B26:"      Month
>F25:" Principal
>E25:" Principal
>D25:"  Interest
>C25:" Principal
>F24:" Remaining
>C24:" Beginning
>G23:/-=
>F23:/-=
```

LOAN PAYOFF CALCULATOR

The formulas used to calculate each number are listed below. They are read from bottom to top and right to left and are referenced by their location in the model.

```
>G48:" (CR)
>F48:"R) /PPH31
>E48:": >A10 (C
>D48:"by typing
>C48:"4) PRINT
>F47:"ame (CR)
>E47:" /SSFilen
>D47:"y typing:
>C47:"3) SAVE b
>E46:"typing: !
>D46:"ULATE by
>C46:"2) RECALC
>E45:"NS (>A10)
>D45:"ASSUMPTIO
>C45:"1) Enter
>H42:/-=
>G42:/-=
>F42:/-=
>E42:/-=
>D42:/-=
>C42:/-=
>B42:/-=
>A42:/-=
>H41:"Sheet 3.1
>B41:"ONS
>A41:"INSTRUCTI
>F31:"  ======
>F30:/F$+F27-F28
>E30:"Loan:   $
>D30:"o Retire
>C30:"equired t
>B30:"Payment R
>F29:"  ------
see formula below
>E28:/FR"$
>D28:"e:
>C28:"Rebate Du
>B28:"Interest
>F27:/F$(F16-F17)*F18
>E27:":        $
>D27:" Payments
>C27:"Remaining
>B27:"Total of
>F25:/F$(F18*F16)-F14
>E25:" Term:  $
>D25:"d at Full
>C25:"erest Pai
>B25:"Total Int
>H23:/-=
>G23:/-=
>F23:/-=
>E23:/-=
>D23:/-=
>C23:/-=
>B23:/-=
>A23:/-=
>H22:"Sheet 2.1
>A22:"SOLUTIONS
>F18:71.14
>E18:/FR"$
>C18:"ayment:
>B18:"Monthly P
>F17:19
>E17:"r:
>D17:"was Numbe
>C17:"ent Made
>B17:"Last Paym
>F16:24
>C16:"onths:
>B16:"Term in M
>G15:" %
>F15:12.75
>E15:/FR"$
>D15:"te:
>C15:"terest Ra
>B15:"Annual In
>F14:1500
>E14:/FR"$
>C14:" Amount:
>B14:"Principal
>H11:/-=
>G11:/-=
>F11:/-=
>E11:/-=
>D11:/-=
>C11:/-=
>B11:/-=
>A11:/-=
>H10:"Sheet 1.1
>B10:"NS
>A10:"ASSUMPTIO
>H9:/-=
>G9:/-=
>F9:/-=
>E9:/-=
>D9:/-=
>C9:/-=
>B9:/-=
>A9:/-=
>D7:"A41
>C7:"UCTIONS >
>B7:"3.1 INSTR
>G6:"IONS >A22
>F6:"2.1 SOLUT
>D6:"10
>C6:"PTIONS >A
>B6:"1.1 ASSUM
>E4:"ENTS
>D4:"       CONT
>H3:/-=
>G3:/-=
>F3:/-=
>E3:/-=
>D3:/-=
>C3:/-=
>B3:/-=
>A3:/-=
>H2:"orp. 1983
>G2:"(C) Que C
>F2:"opyright
>E2:"        C
>C2:"ATOR
>B2:"FF CALCUL
>A2:"LOAN PAYO
>H1:/-=
>G1:/-=
>F1:/-=
>E1:/-=
>D1:/-=
>C1:/-=
>B1:/-=
>A1:/-=
/W1
/GOC
/GRA
/GC9
/X>A1:>A9:/TH
/X>A1:>A1:

>F28:/F$((F16-F17+1)*(F16-F17))/((F16^2)+F16)*F25
```

```
>E23:/-=
>D23:/-=
>C23:/-=
>B23:/-=
>A23:/-=
>G22:" Sheet 2.1
>D22:"to row 67)
>C22:"Continues
>B22:"ON TABLE (
>A22:"AMORTIZATI
>F17:(F14/(100*12))/(1-((1+(F14/(100*12)))^(-F16)))*F15
>E17:/FR"$
>C17:"yment:
>B17:"Monthly Pa
>F16:1
>C16:"nths:
>B16:"Term in Mo
>F15:/F$0
>E15:/FR"$
>C15:"Amount:
>B15:"Principal
>G14:" %
>F14:1
>D14:":
>C14:"erest Rate
>B14:"Annual Int
>G11:/-=
>F11:/-=
>E11:/-=
>D11:/-=
>C11:/-=
>B11:/-=
>A11:/-=
>G10:"Sheet 1.1
>B10:"S
>A10:"ASSUMPTION
>G9:/-=
>F9:/-=
>E9:/-=
>D9:/-=
>C9:/-=
>B9:/-=
>A9:/-=
>D7:"1
>C7:"CTIONS >A9
>B7:"3.1 INSTRU
>G6:"LE >A22
>F6:"ZATION TAB
>E6:"2.1 AMORTI
>C6:"TIONS >A10
>B6:"1.1 ASSUMP
>D4:" CONTENTS
>G3:/-=
>F3:/-=
>E3:/-=
>D3:/-=
>C3:/-=
>B3:/-=
>A3:/-=
>G2:"Corp. 1983
>F2:"t (C) QUE
>E2:"  Copyrigh
>C2:"LCULATOR
>B2:"IZATION CA
>A2:"LOAN AMORT
>G1:/-=
>F1:/-=
>E1:/-=
>D1:/-=
>C1:/-=
>B1:/-=
>A1:/-=
/W1
/GOR
/GRM
/GF$
/GC10
/X>A1:>A9:/TH
/X>A1:>A1:
```

LOAN AMORTIZATION CALCULATOR Copyright (C) QUE Corp. 1983

CONTENTS

ASSUMPTIONS Sheet 1.1

Annual Interest Rate:		1.00 %
Principal Amount:	$	0.00
Term in Months:		1.00
Monthly Payment:	$	0.00

AMORTIZATION TABLE (Continues to row 67) Sheet 2.1

Month	Beginning Principal Balance	Interest Paid	Principal Paid	Remaining Principal Balance
1	0.00	0.00	0.00	0.00
2	0.00	0.00	0.00	0.00
3	0.00	0.00	0.00	0.00
4	0.00	0.00	0.00	0.00
5	0.00	0.00	0.00	0.00
6	0.00	0.00	0.00	0.00
7	0.00	0.00	0.00	0.00
8	0.00	0.00	0.00	0.00
9	0.00	0.00	0.00	0.00
10	0.00	0.00	0.00	0.00
11	0.00	0.00	0.00	0.00
12	0.00	0.00	0.00	0.00
13	0.00	0.00	0.00	0.00
14	0.00	0.00	0.00	0.00
15	0.00	0.00	0.00	0.00
16	0.00	0.00	0.00	0.00
17	0.00	0.00	0.00	0.00
18	0.00	0.00	0.00	0.00
19	0.00	0.00	0.00	0.00
20	0.00	0.00	0.00	0.00
21	0.00	0.00	0.00	0.00
22	0.00	0.00	0.00	0.00
23	0.00	0.00	0.00	0.00
24	0.00	0.00	0.00	0.00
25	0.00	0.00	0.00	0.00
26	0.00	0.00	0.00	0.00
27	0.00	0.00	0.00	0.00
28	0.00	0.00	0.00	0.00
29	0.00	0.00	0.00	0.00
30	0.00	0.00	0.00	0.00
31	0.00	0.00	0.00	0.00
32	0.00	0.00	0.00	0.00
33	0.00	0.00	0.00	0.00
34	0.00	0.00	0.00	0.00
35	0.00	0.00	0.00	0.00
36	0.00	0.00	0.00	0.00
37	0.00	0.00	0.00	0.00
38	0.00	0.00	0.00	0.00
39	0.00	0.00	0.00	0.00
40	0.00	0.00	0.00	0.00
41	0.00	0.00	0.00	0.00
42	0.00	0.00	0.00	0.00
43	0.00	0.00	0.00	0.00
44	0.00	0.00	0.00	0.00
45	0.00	0.00	0.00	0.00
46	0.00	0.00	0.00	0.00
47	0.00	0.00	0.00	0.00
48	0.00	0.00	0.00	0.00
49	0.00	0.00	0.00	0.00
50	0.00	0.00	0.00	0.00
51	0.00	0.00	0.00	0.00
52	0.00	0.00	0.00	0.00
53	0.00	0.00	0.00	0.00
54	0.00	0.00	0.00	0.00
55	0.00	0.00	0.00	0.00
56	0.00	0.00	0.00	0.00
57	0.00	0.00	0.00	0.00
58	0.00	0.00	0.00	0.00
59	0.00	0.00	0.00	0.00
60	0.00	0.00	0.00	0.00

INSTRUCTIONS Sheet 3.1

1) Enter ASSUMPTIONS (>A10)
2) RECALCULATE by typing: !
3) PRINT by typing: >A10 (CR) /PPG87 (CR)
4) If loan term exceeds 60 periods:
   a) RECALCULATE again by typing: !
   b) PRINT by typing: >A28 (CR) /PPG87 (CR)
   c) Repeat a) and b) until finished
5) To CLEAR model, enter "0" at cell F15

```
========================================================================
LOAN PAYOFF CALCULATOR                       Copyright (C) Que Corp. 1983
========================================================================
                              CONTENTS

         1.1 ASSUMPTIONS >A10                2.1 SOLUTIONS >A22
         3.1 INSTRUCTIONS >A41

========================================================================
ASSUMPTIONS                                                    Sheet 1.1
========================================================================


         Principal Amount:                   $      1500
         Annual Interest Rate:               $     12.75 %
         Term in Months:                              24
         Last Payment Made was Number:                19
         Monthly Payment:                    $     71.14


SOLUTIONS                                                      Sheet 2.1
========================================================================

         Total Interest Paid at Full Term:   $    207.36

         Total of Remaining Payments:        $    355.70
         Interest Rebate Due:                $     10.37
                                                  ------
         Payment Required to Retire Loan:    $    345.33
                                                  ======



INSTRUCTIONS                                                   Sheet 3.1
========================================================================


                  1) Enter ASSUMPTIONS (>A10)
                  2) RECALCULATE by typing: !
                  3) SAVE by typing: /SSFilename (CR)
                  4) PRINT by typing: >A10 (CR) /PPH31 (CR)
```

LINE-OF-CREDIT TRACKER

The formulas used to calculate each number are listed below. They are read from bottom to top and right to left and are referenced by their location in the model.

```
>G72:" (CR)
>F72:"R) /PPH60
>E72:": >A10 (C
>D72:"by typing
>C72:"4) PRINT
>F71:"ame (CR)
>E71:" /SSFilen
>D71:"y typing:
>C71:"3) SAVE b
>E70:"typing: !
>D70:"ULATE by
>C70:"2) RECALC
>F69:"10)
>E69:"IVITY (>A
>D69:"DAILY ACT
>C69:"1) Enter
>H66:/-=
>G66:/-=
>F66:/-=
>E66:/-=
>D66:/-=
>C66:/-=
>B66:/-=
>A66:/-=
>H65:"Sheet 3.1
>B65:"ONS
>A65:"INSTRUCTI
>G56:@SUM(H17...H47)/@ABS(B47)
>F56:/FR"ance:    $
>E56:"redit Bal
>D56:"tanding C
>C56:"aily Outs
>B56:"Average D
>G54:@SUM(G17...G47)
>F54:/FR"$
>D54:"ense:
>C54:"erest Exp
>B54:"Total Int
>H52:/-=
>G52:/-=
>F52:/-=
>E52:/-=
>D52:/-=
>C52:/-=
>B52:/-=
>A52:/-=
>H51:"Sheet 2.1
>C51:"S
>B51:"D AVERAGE
>A51:"TOTALS AN
>B48:/FL
>H47:+C47+D47-E47+G47
>G47:(F47/365)*(C47+D47-E47)
>F47:/FG+F46
>C47:+H46
>B47:/FL+B46-1
>H46:+C46+D46-E46+G46
>G46:(F46/365)*(C46+D46-E46)
>F46:/FG+F45
>C46:+H45
>B46:/FL+B45-1
>H45:+C45+D45-E45+G45
>G45:(F45/365)*(C45+D45-E45)
>F45:/FG+F44
>C45:+H44
>B45:/FL+B44-1
>H44:+C44+D44-E44+G44
>G44:(F44/365)*(C44+D44-E44)
>F44:/FG+F43
>C44:+H43
>B44:/FL+B43-1
>H43:+C43+D43-E43+G43
>G43:(F43/365)*(C43+D43-E43)
>F43:/FG+F42
>C43:+H42
>B43:/FL+B42-1
>H42:+C42+D42-E42+G42
>G42:(F42/365)*(C42+D42-E42)
>F42:/FG+F41
>C42:+H41
>B42:/FL+B41-1
>H41:+C41+D41-E41+G41
>G41:(F41/365)*(C41+D41-E41)
>F41:/FG+F40
>C41:+H40
>B41:/FL+B40-1
>H40:+C40+D40-E40+G40
>G40:(F40/365)*(C40+D40-E40)
>F40:/FG+F39
>C40:+H39
>B40:/FL+B39-1
>H39:+C39+D39-E39+G39
>G39:(F39/365)*(C39+D39-E39)
>F39:/FG.165
>C39:+H38
>B39:/FL+B38-1
>H38:+C38+D38-E38+G38
>G38:(F38/365)*(C38+D38-E38)
>F38:/FG+F37
>C38:+H37
>B38:/FL+B37-1
>H37:+C37+D37-E37+G37
>G37:(F37/365)*(C37+D37-E37)
>F37:/FG+F36
>C37:+H36
>B37:/FL+B36-1
>H36:+C36+D36-E36+G36
>G36:(F36/365)*(C36+D36-E36)
>F36:/FG+F35
>C36:+H35
>B36:/FL+B35-1
>H35:+C35+D35-E35+G35
>G35:(F35/365)*(C35+D35-E35)
>F35:/FG+F34
>C35:+H34
>B35:/FL+B34-1
>H34:+C34+D34-E34+G34
>G34:(F34/365)*(C34+D34-E34)
>F34:/FG+F33
>D34:2200
>C34:+H33
>B34:/FL+B33-1
>H33:+C33+D33-E33+G33
>G33:(F33/365)*(C33+D33-E33)
>F33:/FG+F32
>C33:+H32
>B33:/FL+B32-1
>H32:+C32+D32-E32+G32
>G32:(F32/365)*(C32+D32-E32)
>F32:/FG+F31
>C32:+H31
>B32:/FL+B31-1
>H31:+C31+D31-E31+G31
>G31:(F31/365)*(C31+D31-E31)
>F31:/FG+F30
>E31:1506.39
>C31:+H30
>B31:/FL+B30-1
>H30:+C30+D30-E30+G30
>G30:(F30/365)*(C30+D30-E30)
>F30:/FG+F29
>C30:+H29
>B30:/FL+B29-1
>H29:+C29+D29-E29+G29
>G29:(F29/365)*(C29+D29-E29)
>F29:/FG+F28
>C29:+H28
>B29:/FL+B28-1
>H28:+C28+D28-E28+G28
>G28:(F28/365)*(C28+D28-E28)
>F28:/FG+F27
>C28:+H27
>B28:/FL+B27-1
>H27:+C27+D27-E27+G27
>G27:(F27/365)*(C27+D27-E27)
>F27:/FG+F26
>C27:+H26
>B27:/FL+B26-1
>H26:+C26+D26-E26+G26
>G26:(F26/365)*(C26+D26-E26)
>F26:/FG+F25
>C26:+H25
>B26:/FL+B25-1
>H25:+C25+D25-E25+G25
>G25:(F25/365)*(C25+D25-E25)
>F25:/FG+F24
>C25:+H24
>B25:/FL+B24-1
>H24:+C24+D24-E24+G24
>G24:(F24/365)*(C24+D24-E24)
>F24:/FG+F23
>C24:+H23
>B24:/FL+B23-1
>H23:+C23+D23-E23+G23
>G23:(F23/365)*(C23+D23-E23)
>F23:/FG+F22
>C23:+H22
>B23:/FL+B22-1
>H22:+C22+D22-E22+G22
>G22:(F22/365)*(C22+D22-E22)
>F22:/FG+F21
>C22:+H21
>B22:/FL+B21-1
>H21:+C21+D21-E21+G21
>G21:(F21/365)*(C21+D21-E21)
>F21:/FG+F20
>D21:1500
>C21:+H20
>B21:/FL+B20-1
>H20:+C20+D20-E20+G20
>G20:(F20/365)*(C20+D20-E20)
>F20:/FG+F19
>C20:+H19
>B20:/FL+B19-1
>H19:+C19+D19-E19+G19
>G19:(F19/365)*(C19+D19-E19)
>F19:/FG+F18
>E19:3502.97
>C19:+H18
>B19:/FL+B18-1
>H18:+C18+D18-E18+G18
>G18:(F18/365)*(C18+D18-E18)
>F18:/FG+F17
>C18:+H17
>B18:/FL-2
>H17:+C17+D17-E17+G17
>G17:(F17/365)*(C17+D17-E17)
>F17:/FG.155
>C17:3500
>B17:/FL"9-1
>H16:" --------
>G16:" --------
>F16:" --------
>E16:" --------
>D16:" --------
>C16:" --------
>B16:"----
>H15:" Balance
>G15:" Expense
>F15:"    Rate
>E15:"Repayment
>D15:"  Credit
>C15:" Balance
>B15:"Date
>H14:"  Credit
>G14:" Interest
>F14:" Interest
>D14:"    New
>C14:"  Day's
>H13:"  Total
>F13:"  Annual
>C13:" Previous
>H11:/-=
>G11:/-=
>F11:/-=
>E11:/-=
>D11:/-=
>C11:/-=
>B11:/-=
>A11:/-=
>H10:"Sheet 1.1
>D10:"o A47)
>C10:"ntinues t
>B10:"IVITY (Co
>A10:"DAILY ACT
>H9:/-=
>G9:/-=
>F9:/-=
>E9:/-=
>D9:/-=
>C9:/-=
>B9:/-=
>A9:/-=
>D7:"A65
>C7:"UCTIONS >
>B7:"3.1 INSTR
>H6:" >A51
>G6:" AVERAGES
>F6:"OTALS AND
>E6:"    2.1 T
>D6:" >A10
>C6:" ACTIVITY
>B6:"1.1 DAILY
>E4:"ENTS
>D4:"       CONT
>H3:/-=
>G3:/-=
>F3:/-=
>E3:/-=
>D3:/-=
>C3:/-=
>B3:/-=
>A3:/-=
>H2:"orp. 1983
>G2:"(C) Que C
>F2:"opyright
>E2:"          C
>C2:"CKER
>B2:"REDIT TRA
>A2:"LINE OF C
>H1:/-=
>G1:/-=
>F1:/-=
>E1:/-=
>D1:/-=
>C1:/-=
>B1:/-=
>A1:/-=
/W1
/GOR
/GRM
/GF$
/GC9
/X>A1:>A9:/TH
/X>A59:>C79:
```

LINE OF CREDIT TRACKER — Copyright (C) Que Corp. 1983

CONTENTS

DAILY ACTIVITY (Continues to A47) — Sheet 1.1

Date	Previous Day's Balance	New Credit	Repayment	Annual Interest Rate	Interest Expense	Total Credit Balance
9-1	3500.00			.155	1.49	3501.49
-2	3501.49			.155	1.49	3502.97
-3	3502.97		3502.97	.155	0.00	0.00
-4	0.00			.155	0.00	0.00
-5	0.00	1500.00		.155	0.64	1500.64
-6	1500.64			.155	0.64	1501.28
-7	1501.28			.155	0.64	1501.92
-8	1501.92			.155	0.64	1502.55
-9	1502.55			.155	0.64	1503.19
-10	1503.19			.155	0.64	1503.83
-11	1503.83			.155	0.64	1504.47
-12	1504.47			.155	0.64	1505.11
-13	1505.11			.155	0.64	1505.75
-14	1505.75			.155	0.64	1506.39
-15	1506.39		1506.39	.155	0.00	0.00
-16	0.00			.155	0.00	0.00
-17	0.00			.155	0.00	0.00
-18	0.00	2200.00		.155	0.93	2200.93
-19	2200.93			.155	0.93	2201.86
-20	2201.86			.155	0.94	2202.80
-21	2202.80			.155	0.94	2203.73
-22	2203.73			.155	0.94	2204.67
-23	2204.67			.165	1.00	2205.67
-24	2205.67			.165	1.00	2206.66
-25	2206.66			.165	1.00	2207.66
-26	2207.66			.165	1.00	2208.66
-27	2208.66			.165	1.00	2209.66
-28	2209.66			.165	1.00	2210.66
-29	2210.66			.165	1.00	2211.66
-30	2211.66			.165	1.00	2212.66
-31	2212.66			.165	1.00	2213.66

TOTALS AND AVERAGES — Sheet 2.1

Total Interest Expense: $ 23.02

Average Daily Outstanding Credit Balance: $ 1707.76

INSTRUCTIONS — Sheet 3.1

1) Enter DAILY ACTIVITY (>A10)
2) RECALCULATE by typing: !
3) SAVE by typing: /SSFilename (CR)
4) PRINT by typing: >A10 (CR) /PPH60 (CR)

ACRS DEPRECIATION CALCULATOR

The formulas used to calculate each number are listed below. They are read from bottom to top and right to left and are referenced by their location in the model.

```
>G52:" (CR)
>F52:"R) /PPH42
>E52:": >A10 (C
>D52:"by typing
>C52:"4) PRINT
>F51:"ame (CR)
>E51:" /SSFilen
>D51:"y typing:
>C51:"3) SAVE b
>E50:"typing: l
>D50:"ULATE by
>C50:"2) RECALC
>E49:"NS (>A10)
>D49:"ASSUMPTIO
>C49:"1) Enter
>H46:/-=
>G46:/-=
>F46:/-=
>E46:/-=
>D46:/-=
>C46:/-=
>B46:/-=
>A46:/-=
>H45:"Sheet 3.1
>B45:"ONS
>A45:"INSTRUCTI
>C43:/FL
>B43:/FL
>H42:/F$+H41-E42
>E42:/F$@LOOKUP(C42,K8...K23)*(G14-D27)/100
>C42:/FL16
>B42:/FL+B41+1
>H41:/F$+H40-E41
>E41:/F$@LOOKUP(C41,K8...K23)*(G14-D27)/100
>C41:/FL15
>B41:/FL+B40+1
>H40:/F$+H39-E40
>E40:/F$@LOOKUP(C40,K8...K23)*(G14-D27)/100
>C40:/FL14
>B40:/FL+B39+1
>H39:/F$+H38-E39
>E39:/F$@LOOKUP(C39,K8...K23)*(G14-D27)/100
>C39:/FL13
>B39:/FL+B38+1
>H38:/F$+H37-E38
>E38:/F$@LOOKUP(C38,K8...K23)*(G14-D27)/100
>C38:/FL12
>B38:/FL+B37+1
>H37:/F$+H36-E37
>E37:/F$@LOOKUP(C37,K8...K23)*(G14-D27)/100
>C37:/FL11
>B37:/FL+B36+1
>H36:/F$+H35-E36
>E36:/F$@LOOKUP(C36,K8...K23)*(G14-D27)/100
>C36:/FL10
>B36:/FL+B35+1
>H35:/F$+H34-E35
>E35:/F$@LOOKUP(C35,K8...K23)*(G14-D27)/100
>C35:/FL9
>B35:/FL+B34+1
>H34:/F$+H33-E34
>E34:/F$@LOOKUP(C34,K8...K23)*(G14-D27)/100
>C34:/FL8
>B34:/FL+B33+1
>H33:/F$+H32-E33
>E33:/F$@LOOKUP(C33,K8...K23)*(G14-D27)/100
>C33:/FL7
>B33:/FL+B32+1
>H32:/F$+H31-E32
>E32:/F$@LOOKUP(C32,K8...K23)*(G14-D27)/100
>C32:/FL6
>B32:/FL+B31+1
>H31:/F$+H30-E31
>E31:/F$@LOOKUP(C31,K8...K23)*(G14-D27)/100
>C31:/FL5
>B31:/FL+B30+1
>H30:/F$+H29-E30
>E30:/F$@LOOKUP(C30,K8...K23)*(G14-D27)/100
>C30:/FL4
>B30:/FL+B29+1
>H29:/F$+H28-E29
>E29:/F$@LOOKUP(C29,K8...K23)*(G14-D27)/100
>C29:/FL3
>B29:/FL+B28+1
>H28:/F$+H27-E28
>E28:/F$@LOOKUP(C28,K8...K23)*(G14-D27)/100
>C28:/FL2
>B28:/FL+B27+1
>H27:/F$+G14-D27-E27
>G27:/F$@IF(G15>3,(G14-D27)*.1,(G14-D27*.06)
>E27:/F$@LOOKUP(C27,K8...K23)*(G14-D27)/100
>D27:/F$@IF(G19>G14,G14,G19)
>C27:/FL1
>B27:/FL+G16
>H26:" --------
>G26:" --------
>F26:"----
>E26:" --------
>D26:"---------
>C26:"----
>B26:"------ --
>H25:"  Basis
>G25:"   ITC
>F25:"se
>E25:"     Expen
>D25:" Expense
>C25:"riod
>B25:" Year  Pe
>N24:/-#
>M24:/-#
>L24:/-#
>K24:/-#
>J24:/-#
>H24:"Remaining
>F24:"tion
>E24:" Deprecia
>D24:"irst Year
>C24:"         F
>N23:" ########
>M23:" %
see formula below
>K23:16
>J23:/-#
>H23:/-=
>G23:/-=
>F23:/-=
>E23:/-=
>D23:/-=
>C23:/-=
>B23:/-=
>A23:/-=
>N22:" ########
>M22:" %
>L22:@IF(G15=3,0,@IF(G15=5,0,@IF(G15=10,0,@IF(G18=2,.06,.05))))*100
>K22:15
>J22:/-#
>H22:"Sheet 2.1
>E22:" 42)
>D22:"es to row
>C22:" (Continu
>B22:"ION TABLE
>A22:"DEPRECIAT
>N21:" ########
>M21:" %
>L21:@IF(G15=3,0,@IF(G15=5,0,@IF(G15=10,0,@IF(G18=2,.06,.05))))*100
>K21:14
>J21:/-#
>N20:" ########
>M20:" %
>L20:@IF(G15=3,0,@IF(G15=5,0,@IF(G15=10,0,@IF(G18=2,.06,.05))))*100
>K20:13
>J20:/-#
>N19:" ########
>M19:" %
>L19:@IF(G15=3,0,@IF(G15=5,0,@IF(G15=10,0,@IF(G18=2,.06,.05))))*100
>K19:12
>J19:/-#
>G19:/F$5000
>F19:"):        $
>E19:"e (If Any
>D19:" Availabl
>C19:"r Expense
>B19:"First Yea
>N18:" ########
>M18:" %
>L18:@IF(G15=3,0,@IF(G15=5,0,@IF(G15=10,0,@IF(G18=2,.06,.05))))*100
>K18:11
>J18:/-#

>L23:@IF(G18=2,0,@IF(G17=12,.05,@IF(G17>8,.04,@IF(G17>6,.03,@IF(G17>4,.02,@IF(G17>2,.01,0))))))*100
>L17:@IF(G15=3,0,@IF(G15=5,0,@IF(G15=10,.09,@IF(G18=2,.06,@IF(@OR(G17=2,@OR(G17=4,G17=11)),.06,.05)))))*100
>L16:@IF(G15=3,0.@IF(G15=5,0,@IF(G15=10,.09,@IF(G18=2,.06,@IF(@OR(G17=5,@AND(G17<10,G17>6)),.05,.06)))))*100
>L15:@IF(G15=3,0,@IF(G15=5,0,@IF(G15=10,.09,@IF(G18=2,.06,@IF(G17=7,.05,.06)))))*100
>L13:@IF(G15=3,0,@IF(G15=5,0,@IF(G15=10,.1,@IF(G18=2,.07,@IF(G17<5,.06,.07)))))*100
```

```
>G18:2
>F18:",2=No)
>E18:" ? (1=Yes
>D18:" Property
>C18:"sset Real
>B18:"Is this A
>N17:" ########
>M17:" %
see formula below
>K17:10
>J17:/-#
>G17:6
>D17:"rvice:
>C17:"ced in Se
>B17:"Month Pla
>N16:" ########
>M16:" %
see formula below
>K16:9
>J16:/-#
>G16:1982
>D16:"vice:
>C16:"ed in Ser
>B16:"Year Plac
>N15:" ########
>M15:" %
see formula below
>K15:8
>J15:/-#
>G15:5
>D15:":
>C15:" of Asset
>B15:"ACRS Life
>N14:" ########
>M14:" %
>L14:@IF(G15=3,0,@IF(G15=5,0,@IF(G15=10,.09,.06)))*100
>K14:7
>J14:/-#
>G14:/F$8900
>F14:/FR"$
>D14:"of Asset:
>C14:"ase Cost
>B14:"Net Purch
>N13:" ########
>M13:" %
see formula below
>K13:6
>J13:/-#
>G13:/FR"Computer
>D13:"et:
>C13:"on of Ass
>B13:"Descripti
>N12:" ########
>M12:" %
see formula below
>K12:5
>J12:/-#
>N11:" ########
>M11:" %
see formula below
>K11:4
>J11:/-#
>H11:/-=
>G11:/-=
>F11:/-=
>E11:/-=
>D11:/-=
>C11:/-=
>B11:/-=
>A11:/-=
>N10:" ########
>M10:" %
see formula below
>K10:3
>J10:/-#
>H10:"Sheet 1.1
>B10:"NS
>A10:"ASSUMPTIO
>N9:" ########
>M9:" %
see formula below
>K9:2
>J9:/-#
>H9:/-=
```

```
>G9:/-=
>F9:/-=
>E9:/-=
>D9:/-=
>C9:/-=
>B9:/-=
>A9:/-=
>N8:" ########
>M8:" %
see formula below
>K8:1
>J8:/-#
>N7:" ########
>M7:"---
>L7:"      ----
>K7:"      ----
>J7:/-#
>D7:"A45
>C7:"UCTIONS >
>B7:"3.1 INSTR
>N6:" ########
>M6:"ent
>L6:"      Perc
>K6:"      Year
>J6:/-#
>G6:"ABLE >A22
>F6:"CIATION T
>E6:"    DEPRE
>D6:"10
>C6:"PTIONS >A
>B6:"1.1 ASSUM
>N5:"=########
>M5:/-=
>L5:/-=
>K5:/-=
>J5:/-#
>N4:" ########
>L4:"  TABLE
>J4:/-#
>E4:"ENTS
>D4:"      CONT
>N3:" ########
>M3:"N
>L3:"PRECIATIO
>K3:"        DE
>J3:/-#
>H3:/-=
>G3:/-=
>F3:/-=
>E3:/-=
>D3:/-=
>C3:/-=
>B3:/-=
>A3:/-=
>N2:" ########
>L2:"  ACRS
>J2:/-#
>H2:"orp. 1983
>G2:"(C) Que C
>F2:"opyright
>E2:"        C
>D2:"R
>C2:"CALCULATO
>B2:"ECIATION
>A2:"ACRS DEPR
>N1:/-#
>M1:/-#
>L1:/-#
>K1:/-#
>J1:/-#
>H1:/-=
>G1:/-=
>F1:/-=
>E1:/-=
>D1:/-=
>C1:/-=
>B1:/-=
>A1:/-=
/W1
/GOC
/GRM
/GC9
/X>A1:>A9:/TH
/X>A1:>A1:
```

```
>L12:@IF(G15=3,0,@IF(G15=5,.21,@IF(G15=10,.1,@IF(G18=2,.07,@IF(G17<7,.07,.08)))))*100
>L11:@IF(G15=3,0,@IF(G15=5,.21,@IF(G15=10,.1,@IF(G18=2,.08,@IF(G17<7,.08,.09)))))*100
>L10:@IF(G15=3,.37,@IF(G15=5,.21,@IF(G15=10,.12,@IF(G18=2,.09,@IF(G17<5,.09,.1)))))*100
>L9:@IF(G15=3,.38,@IF(G15=5,.22,@IF(G15=10,.14,@IF(G18=2,.1,@IF(G17<3,.1,@IF(G17=12,.12,.11))))))*100
>L8:@IF(G15=3,.25,@IF(G15=5,.15,@IF(G15=10,.08,@IF(G18=2,.05,(12-(G17-1))/100))))*100
```

```
===========================================================================
ACRS DEPRECIATION CALCULATOR                         Copyright (C) Que Corp. 1983
===========================================================================
                              CONTENTS

      1.1 ASSUMPTIONS >A10             DEPRECIATION TABLE >A22
      3.1 INSTRUCTIONS >A45

===========================================================================
ASSUMPTIONS                                                        Sheet 1.1
===========================================================================

      Description of Asset:                                   Computer
      Net Purchase Cost of Asset:                          $   8900.00
      ACRS Life of Asset:                                            5
      Year Placed in Service:                                     1982
      Month Placed in Service:                                       6
      Is this Asset Real Property ? (1=Yes,2=No)                     2
      First Year Expense Available (If Any):               $   5000.00


DEPRECIATION TABLE (Continues to row 42)                           Sheet 2.1
===========================================================================
                          First Year Depreciation                Remaining
        Year  Period        Expense     Expense           ITC      Basis
       ------ ------      --------- -----------      -------- --------
        1982     1         5000.00    585.00           390.00  3315.00
        1983     2                    858.00                   2457.00
        1984     3                    819.00                   1638.00
        1985     4                    819.00                    819.00
        1986     5                    819.00                      0.00
        1987     6                      0.00                      0.00
        1988     7                      0.00                      0.00
        1989     8                      0.00                      0.00
        1990     9                      0.00                      0.00
        1991    10                      0.00                      0.00
        1992    11                      0.00                      0.00
        1993    12                      0.00                      0.00
        1994    13                      0.00                      0.00
        1995    14                      0.00                      0.00
        1996    15                      0.00                      0.00
        1997    16                      0.00                      0.00


INSTRUCTIONS                                                       Sheet 3.1
===========================================================================

               1) Enter ASSUMPTIONS (>A10)
               2) RECALCULATE by typing: !
               3) SAVE by typing: /SSFilename (CR)
               4) PRINT by typing: >A10 (CR) /PPH42 (CR)
```

```
################################################
#########           ACRS              #########
#########       DEPRECIATION          #########
#########           TABLE             #########
#########=============================#########
#########     Year       Percent      #########
#########     ----       --------     #########
#########        1         15 %       #########
#########        2         22 %       #########
#########        3         21 %       #########
#########        4         21 %       #########
#########        5         21 %       #########
#########        6          0 %       #########
#########        7          0 %       #########
#########        8          0 %       #########
#########        9          0 %       #########
#########       10          0 %       #########
#########       11          0 %       #########
#########       12          0 %       #########
#########       13          0 %       #########
#########       14          0 %       #########
#########       15          0 %       #########
#########       16          0 %       #########
################################################
```

[illegible] DEPRECIATION [illegible]

[illegible]

1. ASSUMPTIONS [illegible]
2. [illegible]

ASSUMPTIONS

[illegible] Inflation [illegible]
Net [illegible] Cost of Asset [illegible] 4000.00
[illegible] Life of Asset [illegible]
Year Placed in Service [illegible]
Month Placed in Service [illegible]
Is This Asset [illegible]
First Year [illegible]

DEPRECIATION TABLE [illegible]

Year	Period	[illegible]	[illegible]
[illegible]	1	[illegible]	[illegible]
[illegible]	2	[illegible]	[illegible]
[illegible]	3	[illegible]	[illegible]
[illegible]	4	[illegible]	[illegible]
[illegible]	5	[illegible]	[illegible]
[illegible]	6	[illegible]	[illegible]
[illegible]	7	[illegible]	[illegible]
[illegible]	8	[illegible]	[illegible]
[illegible]	9	[illegible]	[illegible]
[illegible]	10	[illegible]	[illegible]
[illegible]	11	[illegible]	[illegible]
[illegible]	12	[illegible]	[illegible]
[illegible]	13	[illegible]	[illegible]
[illegible]	14	[illegible]	[illegible]
[illegible]	15	[illegible]	[illegible]
[illegible]	16	[illegible]	[illegible]

[illegible]

1) [illegible] ASSUMPTIONS [illegible]
2) [illegible] CALCULATE [illegible]
3) SAVE [illegible]
4) PRINT [illegible]

INTERNAL RATE OF RETURN CALCULATOR

The formulas used to calculate each number are listed below. They are read from bottom to top and right to left and are referenced by their location in the model.

```
>G68:" (CR)
>F68:"R) /PPH50
>E68:": >A10 (C
>D68:"by typing
>C68:"4) PRINT
>F67:"ame (CR)
>E67:" /SSFilen
>D67:"y typing:
>C67:"3) SAVE b
>E66:"typing: !
>D66:"ULATE by
>C66:"2) RECALC
>E65:"NS (>A10)
>D65:"ASSUMPTIO
>C65:"1) Enter
>H62:/-=
>G62:/-=
>F62:/-=
>E62:/-=
>D62:/-=
>C62:/-=
>B62:/-=
>A62:/-=
>H61:"Sheet 3.1
>B61:"ONS
>A61:"INSTRUCTI
>H50:" %
>G50:/FG+X12*100
>D50:"eturn:
>C50:"Rate of R
>B50:"Internal
>H46:/-=
>G46:/-=
>F46:/-=
>E46:/-=
>D46:/-=
>C46:/-=
>B46:/-=
>A46:/-=
>H45:"Sheet 2.1
>A45:"SOLUTIONS
>E40:0
>C40:/FL+C39+1
>E39:0
>C39:/FL+C38+1
>E38:0
>C38:/FL+C37+1
>E37:0
>C37:/FL+C36+1
>E36:0
>C36:/FL+C35+1
>E35:0
>C35:/FL+C34+1
>E34:0
>C34:/FL+C33+1
>E33:0
>C33:/FL+C32+1
>E32:0
>C32:/FL+C31+1
>E31:0
>C31:/FL+C30+1
>E30:0
>C30:/FL+C29+1
>E29:0
>C29:/FL+C28+1
>E28:0
>C28:/FL+C27+1
>E27:0
>C27:/FL+C26+1
>E26:0
>C26:/FL+C25+1
>E25:12000
>C25:/FL+C24+1
>E24:12000
>C24:/FL+C23+1
>E23:12000
>C23:/FL+C22+1
>E22:12000
>C22:/FL+C21+1
>E21:12000
>C21:/FL+C20+1
>E20:12000
>C20:/FL+C19+1
>E19:12000
>C19:/FL+C18+1
>E18:12000
>C18:/FL+C17+1
>E17:12000
>C17:/FL+C16+1
>E16:12000
>D16:/FL45000
>C16:/FL1982
>E15:"  -------
>D15:"--------
>C15:" ---- --
>Y14:/-#
>X14:/-#
>W14:/-#
>V14:/-#
>U14:/-#
>T14:/-#
>S14:/-#
>R14:/-#
>Q14:/-#
>P14:/-#
>O14:/-#
>N14:/-#
>M14:/-#
>L14:/-#
>K14:/-#
>J14:/-#
>E14:"  Inflows
>D14:"vestment
>C14:" Year  In
>Y13:" ########
>J13:/-#
>E13:"    Cash
>Y12:" ########
>X12:/FG@LOOKUP(D16,M11...W11)
>W12:/FG+V12-.001
>V12:/FG+U12-.001
>U12:/FG+T12-.001
>T12:/FG+S12-.001
>S12:/FG+R12-.001
>R12:/FG+Q12-.001
>Q12:/FG+P12-.001
>P12:/FG+O12-.001
>O12:/FG+N12-.001
>N12:/FG+M12-.001
>M12:/FG+X9
>L12:"RATE
>J12:/-#
>E12:"   Annual
>Y11:" ########
>W11:@NPV(X9-.01,E16...E40)
>V11:@NPV(X9-.009,E16...E40)
>U11:@NPV(X9-.008,E16...E40)
>T11:@NPV(X9-.007,E16...E40)
>S11:@NPV(X9-.006,E16...E40)
>R11:@NPV(X9-.005,E16...E40)
>Q11:@NPV(X9-.004,E16...E40)
>P11:@NPV(X9-.003,E16...E40)
>O11:@NPV(X9-.002,E16...E40)
>N11:@NPV(X9-.001,E16...E40)
>M11:@NPV(X9,E16...E40)
>L11:"NPV
>K11:" Pass 3
>J11:/-#
>H11:/-=
>G11:/-=
>F11:/-=
>E11:/-=
>D11:/-=
>C11:/-=
>B11:/-=
>A11:/-=
>Y10:" ########
>J10:/-#
>H10:"Sheet 1.1
>D10:"ow 41)
>C10:"nues to r
>B10:"NS (Conti
>A10:"ASSUMPTIO
>Y9:" ########
>X9:/F$@LOOKUP(D16,M8...W8)
>W9:+V9-.01
>V9:+U9-.01
>U9:+T9-.01
>T9:+S9-.01
>S9:+R9-.01
>R9:+Q9-.01
>Q9:+P9-.01
>P9:+O9-.01
>O9:+N9-.01
>N9:+M9-.01
>M9:+X6
>L9:"RATE
>J9:/-#
>H9:/-=
>G9:/-=
>F9:/-=
>E9:/-=
>D9:/-=
>C9:/-=
>B9:/-=
>A9:/-=
>Y8:" ########
>W8:@NPV(X6-.1,E16...E40)
>V8:@NPV(X6-.09,E16...E40)
>U8:@NPV(X6-.08,E16...E40)
>T8:@NPV(X6-.07,E16...E40)
>S8:@NPV(X6-.06,E16...E40)
>R8:@NPV(X6-.05,E16...E40)
>Q8:@NPV(X6-.04,E16...E40)
>P8:@NPV(X6-.03,E16...E40)
>O8:@NPV(X6-.02,E16...E40)
>N8:@NPV(X6-.01,E16...E40)
>M8:@NPV(X6,E16...E40)
>L8:"NPV
>K8:" Pass 2
>J8:/-#
>Y7:" ########
>J7:/-#
>D7:"A61
>C7:"UCTIONS >
>B7:"3.1 INSTR
>Y6:" ########
>X6:/F$@LOOKUP(D16,M5...W5)
>W6:0
>V6:.1
>U6:.2
>T6:.3
>S6:.4
>R6:.5
>Q6:.6
>P6:.7
>O6:.8
>N6:.9
>M6:1
>L6:"RATE
>J6:/-#
>G6:"ION >A45
>F6:"2.1 SOLUT
>D6:"10
>C6:"PTIONS >A
>B6:"1.1 ASSUM
>Y5:" ########
>W5:/FI@NPV(W6,E16...E40)
>V5:@NPV(V6,E16...E40)
>U5:@NPV(U6,E16...E40)
>T5:@NPV(T6,E16...E40)
>S5:@NPV(S6,E16...E40)
>R5:@NPV(R6,E16...E40)
>Q5:@NPV(Q6,E16...E40)
>P5:@NPV(P6,E16...E40)
>O5:@NPV(O6,E16...E40)
>N5:@NPV(N6,E16...E40)
>M5:@NPV(M6,E16...E40)
>L5:"NPV
>K5:" Pass 1
>J5:/-#
>Y4:" ########
>J4:/-#
>E4:"ENTS
>D4:"      CONT
>Y3:" ########
>X3:/-=
>W3:/-=
>V3:/-=
>U3:/-=
>T3:/-=
>S3:/-=
>R3:/-=
>Q3:/-=
>P3:/-=
>O3:/-=
>N3:/-=
>M3:/-=
>L3:/-=
>K3:/-=
>J3:/-#
>H3:/-=
>G3:/-=
>F3:/-=
>E3:/-=
>D3:/-=
>C3:/-=
>B3:/-=
>A3:/-=
>Y2:" ########
>N2:"le
>M2:"eturn Tab
>L2:"Rate of R
>K2:"Internal
>J2:/-#
>H2:"orp. 1983
>G2:"(C) Que C
>F2:"opyright
>E2:"         C
>D2:"CULATOR
>C2:"ETURN CAL
>B2:"RATE OF R
>A2:"INTERNAL
>Y1:/-#
>X1:/-#
>W1:/-#
>V1:/-#
>U1:/-#
>T1:/-#
>S1:/-#
>R1:/-#
>Q1:/-#
>P1:/-#
>O1:/-#
>N1:/-#
>M1:/-#
>L1:/-#
>K1:/-#
>J1:/-#
>H1:/-=
>G1:/-=
>F1:/-=
>E1:/-=
>D1:/-=
>C1:/-=
>B1:/-=
>A1:/-=
/W1
/GOR
/GRM
/GF$
/GC9
/X>A1:>A9:/TH
/X>R1:>R1:
```

INTERNAL RATE OF RETURN CALCULATOR Copyright (C) Que Corp. 1983

CONTENTS

ASSUMPTIONS (Continues to row 41) Sheet 1.1

Year	Investment	Annual Cash Inflows
1982	45000	12000.00
1983		12000.00
1984		12000.00
1985		12000.00
1986		12000.00
1987		12000.00
1988		12000.00
1989		12000.00
1990		12000.00
1991		12000.00
1992		0.00
1993		0.00
1994		0.00
1995		0.00
1996		0.00
1997		0.00
1998		0.00
1999		0.00
2000		0.00
2001		0.00
2002		0.00
2003		0.00
2004		0.00
2005		0.00
2006		0.00

SOLUTIONS Sheet 2.1

Internal Rate of Return: 23.5 %

INSTRUCTIONS Sheet 3.1

1) Enter ASSUMPTIONS (>A10)
2) RECALCULATE by typing: !
3) SAVE by typing: /SSFilename (CR)
4) PRINT by typing: >A10 (CR) /PPH50 (CR)

Internal Rate of Return Table

Pass 1	NPV	11988.28	13311.59	14957.99	17057.82	19818.10	23583.80	28962.85	37098.47	50309.67	73734.81	120000	
	RATE	1.00	0.90	0.80	0.70	0.60	0.50	0.40	0.30	0.20	0.10	0.00	0.30
Pass 2	NPV	37098.47	38136.76	39227.00	40372.70	41577.67	42846.04	44182.28	45591.24	47078.21	48648.94	50309.67	
	RATE	0.30	0.29	0.28	0.27	0.26	0.25	0.24	0.23	0.22	0.21	0.20	0.24
Pass 3	NPV	44182.28	44319.82	44458.09	44597.10	44736.85	44877.35	45018.60	45160.61	45303.38	45446.92	45591.24	
	RATE	.24	.239	.238	.237	.236	.235	.234	.233	.232	.231	.23	.235

INTERNAL RATE OF RETURN CALCULATION

[illegible]

[illegible]

[illegible]

[illegible]

[illegible]

ACCOUNTS RECEIVABLE COLLECTIONS TRACKER   Copyright (C) Que Corp. 1983

CONTENTS

SALES DATA   Sheet 1.1

Report for month of: August 83

		Total Sales	Returns	Cash Sales	Net Credit Sales
Last Month:	$	100000	1000	5000	94000
Month before Last:	$	96000	4000	4000	88000

COLLECTIONS DATA (Continues to row 66)   Sheet 2.1

	Amount Collected			Total Collections		
	Last Month	Month Before Last	All Previous Months	Amount	Percent	Cumulative Percent
8-1	1000	250	0	1250	2	2
-2	2000	400	0	2400	3	5
-3	0	350	0	350	0	5
-4	1675	350	0	2025	3	8
-5	2608	200	255	3063	4	12
-6	1665	0	378	2043	3	15
-7	966	180	118	1264	2	16
-8	1788	430	1000	3218	4	20
-9	1009	505	0	1514	2	22
-10	0	0	0	0	0	22
-11	2445	550	244	3239	4	27
-12	768	348	477	1593	2	29
-13	2278	0	0	2278	3	32
-14	120	543	0	663	1	33
-15	2455	612	244	3311	4	37
-16	4167	213	0	4380	6	43
-17	0	355	0	355	0	43
-18	5346	288	117	5751	8	51
-19	4678	666	0	5344	7	58
-20	4212	0	0	4212	6	63
-21	4867	476	0	5343	7	70
-22	2213	356	0	2569	3	73
-23	2440	305	0	2745	4	77
-24	0	678	0	678	1	78
-25	795	380	0	1175	2	79
-26	3356	587	0	3943	5	85
-27	2667	0	0	2667	3	88
-28	378	950	400	1728	2	90
-29	1478	704	0	2182	3	93
-30	4590	345	0	4935	6	100
-31	0	307	0	307	0	100
Total Collections	61964	11328	3233	76525	100 %	
Percent of Sales	65.92	12.87				

INSTRUCTIONS   Sheet 3.1

1) Enter SALES DATA (>A10)
2) Daily, Enter COLLECTIONS DATA (>A22)
3) RECALCULATE by typing: !
4) SAVE by typing: /SSFilename (CR)
5) PRINT by typing: >A10 (CR) /PPH66 (CR)

EOQ INVENTORY ORDERING CALCULATOR

The formulas used to calculate each number are listed below. They are read from bottom to top and right to left and are referenced by their location in the model.

```
>E43:"
>G42:" (CR)
>F42:"R) /PPH28
>E42:": >A10 (C
>D42:"by typing
>C42:"4) PRINT
>F41:"ame (CR)
>E41:" /SSFilen
>D41:"y typing:
>C41:"3) SAVE b
>E40:"typing: !
>D40:"ULATE by
>C40:"2) RECALC
>E39:"NS (>A10)
>D39:"ASSUMPTIO
>C39:"1) Enter
>H36:/-=
>G36:/-=
>F36:/-=
>E36:/-=
>D36:/-=
>C36:/-=
>B36:/-=
>A36:/-=
>H35:"Sheet 3.1
>B35:"ONS
>A35:"INSTRUCTI
>G28:" Units
>F28:+F13*F16
>D28:"ck:
>C28:"afety Sto
>B28:"Minimum S
>G27:" Days
>F27:/FI(F26/F13)*7
>D27:"y:
>C27:"aced Ever
>B27:"Orders Pl
>G26:" Units
>F26:/FI@SQRT((2*F15*F13)/F25)
>D26:" Order:
>C26:" Units to
>B26:"Number of
>F25:/F$(((F17+F18)/100)/52)*F14
>E25:/FR"$
>D25:"Unit:
>C25:"Cost per
>B25:"Carrying
>H23:/-=
>G23:/-=
>F23:/-=
>E23:/-=
>D23:/-=
>C23:/-=
>B23:/-=
>A23:/-=
>H22:"Sheet 2.1
>A22:"SOLUTIONS
>G18:" %
>F18:3
>D18:"llowance:
>C18:"rinkage A
>B18:"Annual Sh
>G17:" %
>F17:14
>D17:"te:
>C17:"terest Ra
>B17:"Annual In
>G16:" weeks
>F16:3
>D16:" Weeks:
>C16:"d Time in
>B16:"Order Lea
>F15:/F$9
>E15:/FR"$
>C15:"Cost:
>B15:"Ordering
>F14:/F$20
>E14:/FR"$
>D14:" Unit:
>C14:"Price per
>B14:"Purchase
>F13:400
>E13:"ek:
>D13:"ld per We
>C13:" Units So
>B13:"Number of
>H11:/-=
>G11:/-=
>F11:/-=
>E11:/-=
>D11:/-=
>C11:/-=
>B11:/-=
>A11:/-=
>H10:"Sheet 1.1
>B10:"NS
>A10:"ASSUMPTIO
>H9:/-=
>G9:/-=
>F9:/-=
>E9:/-=
>D9:/-=
>C9:/-=
>B9:/-=
>A9:/-=
>D7:"A35
>C7:"UCTIONS >
>B7:"3.1 INSTR
>G6:"IONS >A22
>F6:"2.1 SOLUT
>D6:"10
>C6:"PTIONS >A
>B6:"1.1 ASSUM
>E4:"ENTS
>D4:"      CONT
>H3:/-=
>G3:/-=
>F3:/-=
>E3:/-=
>D3:/-=
>C3:/-=
>B3:/-=
>A3:/-=
>H2:"orp. 1983
>G2:"(C) Que C
>F2:"opyright
>E2:"         C
>D2:"ULATOR
>C2:"RING CALC
>B2:"TORY ORDE
>A2:"EOQ INVEN
>H1:/-=
>G1:/-=
>F1:/-=
>E1:/-=
>D1:/-=
>C1:/-=
>B1:/-=
>A1:/-=
/W1
/GOC
/GRA
/GC9
/X>A1:>A9:/TH
/X>A1:>A1:
```

```
======================================================================
EOQ INVENTORY ORDERING CALCULATOR          Copyright (C) Que Corp. 1983
======================================================================
                              CONTENTS

        1.1 ASSUMPTIONS >A10                2.1 SOLUTIONS >A22
        3.1 INSTRUCTIONS >A35

======================================================================
ASSUMPTIONS                                                  Sheet 1.1
======================================================================

        Number of Units Sold per Week:                 400
        Purchase Price per Unit:             $       20.00
        Ordering Cost:                       $        9.00
        Order Lead Time in Weeks:                        3 weeks
        Annual Interest Rate:                           14 %
        Annual Shrinkage Allowance:                      3 %


SOLUTIONS                                                    Sheet 2.1
======================================================================

        Carrying Cost per Unit:              $        0.07
        Number of Units to Order:                      332 Units
        Orders Placed Every:                             6 Days
        Minimum Safety Stock:                         1200 Units



INSTRUCTIONS                                                 Sheet 3.1
======================================================================

                 1) Enter ASSUMPTIONS (>A10)
                 2) RECALCULATE by typing: !
                 3) SAVE by typing: /SSFilename (CR)
                 4) PRINT by typing: >A10 (CR) /PPH28 (CR)
```

```
>C203:" Earnings
>B203:" Retained
>H202:+F127
>G202:+F123
>C202:"tock
>B202:" Common S
>D201:"ty
>C201:"ers' Equi
>B201:"Stockhold
>H199:+H190+H195+H197
>G199:+G190+G195+G197
>C199:"bilities
>B199:"Total Lia
>H198:"  ------
>G198:"  ------
>H197:2500
>G197:7000
>C197:"bilities
>B197:"Other Lia
>H195:@SUM(H193...H194)
>G195:@SUM(G193...G194)
>E195:"s
>D195:"iabilitie
>C195:"current L
>B195:"Total Non
>H194:"  ------
>G194:"  ------
>H193:135744
>G193:245822
>C193:"m Debt
>B193:" Long-Ter
>D192:"ties
>C192:"t Liabili
>B192:"Noncurren
>H190:@SUM(H184...H189)
>G190:@SUM(G184...G189)
>D190:"ilities
>C190:"rent Liab
>B190:"Total Cur
>H189:"  ------
>G189:"  ------
>H188:0
>G188:700
>D188:"bilites
>C188:"rrent Lia
>B188:" Other Cu
>H187:24540
>G187:29900
>C187:"Expenses
>B187:" Accrued
>H186:42700
>G186:39890
>C186:" Payable
>B186:" Accounts
>H185:12366
>G185:9055
>C185:"yable
>B185:" Taxes Pa
>H184:23567
>G184:23567
>F184:/FR"$
>E184:"m Debt
>D184:" Long-Ter
>C184:"Portion -
>B184:" Current
>D183:"s
>C183:"iabilitie
>B183:"Current L
>H182:" -------
>G182:" -------
>H181:"    19XY
>G181:"    19XX
>H180:/--
>G180:" -------
>H179:" Day
>G179:"       Any
>G177:"uity
>F177:"lders' Eq
>E177:"d Stockho
>D177:"lities an
>C177:"    Liabi
>F175:"nd 19XY
>E175:"y, 19XX a
>D175:"At Any Da
>E174:"nce Sheet
>D174:"     Bala
>E173:" COMPANY
>D173:"       ANY
>H172:/-=
>G172:/-=
>F172:/-=
>E172:/-=
>D172:/-=
>C172:/-=
>B172:/-=
>A172:/-=
>H171:"Sheet 5.2
>F171:" 208)
>E171:"es to row
>D171:" (Continu
>C171:"ABILITIES
```

```
>F145:/FR"$
>B145:" Cash
>D144:"s
>C144:"iabilitie
>B144:"Current L
>H143:"  -------
>G143:"  -------
>H142:"    19XY
>G142:"    19XX
>H141:/--
>G141:"  -------
>H140:" Day
>G140:"       Any
>E138:"ssets
>D138:"         A
>F136:"nd 19XY
>E136:"y, 19XX a
>D136:"At Any Da
>E135:"nce Sheet
>D135:"     Bala
>E134:" COMPANY
>D134:"       ANY
>H133:/-=
>G133:/-=
>F133:/-=
>E133:/-=
>D133:/-=
>C133:/-=
>B133:/-=
>A133:/-=
>H132:"Sheet 5.1
>E132:" row 167)
>D132:"tinues to
>C132:"SETS (Con
>B132:"HEET - AS
>A132:"BALANCE S
>H128:"  ======
>F128:"  ======
>H127:+H123+H125
>G127:/FR"$
>F127:+F123+F125
>E127:/FR"$
>D127:", 19XY
>C127:"t Any Day
>B127:"Balance at
>H126:"  ------
>F126:"  ------
>H125:+H103
>F125:0
>D125:"Y
>C125:"e for 19X
>B125:"Net Incom
>H123:+H119+H121
>F123:+F119+F121
>D123:", 19XX
>C123:"t Any Day
>B123:"Balance at
>H122:"  ------
>F122:"  ------
>H121:+G103
>F121:0
>D121:"X
>C121:"e for 19X
>B121:"Net Incom
>H119:132954
>G119:/FR"$
>F119:100000
>E119:/FR"$
>D119:", 19XW
>C119:"t Any Day
>B119:"Balance at
>H118:" --------
>F118:" --------
>H117:" Earnings
>F117:"   Stock
>H116:" Retained
>F116:"  Common
>G112:"d 19XY
>F112:", 19XX an
>E112:"d Any Day
>D112:"ears Ende
>C112:"For the Y
>F111:"Earnings
>E111:"Retained
>D111:"ement of
>C111:"      Stat
>E110:" COMPANY
>D110:"       ANY
>H109:/-=
>G109:/-=
>F109:/-=
>E109:/-=
>D109:/-=
>C109:/-=
>B109:/-=
>A109:/-=
>H108:"Sheet 4.1
>F108:"row 128)
>E108:"inues to
>D108:"NGS (Cont
>C108:"NED EARNI
```

```
>D74:/-=
>C74:/-=
>B74:/-=
>A74:/-=
>H73:"Sheet 3.1
>E73:"04)
>D73:" to row 1
>C73:"Continues
>B73:"ATEMENT (
>A73:"INCOME ST
>H68:"  ======
>G68:"  ======
>H67:+H61+H63+H65
>G67:+G61+G63+G65
>F67:/FR"$
>D67:"s Sold
>C67:"t of Good
>B67:"Total Cos
>H66:"  ------
>G66:"  ------
>H65:63750
>G65:50000
>C65:"verhead
>B65:"Factory O
>H63:272000
>G63:234500
>C63:"bor
>B63:"Direct La
>H61:+H57-H59
>G61:+G57-G59
>D61:"xpense
>C61:"terials E
>B61:"Direct Ma
>H60:"  ------
>G60:"  ------
>H59:327000
>G59:354000
>C59:"ventory
>B59:"Ending In
>H57:+H53+H54-H55
>G57:+G53+G54-G55
>D57:"ailable
>C57:"erials Av
>B57:"Total Mat
>H56:"  ------
>G56:"  ------
>H55:10250
>G55:3400
>E55:"es
>D55:" Allowanc
>C55:"turns and
>B55:" Less: Re
>H54:431520
>G54:375000
>C54:"rchases
>B54:" Plus: Pu
>H53:+G59
>G53:327000
>F53:/FR"$
>D53:"ry
>C53:"g Invento
>B53:" Beginnin
>C52:"terials
>B52:"Direct Ma
>H51:"  -------
>G51:"  -------
>H50:"    19XY
>G50:"    19XX
>G46:"d 19XY
>F46:", 19XX an
>E46:"d Any Day
>D46:"ears Ende
>C46:"For the Y
>F45:"oods Sold
>E45:"Cost of G
>D45:"ement of
>C45:"      Stat
>E44:" COMPANY
>D44:"       ANY
>H43:/-=
>G43:/-=
>F43:/-=
>E43:/-=
>D43:/-=
>C43:/-=
>B43:/-=
>A43:/-=
>H42:"Sheet 2.1
>F42:" row 68)
>E42:"tinues to
>D42:"SOLD (Con
>C42:"OF GOODS
>B42:" OF COST
>A42:"STATEMENT
>H38:"  ======
>G38:"  ======
>H37:@SUM(H19...H36)
>G37:@SUM(G19...G36)
>F37:/FR"$
>D37:"penses
>C37:"rating Ex
```

```
>G11:"s
>F11:"g Expenses
>E11:" Operatin
>D11:"tement of
>C11:"        Sta
>E10:" COMPANY
>D10:"       ANY
>H9:/-=
>G9:/-=
>F9:/-=
>E9:/-=
>D9:/-=
>C9:/-=
>B9:/-=
>A9:/-=
>H8:"Sheet 1.1
>F8:" row 38)
>E8:"tinues to
>D8:"NSES (Con
>C8:"TING EXPE
>B8:" OF OPERA
>A8:"STATEMENT
>H7:/-=
>G7:/-=
>F7:/-=
>E7:/-=
>D7:/-=
>C7:/-=
>B7:/-=
>A7:/-=
>G5:">A226
>F5:"CONTENTS
>C5:"ONS >A212
>B5:"INSTRUCTI
>H3:/-=
>G3:/-=
>F3:/-=
>E3:/-=
>D3:/-=
>C3:/-=
>B3:/-=
>A3:/-=
>H2:"orp. 1983
>G2:"(C) Que C
>F2:"opyright
>E2:"         C
>D2:"MENTS
>C2:"IAL STATE
>B2:"NE FINANC
>A2:"FIVE-IN-O
>H1:/-=
>G1:/-=
>F1:/-=
>E1:/-=
>D1:/-=
>C1:/-=
>B1:/-=
>A1:/-=
/W1
/GOR
/GRM
/GC9
/X>A1:>A7:/TH
/X>A1:>A1:
```

FIVE-IN-ONE FINANCIAL STATEMENT

The formulas used to calculate each number are listed below. They are read from bottom to top and right to left and are referenced by their location in the model.

```
>G113:"(CR)
>F113:") /PPG101
>E113:": >A10 (CR
>D113:"y typing:
>C113:"4) PRINT b
>F112:" (CR)
>E112:"SSFilename
>D112:" typing: /
>C112:"3) SAVE by
>E111:"ping: |
>D111:"LATE by ty
>C111:"2) RECALCU
>F110:"data
>E110:"T  (>A35)
>D110:"LANCE SHEE
>C110:"    and BA
>F109:"O)
>E109:"EMENT (>A1
>D109:"NCOME STAT
>C109:"1) Enter I
>H106:"=
>G106:/-=
>F106:/-=
>E106:/-=
>D106:/-=
>C106:/-=
>B106:/-=
>A106:/-=
>H105:"Sheet 3.1
>G105:" Sheet 4.1
>B105:"NS
>A105:"INSTRUCTIO
>G101:" %
>F101:/F$+E28/E66*100
>D101:"y
>C101:"ers' Equit
>B101:" Stockhold
>A101:" Return on
>G100:" %
>F100:/F$+E28/E52*100
>C100:"ets
>B100:" Total Ass
>A100:" Return on
>G99:" %
>F99:/F$+E28/E14*100
>B99:" Sales
>A99:" Return on
>B98:"ITY RATIOS
>A98:"PROFITABIL
>F96:/F$+E14/E50
>B96:"ed Assets
>A96:" Sales/Fix
>G95:" Days
>F95:/FI(E43/E15)*365
>C95:"tory
>B95:"s in Inven
>A95:" Days Sale
>F94:/F$+E15/E43
>B94:" Turnover
>A94:" Inventory
>G93:" Days
>F93:/FI+F92*365
>C93:"ayables
>B93:"hases in P
>A93:" Days Purc
>F92:/F$+E57/E15
>C92:"ods Sold
>B92:"Cost of Go
>A92:" Payables/
>G91:" Days
>F91:/FI+F90*365
>C91:"ing
>B91:"s Outstand
>A91:" Days Sale
>F90:/F$+E42/E14
>B90:"es/Sales
>A90:" Receivabl
>F89:/F$
>C89:"IOS
>B89:"GEMENT RAT
>A89:"FUNDS MANA
>F88:/F$
>F87:/F$+E41/E59
>B87:"o
>A87:" Cash Ratio
>F86:/F$(E45-E43)/E59
>B86:"io
>A86:" Quick Rat
>F85:/F$+E45/E59
>B85:"atio
>A85:" Current R
>F84:/F$+F83/E52
>B84:"ng/Assets
>A84:" Net Worki
>F83:+E45-E59
>E83:/FR"$
>B83:"ng Capital
>A83:" Net Worki
>F82:/F$
>C82:"ITY
>B82:" OF LIQUID
>A82:"INDICATORS
>F81:/F$
>G80:" Times
>F80:/F$+E22/E23
>C80:"ed
>B80:"erest Earn
>A80:" Times Int
>F79:/F$(E59+E61)/E66
>B79:"ty Ratio
>A79:" Debt/Equi
>C78:"CY
>B78:" OF SOLVEN
>A78:"INDICATORS
>G76:/-=
>F76:/-=
>E76:/-=
>D76:/-=
>C76:/-=
>B76:/-=
>A76:/-=
>G75:" Sheet 3.1
>D75:"ow 101)
>C75:"inues to r
>B75:"YSIS (Cont
>A75:"RATIO ANAL
>F69:"   =======
>E69:"   =======
>G68:" %
>F68:+F59+F61+F66
>E68:+E59+E61+E66
>C68:"d Equity
>B68:"ilities an
>A68:"Total Liab
>F67:"   -------
>E67:"   -------
>G66:" %
>F66:/FI+F63+F64
>E66:+E63+E64
>C66:"s Equity
>B66:"ockholder'
>A66:"  Total St
>F65:"   -------
>E65:"   -------
>G64:" %
>F64:/FI+E64/E68*100
>E64:45000
>B64:"Surplus
>A64:" Retained
>G63:" %
>F63:/FI+E63/E68*100
>E63:75000
>B63:"ock
>A63:" Common St
>G61:" %
>F61:/FI+E61/E68*100
>E61:100000
>B61:" Debt
>A61:" Long-Term
>G59:" %
>F59:/FI+F56+F57
>E59:+E56+E57
>C59:"ilities
>B59:"rrent Liab
>A59:"  Total Cu
>F58:"   -------
>E58:"   -------
>G57:" %
>F57:/FI+E57/E68*100
>E57:11000
>B57:"Payable
>A57:" Accounts
>G56:" %
>F56:/FI+E56/E68*100
>E56:25000
>C56:"s Payable
>B56:"s and Note
>A56:" Bank Loan
>B55:"s
>A55:"Liabilities
>F53:"   =======
>E53:"   =======
>G52:" %
>F52:+F50+F45
>E52:+E50+E45
>B52:"ts
>A52:"Total Asse
>F51:"   -------
>E51:"   -------
>G50:" %
>F50:/FI+F47-F48
>E50:+E47-E48
>B50:"d Assets
>A50:"  Net Fixe
>F49:"   -------
>E49:"   -------
>G48:" %
>F48:/FI+E48/E52*100
>E48:45000
>C48:"ation
>B48:"ed Depreci
>A48:" Accumulat
>G47:" %
>F47:/FI+E47/E52*100
>E47:250000
>B47:"ed Assets
>A47:" Gross Fix
>G45:" %
>F45:/FI@SUM(F41...F44)
>E45:@SUM(E41...E44)
>C45:"ts
>B45:"rrent Assets
>A45:"  Total Cu
>F44:"   -------
>E44:"   -------
>G43:" %
>F43:/FI+E43/E52*100
>E43:18000
>B43:"es
>A43:" Inventorie
>G42:" %
>F42:/FI+E42/E52*100
>E42:24000
>B42:"Receivable
>A42:" Accounts
>G41:" %
>F41:/FI+E41/E52*100
>E41:9000
>D41:"s
>C41:" Securitie
>B41:"Marketable
>A41:" Cash and
>A40:"Assets
>F39:" ---------
>E39:"  --------
>F38:"  Percent
>E38:"   Amount
>G36:/-=
>F36:/-=
>E36:/-=
>D36:/-=
>C36:/-=
>B36:/-=
>A36:/-=
>G35:" Sheet 3.1
>D35:"w 69)
>C35:"nues to ro
>B35:"EET (Conti
>A35:"BALANCE SH
>F32:"   =======
>E32:"   =======
>G31:" %
>F31:+F28-F29
>E31:+E28-E29
>B31:"arnings
>A31:"Retained E
>F30:"   -------
>E30:"   -------
>G29:" %
>F29:/FI+E29/E14*100
>E29:3500
>A29:"Dividends
>G28:" %
>F28:/FI+F25-F26
>E28:+E25-E26
>B28:"fter Taxes
>A28:"Earnings A
>F27:"   -------
>E27:"   -------
>G26:" %
>F26:/FI+E26/E14*100
>E26:7050
>B26:"es
>A26:"Income Tax
>G25:" %
>F25:/FI+F22-F23
>E25:+E22-E23
>C25:"s
>B25:"efore Taxe
>A25:"Earnings B
>F24:"   -------
>E24:"   -------
>G23:" %
>F23:/FI+E23/E14*100
>E23:2550
>A23:"Interest
>G22:" %
>F22:/FI+F17-F19-F20
>E22:+E17-E19-E20
>D22:"axes
>C22:"rest and T
>B22:"efore Inte
>A22:"Earnings B
>F21:"   -------
>E21:"   -------
>G20:" %
>F20:/FI+E20/E14*100
>E20:1000
>B20:"on
>A20:"Depreciati
>G19:" %
>F19:/FI+E19/E14*100
>E19:7500
>C19:"penses
>B19:"trative Ex
>A19:"   Adminis
>C18:"d
>B18:"eneral, an
>A18:"Selling, G
>G17:" %
>F17:/FI+F14-F15
>E17:+E14-E15
>B17:"in
>A17:"Gross Marg
>F16:"   -------
>E16:"   -------
>G15:" %
>F15:/FI+E15/E14*100
>E15:72400
>B15:"ods Sold
>A15:"Cost of Go
>G14:" %
>F14:/FI+E14/E14*100
>E14:100000
>A14:"Sales
>F13:" ---------
>E13:"  --------
>F12:"  Percent
>E12:"   Amount
>H11:/-=
>G11:/-=
>F11:/-=
>E11:/-=
>D11:/-=
>C11:/-=
>B11:/-=
>A11:/-=
>H10:"Sheet 1.1
>G10:" Sheet 1.1
>D10:" row 32)
>C10:"ntinues to
>B10:"TEMENT (Co
>A10:"INCOME STA
>H9:/-=
>G9:/-=
>F9:/-=
>E9:/-=
>D9:/-=
>C9:/-=
>B9:/-=
>A9:/-=
>G7:">A105
>F7:"TRUCTIONS
>E7:"   4.1 INS
>C7:"S >A75
>B7:"IO ANALYSI
>A7:"   3.1 RAT
>G6:" >A35
>F6:"ANCE SHEET
>E6:"   2.1 BAL
>C6:"ENT >A10
>B6:"OME STATEM
>A6:"   1.1 INC
>D4:" CONTENTS
>H3:/-=
>G3:/-=
>F3:/-=
>E3:/-=
>D3:/-=
>C3:/-=
>B3:/-=
>A3:/-=
>H2:"orp. 1983
>G2:"Corp. 1983
>F2:"t (C) QUE
>E2:"  Copyrigh
>B2:"YZER
>A2:"RATIO ANAL
>H1:/-=
>G1:/-=
>F1:/-=
>E1:/-=
>D1:/-=
>C1:/-=
>B1:/-=
>A1:/-=
/W1
/GOC
/GRM
/GC10
/X>A1:>A9:/TH
/X>A1:>A1:
```

RATIO ANALYZER

```
=========================================================================
RATIO ANALYZER                                Copyright (C) QUE Corp. 1983
=========================================================================
                                 CONTENTS

   1.1 INCOME STATEMENT >A10                 2.1 BALANCE SHEET >A35
   3.1 RATIO ANALYSIS >A75                   4.1 INSTRUCTIONS >A105

=========================================================================
INCOME STATEMENT (Continues to row 32)                          Sheet 1.1
=========================================================================
                                              Amount   Percent
                                             -------- ---------
Sales                                          100000       100 %
Cost of Goods Sold                              72400        72 %
                                              -------   -------
Gross Margin                                    27600        28 %
Selling, General, and
   Administrative Expenses                       7500         8 %
Depreciation                                     1000         1 %
                                              -------   -------
Earnings Before Interest and Taxes              19100        19 %
Interest                                         2550         3 %
                                              -------   -------
Earnings Before Taxes                           16550        17 %
Income Taxes                                     7050         7 %
                                              -------   -------
Earnings After Taxes                             9500        10 %
Dividends                                        3500         4 %
                                              -------   -------
Retained Earnings                                6000         6 %
                                              =======   =======

BALANCE SHEET (Continues to row 69)                             Sheet 3.1
=========================================================================

                                              Amount   Percent
                                             -------- ---------
Assets
 Cash and Marketable Securities                  9000         4 %
 Accounts Receivable                            24000         9 %
 Inventories                                    18000         7 %
                                              -------   -------
  Total Current Assets                          51000        20 %

 Gross Fixed Assets                            250000        98 %
 Accumulated Depreciation                       45000        18 %
                                              -------   -------
  Net Fixed Assets                             205000        80 %
                                              -------   -------
Total Assets                                   256000       100 %
                                              =======   =======

Liabilities
 Bank Loans and Notes Payable                   25000        10 %
 Accounts Payable                               11000         4 %
                                              -------   -------
  Total Current Liabilities                     36000        14 %

 Long-Term Debt                                100000        39 %

 Common Stock                                   75000        29 %
 Retained Surplus                               45000        18 %
                                              -------   -------
  Total Stockholder's Equity                   120000        47 %
                                              -------   -------
Total Liabilities and Equity                   256000       100 %
                                              =======   =======



RATIO ANALYSIS (Continues to row 101)                           Sheet 3.1
=========================================================================

INDICATORS OF SOLVENCY
 Debt/Equity Ratio                                       1.13
 Times Interest Earned                                   7.49 Times

INDICATORS OF LIQUIDITY
 Net Working Capital                           $        15000
 Net Working/Assets                                      0.06
 Current Ratio                                           1.42
 Quick Ratio                                             0.92
 Cash Ratio                                              0.25

FUNDS MANAGEMENT RATIOS
 Receivables/Sales                                       0.24
 Days Sales Outstanding                                    88 Days
 Payables/Cost of Goods Sold                             0.15
 Days Purchases in Payables                                55 Days
 Inventory Turnover                                      4.02
 Days Sales in Inventory                                   91 Days
 Sales/Fixed Assets                                      0.49

PROFITABILITY RATIOS
 Return on Sales                                         9.50 %
 Return on Total Assets                                  3.71 %
 Return on Stockholders' Equity                          7.92 %


INSTRUCTIONS                                                    Sheet 4.1
=========================================================================


                    1) Enter INCOME STATEMENT (>A10)
                         and BALANCE SHEET  (>A35) data
                    2) RECALCULATE by typing: !
                    3) SAVE by typing: /SSFilename (CR)
                    4) PRINT by typing: : >A10 (CR) /PPG101 (CR)
```

RATIO ANALYSIS [illegible]

CONTENTS

[illegible] INCOME STATEMENT [illegible] BALANCE SHEET [illegible]
[illegible] RATIO [illegible] TITLE [illegible]

INCOME STATEMENT [illegible]

Amount Percent

[illegible]

[illegible]

[illegible]

[illegible]

```
>F121:"  ------
>E121:"  ------
>H120:14000
>G120:16000
>F120:18000
>E120:20000
>B120:"rm Debt
>A120:" Long-Te
>C119:"ities
>B119:"nt Liabi
>A119:"Noncurre
>H117:@SUM(H114...H116)
>G117:@SUM(G114...G116)
>F117:@SUM(F114...F116)
>E117:@SUM(E114...E116)
>D117:"s
>C117:"abilitie
>B117:"rrent Li
>A117:"Total Cu
>H116:"  ------
>G116:"  ------
>F116:"  ------
>E116:"  ------
>A116:"
>H115:+H74
>G115:+G74
>F115:+F74
>E115:+E74
>C115:"yable
>B115:"Taxes Pa
>A115:" Income
>H114:+F29/90*H46
>G114:+F29/90*G46
>F114:+F29/90*F46
>E114:+F29/90*E46
>C114:"e
>B114:"s Payabl
>A114:" Account
>C113:"ies
>B113:"Liabilit
>A113:"Current
>H110:"  ======
>G110:"  ======
>F110:"  ======
>E110:"  ======
>H109:+H90+H107
>G109:+G90+G107
>F109:+F90+F107
>E109:+E90+E107
>B109:"sets
>A109:"Total As
>H108:"  ------
>G108:"  ------
>F108:"  ------
>E108:"  ------
>H107:+H102+H104+H105
>G107:+G102+G104+G105
>F107:+F102+F104+F105
>E107:+E102+E104+E105
>C107:"ts
>B107:"xed Asse
>A107:"Total Fi
>H106:"  ------
>G106:"  ------
>F106:"  ------
>E106:"  ------
>H105:300
>G105:300
>F105:300
>E105:300
>A105:" Other
>H104:611
>G104:611
>F104:611
>E104:611
>B104:"s
>A104:" Deposits
>H102:+H99-H100
>G102:+G99-G100
>F102:+F99-F100
>E102:+E99-E100
>B102:"P, & E
>A102:" Net P,
>H101:"  ------
>G101:"  ------
>F101:"  ------
>E101:"  ------
>H100:+G100+H64
>G100:+F100+G64
>F100:+E100+F64
>E100:+F26+E64
>D100:"n
>C100:"reciatio
>B100:"ated Dep
>A100:" Accumul
>H99:@SUM(H94...H98)
>G99:@SUM(G94...G98)
>F99:@SUM(F94...F98)
>E99:@SUM(E94...E98)
```

```
>F82:/-=
>E82:/-=
>D82:/-=
>C82:/-=
>B82:/-=
>A82:/-=
>E81:"129)
>D81:" to row
>C81:"ontinues
>B81:"SHEET (C
>A81:"BALANCE
>I77:"  ======
>H77:"  ======
>G77:"  ======
>F77:"  ======
>E77:"  ======
>I76:@SUM(E76...H76)
>H76:+H72-H74
>G76:+G72-G74
>F76:+F72-F74
>E76:+E72-E74
>B76:"me
>A76:"Net Income
>I75:"  ------
>H75:"  ------
>G75:"  ------
>F75:"  ------
>E75:"  ------
>I74:@SUM(E74...H74)
>H74:@IF(H72>0,F18/100*H72,0)
>G74:@IF(G72>0,F18/100*G72,0)
>F74:@IF(F72>0,F18/100*F72,0)
>E74:@IF(E72>0,F18/100*E72,0)
>B74:"axes
>A74:"Income T
>I72:@SUM(E72...H72)
>H72:+H48-H70
>G72:+G48-G70
>F72:+F48-F70
>E72:+E48-E70
>C72:"xes
>B72:"efore Ta
>A72:"Profit B
>I71:"  ------
>H71:"  ------
>G71:"  ------
>F71:"  ------
>E71:"  ------
>I70:@SUM(E70...H70)
>H70:@SUM(H51...H69)
>G70:@SUM(G51...G69)
>F70:@SUM(F51...F69)
>E70:@SUM(E51...E69)
>C70:"Expenses
>B70:"erating
>A70:"Total Op
>I69:"  ------
>H69:"  ------
>G69:"  ------
>F69:"  ------
>E69:"  ------
>I68:@SUM(E68...H68)
>H68:400
>G68:400
>F68:400
>E68:400
>A68:" Other
>I67:@SUM(E67...H67)
>H67:900
>G67:900
>F67:900
>E67:900
>C67:"l
>B67:"nt Renta
>A67:" Equipment
>I66:@SUM(E66...H66)
>H66:@INT(F15/100/4*H120)
>G66:@INT(F15/100/4*G120)
>F66:@INT(F15/100/4*F120)
>E66:@INT(F15/100/4*E120)
>B66:"t
>A66:" Interes
>I65:@SUM(E65...H65)
>H65:400
>G65:400
>F65:400
>E65:400
>B65:"ance
>A65:" Maintena
>I64:@SUM(E64...H64)
>H64:@INT(H99/F25*3)
>G64:@INT(G99/F25*3)
>F64:@INT(F99/F25*3)
>E64:@INT(E99/F25*3)
>B64:"ation
>A64:" Depreciat
>I63:@SUM(E63...H63)
>H63:750
>G63:750
```

```
>H52:300
>G52:300
>F52:300
>E52:300
>B52:"s
>A52:" Benefit
>I51:@SUM(E51...H51)
>H51:9000
>G51:9000
>F51:9000
>E51:9000
>C51:"ges
>B51:"s and Wa
>A51:" Salaries
>C50:"es
>B50:"g Expens
>A50:"Operatin
>I48:@SUM(E48...H48)
>H48:+H44-H46
>G48:+G44-G46
>F48:+F44-F46
>E48:+E44-E46
>B48:"rgin
>A48:"Gross Ma
>I47:"  ------
>H47:"  ------
>G47:"  ------
>F47:"  ------
>E47:"  ------
>I46:@SUM(E46...H46)
>H46:+F16*H39/100
>G46:+F16*G39/100
>F46:+F16*F39/100
>E46:+F16*E39/100
>C46:"ld
>B46:"Goods So
>A46:"Cost of
>I44:@SUM(E44...H44)
>H44:@SUM(H39...H43)
>G44:@SUM(G39...G43)
>F44:@SUM(F39...F43)
>E44:@SUM(E39...E43)
>C44:"me
>B44:"oss Inco
>A44:"Total Gr
>I43:"  ------
>H43:"  ------
>G43:"  ------
>F43:"  ------
>E43:"  ------
>I42:@SUM(E42...H42)

see formula below

>B42:"t Income
>A42:" Interes
>I41:@SUM(E41...H41)
>H41:1500
>G41:1500
>F41:1500
>E41:1500
>B41:"ales
>A41:" Other S
>I40:@SUM(E40...H40)
>H40:40000
>G40:35000
>F40:32000
>E40:25000
>C40:"vices
>B40:"from Ser
>A40:" Income
>I39:@SUM(E39...H39)
>H39:70000
>G39:60000
>F39:55000
>E39:50000
>B39:" Sales
>A39:" Product
>B38:"come
>A38:"Gross In
>I37:"  ------
>H37:"  ------
>G37:"  ------
>F37:"  ------
>E37:"  ------
>I36:"   Total
>H36:/FR"Qtr 4
>G36:/FR"Qtr 3
>F36:/FR"Qtr 2
>E36:/FR"Qtr 1
>I35:/-=
>H35:/-=
>G35:/-=
>F35:/-=
>E35:/-=
>D35:/-=
>C35:/-=
>B35:/-=
```

```
>A14:"  Earned
>G13:" %
>F13:18
>C13:") Rate:
>B13:" (Income
>A13:"Interest
>I11:/-=
>H11:/-=
>G11:/-=
>F11:/-=
>E11:/-=
>D11:/-=
>C11:/-=
>B11:/-=
>A11:/-=
>I10:"heet 1.1
>H10:"        S
>D10:"t A22)
>C10:"tinued a
>B10:"ONS (Con
>A10:"ASSUMPTI
>I9:/-=
>H9:/-=
>G9:/-=
>F9:/-=
>E9:/-=
>D9:/-=
>C9:/-=
>B9:/-=
>A9:/-=
>H7:" >A131
>G7:"RUCTIONS
>F7:"4.1 INST
>D7:"T >A81
>C7:"NCE SHEE
>B7:"3.1 BALA
>I6:"4
>H6:"MENT >A3
>G6:"ME STATE
>F6:"2.1 INCO
>D6:">A10
>C6:"MPTIONS
>B6:"1.1 ASSUM
>E4:"CONTENTS
>I3:/-=
>H3:/-=
>G3:/-=
>F3:/-=
>E3:/-=
>D3:/-=
>C3:/-=
>B3:/-=
>A3:/-=
>I2:"rp. 1983
>H2:") Que Co
>G2:"        (C
>F2:" SHEET
>E2:" BALANCE
>D2:"MENT AND
>C2:"ME STATE
>B2:"IVE INCO
>A2:"INTERACTI
>I1:/-=
>H1:/-=
>G1:/-=
>F1:/-=
>E1:/-=
>D1:/-=
>C1:/-=
>B1:/-=
>A1:/-=
/W1
/GOC
/GRM
/GFI
/GCB
/X>A1:>A9:/TH
/X>A1:>A1:
```

```
>H42:@IF(@ISERROR(H86),0,@IF(H86>F14,@INT((F13/100/4)*(H86-F14)),0))
>G42:@IF(@ISERROR(G86),0,@IF(G86>F14,@INT((F13/100/4)*(G86-F14)),0))
>F42:@IF(@ISERROR(F86),0,@IF(F86>F14,@INT((F13/100/4)*(F86-F14)),0))
>E42:@IF(@ISERROR(E86),0,@IF(E86>F14,@INT((F13/100/4)*(E86-F14)),0))
```

INTERACTIVE INCOME STATEMENT AND BALANCE SHEET

```
==========================================================================
INTERACTIVE INCOME STATEMENT AND BALANCE SHEET          (C) Que Corp. 1983
==========================================================================
                               CONTENTS

        1.1 ASSUMPTIONS >A10             2.1 INCOME STATEMENT >A34
        3.1 BALANCE SHEET >A81           4.1 INSTRUCTIONS >A131

==========================================================================
ASSUMPTIONS (Continued at A22)                                   Sheet 1.1
==========================================================================

Interest (Income) Rate:                          18 %
  Earned on Cash Balance Over:          $     5000
Interest (Expense) Rate:                         18 %
Cost of Goods Sold:                              75 %
Payroll Taxes:                                   10 %
Income Tax Rate:                                 25 %


ASSUMPTIONS (Continued)                                          Sheet 1.2
==========================================================================

Depreciable Life of Assets:                      60 Months
Beginning Accumulated Depreciation:     $     5000
Days Sales in Receivables:                       45 Days
Days Cost of Goods Sold in Inventory:            30 Days
Days Cost of Goods Sold in Payables:             45 Days
Beginning Retained Earnings:            $     4200


INCOME STATEMENT (Continues to row 77)
==========================================================================
                                     Qtr 1   Qtr 2   Qtr 3   Qtr 4   Total
                                    ------  ------  ------  ------  ------
Gross Income
 Product Sales                       50000   55000   60000   70000  235000
 Income from Services                25000   32000   35000   40000  132000
 Other Sales                          1500    1500    1500    1500    6000
 Interest Income                         0       0       0       0       0
                                    ------  ------  ------  ------  ------
Total Gross Income                   76500   88500   96500  111500  373000

Cost of Goods Sold                   37500   41250   45000   52500  176250
                                    ------  ------  ------  ------  ------
Gross Margin                         39000   47250   51500   59000  196750

Operating Expenses
 Salaries and Wages                   9000    9000    9000    9000   36000
 Benefits                              300     300     300     300    1200
 Health Insurance                      495     495     495     495    1980
 Payroll Taxes                         900     900     900     900    3600
 Office Rent                          1842    1842    1842    1842    7368
 Supplies                              400     400     400     400    1600
 Postage                               120     120     120     120     480
 Telephone                            1050    1050    1050    1050    4200
 Insurance                              75      75      75      75     300
 Dues and Subscriptions                120     120     120     120     480
 Advertising and Promotion            3000    3000    3000    3000   12000
 Travel and Entertainment             1500    1500    1500    1500    6000
 Professional Fees                     750     750     750     750    3000
 Depreciation                         1699    1699    1699    1699    6796
 Maintenance                           400     400     400     400    1600
 Interest                              900     810     720     630    3060
 Equipment Rental                      900     900     900     900    3600
 Other                                 400     400     400     400    1600
                                    ------  ------  ------  ------  ------
Total Operating Expenses             23851   23761   23671   23581   94864
                                    ------  ------  ------  ------  ------
Profit Before Taxes                  15149   23489   27829   35419  101886

Income Taxes                          3787    5872    6957    8855   25472
                                    ------  ------  ------  ------  ------
Net Income                           11362   17617   20872   26564   76415
                                    ======  ======  ======  ======  ======


BALANCE SHEET (Continues to row 129)
==========================================================================
                                     Qtr 1   Qtr 2   Qtr 3   Qtr 4
                                    ------  ------  ------  ------
Current Assets
 Cash                                29138   43164   61445   83355
 Accounts Receivable                 38250   44250   48250   55750
 Inventory                           12499   13749   14999   17499
                                    ------  ------  ------  ------
Total Current Assets                 79887  101163  124694  156604

Fixed Assets
 Plant, Property, and Equipment
  Leasehold Improvements             10000   10000   10000   10000
  Furniture and Fixtures             12500   12500   12500   12500
  Equipment                           7500    7500    7500    7500
  Office Equipment                    4000    4000    4000    4000
                                    ------  ------  ------  ------
 Gross P, P, & E                     34000   34000   34000   34000
 Accumulated Depreciation             6699    8398   10097   11796
                                    ------  ------  ------  ------
 Net P, P, & E                       27301   25602   23903   22204

 Deposits                              611     611     611     611
 Other                                 300     300     300     300
                                    ------  ------  ------  ------
Total Fixed Assets                   28212   26513   24814   23115

Total Assets                        108099  127676  149508  179719
                                    ======  ======  ======  ======


Current Liabilities
 Accounts Payable                    18750   20625   22500   26250
 Income Taxes Payable                 3787    5872    6957    8855
                                    ------  ------  ------  ------
Total Current Liabilities            22537   26497   29457   35105

Noncurrent Liabilities
 Long-Term Debt                      20000   18000   16000   14000
                                    ------  ------  ------  ------
Total Liabilities                    42537   44497   45457   49105

Common Stock                         50000   50000   50000   50000

Retained Earnings                    15562   33179   54050   80615

Total Liabilities and Equity        108099  127676  149508  179719
                                    ======  ======  ======  ======
INSTRUCTIONS                                                     Sheet 3.1
==========================================================================

              1) Enter ASSUMPTIONS (>A10)
              2) Enter other INCOME STATEMENT (>A34) and
                   BALANCE SHEET (>A81) data
              3) RECALCULATE by typing: !!!!!!!!!
              4) SAVE by typing: /SSFilename (CR)
              5) PRINT by typing: >A10 (CR) /PPI128 (CR)
```

The formulas used to calculate each number are listed below. They are read from bottom to top and right to left and are referenced by their location in the model.

```
>H139:"R)
>G139:"PI128 (C
>F139:" (CR) /P
>E139:"ng: >A10
>D139:" by typi
>C139:"5) PRINT
>G138:"CR)
>F138:"lename (
>E138:"g: /SSFi
>D138:"by typin
>C138:"4) SAVE
>G137:"!!!
>F137:": !!!!!!
>E137:"y typing
>D137:"CULATE b
>C137:"3) RECAL
>F136:" data
>E136:"T (>A81)
>D136:"NCE SHEE
>C136:"    BALA
>H135:"nd
>G135:"(>A34) a
>F135:"ATEMENT
>E135:"NCOME ST
>D135:" other I
>C135:"2) Enter
>F134:"10)
>E134:"IONS (>A
>D134:" ASSUMPT
>C134:"1) Enter
>I132:/-=
>H132:/-=
>G132:/-=
>F132:/-=
>E132:/-=
>D132:/-=
>C132:/-=
>B132:/-=
>A132:/-=
>I131:"heet 3.1
>H131:"        S
>B131:"IONS
>A131:"INSTRUCT
>H129:"  ======
>G129:"  ======
>F129:"  ======
>E129:"  ======
>H128:+H122+H124+H126
>G128:+G122+G124+G126
>F128:+F122+F124+F126
>E128:+E122+E124+E126
>D128:"uity
>C128:"s and Eq
>B128:"abilitie
>A128:"Total Li
>H127:"  ------
>G127:"  ------
>F127:"  ------
>E127:"  ------
```

```
>B99:", P, & E
>A99:" Gross P
>H98:"  ------
>G98:"  ------
>F98:"  ------
>E98:"  ------
>H97:4000
>G97:4000
>F97:4000
>E97:4000
>C97:"nt
>B97:" Equipme
>A97:"  Office
>H96:7500
>G96:7500
>F96:7500
>E96:7500
>B96:"ent
>A96:"  Equipm
>H95:12500
>G95:12500
>F95:12500
>E95:12500
>C95:"Fixtures
>B95:"ure and
>A95:"  Furnit
>H94:10000
>G94:10000
>F94:10000
>E94:10000
>C94:"ovements
>B94:"old Impr
>A94:"  Leaseh
>D93:"uipment
>C93:", and Eq
>B93:"Property
>A93:" Plant,
>B92:"sets
>A92:"Fixed As
>H90:@SUM(H86...H89)
>G90:@SUM(G86...G89)
>F90:@SUM(F86...F89)
>E90:@SUM(E86...E89)
>C90:"sets
>B90:"rrent As
>A90:"Total Cu
>H89:"  ------
>G89:"  ------
>F89:"  ------
>E89:"  ------
>H88:@INT(F28/90*H46)
>G88:@INT(F28/90*G46)
>F88:@INT(F28/90*F46)
>E88:@INT(F28/90*E46)
>B88:"ry
>A88:" Invento
>H87:@INT(F27/90*H44)
>G87:@INT(F27/90*G44)
>F87:@INT(F27/90*F44)
>E87:@INT(F27/90*E44)
```

```
>F63:750
>E63:750
>C63:"es
>B63:"ional Fe
>A63:" Professio
>I62:@SUM(E62...H62)
>H62:1500
>G62:1500
>F62:1500
>E62:1500
>D62:"t
>C62:"rtainmen
>B62:"and Ente
>A62:" Travel an
>I61:@SUM(E61...H61)
>H61:3000
>G61:3000
>F61:3000
>E61:3000
>D61:"on
>C61:" Promoti
>B61:"sing and
>A61:" Advertisi
>I60:@SUM(E60...H60)
>H60:120
>G60:120
>F60:120
>E60:120
>C60:"iptions
>B60:"d Subscr
>A60:" Dues and
>I59:@SUM(E59...H59)
>H59:75
>G59:75
>F59:75
>E59:75
>B59:"ce
>A59:" Insurance
>I58:@SUM(E58...H58)
>H58:1050
>G58:1050
>F58:1050
>E58:1050
>B58:"ne
>A58:" Telephone
>I57:@SUM(E57...H57)
>H57:120
>G57:120
>F57:120
>E57:120
>A57:" Postage
>I56:@SUM(E56...H56)
>H56:400
>G56:400
>F56:400
>E56:400
>B56:"s
>A56:" Supplies
>I55:@SUM(E55...H55)
>H55:1842
```

```
>A35:/-=
>E34:"ow 77)
>D34:"ues to r
>C34:" (Contin
>B34:"TATEMENT
>A34:"INCOME S
>F30:4200
>E30:/FR"$
>D30:"ngs:
>C30:"ed Earni
>B30:"g Retain
>A30:"Beginnin
>G29:" Days
>F29:45
>E29:"les:
>D29:"in Payab
>C29:"ds Sold
>B29:"t of Goo
>A29:"Days Cos
>G28:" Days
>F28:30
>E28:"tory:
>D28:"in Inven
>C28:"ds Sold
>B28:"t of Goo
>A28:"Days Cos
>G27:" Days
>F27:45
>D27:"s:
>C27:"ceivable
>B27:"es in Re
>A27:"Days Sal
>F26:5000
>E26:"on:     $
>D26:"preciati
>C26:"lated De
>B26:"g Accumu
>A26:"Beginnin
>G25:" Months
>F25:60
>D25:"ts:
>C25:" of Assets:
>B25:"ble Life
>A25:"Deprecia
>I23:/-=
>H23:/-=
>G23:/-=
>F23:/-=
>E23:/-=
>D23:/-=
>C23:/-=
>B23:/-=
>A23:/-=
>I22:"heet 1.2
>H22:"        S
>C22:"tinued)
>B22:"ONS (Con
>A22:"ASSUMPTI
>G18:" %
>F18:25
>B18:"ax Rate:
```

[illegible]

```
=========================================================================
RATIO ANALYZER                                Copyright (C) QUE Corp. 1983
=========================================================================
                                 CONTENTS

   1.1 INCOME STATEMENT >A10                  2.1 BALANCE SHEET >A35
   3.1 RATIO ANALYSIS >A75                    4.1 INSTRUCTIONS >A105

=========================================================================
INCOME STATEMENT (Continues to row 32)                           Sheet 1.1
=========================================================================
                                              Amount   Percent
                                            -------- ---------
Sales                                         100000       100 %
Cost of Goods Sold                             72400        72 %
                                             -------   -------
Gross Margin                                   27600        28 %
Selling, General, and
   Administrative Expenses                      7500         8 %
Depreciation                                    1000         1 %
                                             -------   -------
Earnings Before Interest and Taxes             19100        19 %
Interest                                        2550         3 %
                                             -------   -------
Earnings Before Taxes                          16550        17 %
Income Taxes                                    7050         7 %
                                             -------   -------
Earnings After Taxes                            9500        10 %
Dividends                                       3500         4 %
                                             -------   -------
Retained Earnings                               6000         6 %
                                             =======   =======

BALANCE SHEET (Continues to row 69)                              Sheet 3.1
=========================================================================

                                              Amount   Percent
                                            -------- ---------
Assets
 Cash and Marketable Securities                 9000         4 %
 Accounts Receivable                           24000         9 %
 Inventories                                   18000         7 %
                                             -------   -------
  Total Current Assets                         51000        20 %

 Gross Fixed Assets                           250000        98 %
 Accumulated Depreciation                      45000        18 %
                                             -------   -------
  Net Fixed Assets                            205000        80 %
                                             -------   -------
Total Assets                                  256000       100 %
                                             =======   =======

Liabilities
 Bank Loans and Notes Payable                  25000        10 %
 Accounts Payable                              11000         4 %
                                             -------   -------
  Total Current Liabilities                    36000        14 %

 Long-Term Debt                               100000        39 %

 Common Stock                                  75000        29 %
 Retained Surplus                              45000        18 %
                                             -------   -------
  Total Stockholder's Equity                  120000        47 %
                                             -------   -------
Total Liabilities and Equity                  256000       100 %
                                             =======   =======


RATIO ANALYSIS (Continues to row 101)                            Sheet 3.1
=========================================================================

INDICATORS OF SOLVENCY
 Debt/Equity Ratio                                      1.13
 Times Interest Earned                                  7.49 Times

INDICATORS OF LIQUIDITY
 Net Working Capital                         $         15000
 Net Working/Assets                                     0.06
 Current Ratio                                          1.42
 Quick Ratio                                            0.92
 Cash Ratio                                             0.25

FUNDS MANAGEMENT RATIOS
 Receivables/Sales                                      0.24
 Days Sales Outstanding                                   88 Days
 Payables/Cost of Goods Sold                            0.15
 Days Purchases in Payables                               55 Days
 Inventory Turnover                                     4.02
 Days Sales in Inventory                                  91 Days
 Sales/Fixed Assets                                     0.49

PROFITABILITY RATIOS
 Return on Sales                                        9.50 %
 Return on Total Assets                                 3.71 %
 Return on Stockholders' Equity                         7.92 %


INSTRUCTIONS                                                     Sheet 4.1
=========================================================================


                 1) Enter INCOME STATEMENT (>A10)
                    and BALANCE SHEET  (>A35) data
                 2) RECALCULATE by typing: !
                 3) SAVE by typing: /SSFilename (CR)
                 4) PRINT by typing: : >A10 (CR) /PPG101 (CR)
```

STATISTICS CALCULATOR

```
>K42:"   =======
>I42:/-#
>C42:"   =======
>B42:"   =======
>N41:" #########
>M41:@SUM(M16...M40)
>L41:@SUM(L16...L40)
>K41:@SUM(K16...K40)
>I41:/-#
>C41:@SUM(C16...C40)
>B41:@SUM(B16...B40)
>N40:" #########
>M40:"   -------
>L40:"   -------
>K40:"   -------
>I40:/-#
>C40:"   -------
>B40:"   -------
>N39:" #########
>M39:+B39*B39
>L39:+B39*C39
>K39:/FI+J39*J39
>J39:/FI+C39-E50
>I39:/-#
>F39:/F$@AVERAGE(C28...C39)
>E39:/F$@AVERAGE(C34...C39)
>D39:/F$@AVERAGE(C37...C39)
>C39:13000
>B39:24
>N38:" #########
>M38:+B38*B38
>L38:+B38*C38
>K38:/FI+J38*J38
>J38:/FI+C38-E50
>I38:/-#
>F38:/F$@AVERAGE(C27...C38)
>E38:/F$@AVERAGE(C33...C38)
>D38:/F$@AVERAGE(C36...C38)
>C38:12698
>B38:23
>N37:" #########
>M37:+B37*B37
>L37:+B37*C37
>K37:/FI+J37*J37
>D31:/F$@AVERAGE(C29...C31)
>C31:11025
>B31:16
>N30:" #########
>M30:+B30*B30
>L30:+B30*C30
>K30:/FI+J30*J30
>J30:/FI+C30-E50
>I30:/-#
>F30:/F$@AVERAGE(C19...C30)
>E30:/F$@AVERAGE(C25...C30)
>D30:/F$@AVERAGE(C28...C30)
>C30:10444
>B30:15
>N29:" #########
>M29:+B29*B29
>L29:+B29*C29
>K29:/FI+J29*J29
>J29:/FI+C29-E50
>I29:/-#
>F29:/F$@AVERAGE(C18...C29)
>E29:/F$@AVERAGE(C24...C29)
>D29:/F$@AVERAGE(C27...C29)
>C29:7656
>B29:14
>N28:" #########
>M28:+B28*B28
>L28:+B28*C28
>K28:/FI+J28*J28
>J28:/FI+C28-E50
>I28:/-#
>F28:/F$@AVERAGE(C17...C28)
>E28:/F$@AVERAGE(C23...C28)
>D28:/F$@AVERAGE(C26...C28)
>C28:10540
>B28:13
>N27:" #########
>M27:+B27*B27
>L27:+B27*C27
>K27:/FI+J27*J27
>J27:/FI+C27-E50
>I27:/-#
>F27:/F$@AVERAGE(C16...C27)
>E27:/F$@AVERAGE(C22...C27)
>C20:2333
>B20:5
>N19:" #########
>M19:+B19*B19
>L19:+B19*C19
>K19:/FI+J19*J19
>J19:/FI+C19-E50
>I19:/-#
>D19:/F$@AVERAGE(C17...C19)
>C19:6554
>B19:4
>N18:" #########
>M18:+B18*B18
>L18:+B18*C18
>K18:/FI+J18*J18
>J18:/FI+C18-E50
>I18:/-#
>D18:/F$@AVERAGE(C16...C18)
>C18:4335
>B18:3
>N17:" #########
>M17:+B17*B17
>L17:+B17*C17
>K17:/FI+J17*J17
>J17:/FI+C17-E50
>I17:/-#
>C17:3467
>B17:2
>N16:" #########
>M16:+B16*B16
>L16:+B16*C16
>K16:/FI+J16*J16
>J16:/FI+C16-E50
>I16:/-#
>C16:2500
>B16:1
>N15:" #########
>M15:" ---------
>L15:" ---------
>K15:" ---------
>J15:" ---------
>I15:/-#
>F15:"   -------
>E15:"   -------
>G6:"ONS >A44
>F6:"2.1 SOLUTI
>E6:"10
>D6:"VERAGES >A
>C6:"D MOVING A
>B6:"A TABLE AN
>A6:"   1.1 DAT
>D4:" CONTENTS
>G3:/-=
>F3:/-=
>E3:/-=
>D3:/-=
>C3:/-=
>B3:/-=
>A3:/-=
>G2:"Corp. 1983
>F2:"t (C) QUE
>E2:"  Copyrigh
>C2:"R
>B2:" CALCULATO
>A2:"STATISTICS
>G1:/-=
>F1:/-=
>E1:/-=
>D1:/-=
>C1:/-=
>B1:/-=
>A1:/-=
/W1
/GOC
/GRM
/GC10
/X>A1:>A9:/TH
/X>A1:>A1:

>E54:/F$((((B41*C41)/E46)-L41)/((B41^2)/E46)-M41))*E53)+((C41/E46)-(((((C41*B41)/E46)-L41)/((B41^2/E46)-M41))*(B41/E46)))
```

```
==============================================================================
STATISTICS CALCULATOR                              Copyright (C) QUE Corp. 1983
==============================================================================
                                CONTENTS

  1.1 DATA TABLE AND MOVING AVERAGES >A10          2.1 SOLUTIONS >A44
  3.1 INSTRUCTIONS >A61

==============================================================================
DATA TABLE AND MOVING AVERAGES (Continues to row 42)                  Sheet 1.1
==============================================================================
                 Data              3-Period  6-Period 12-Period
                 Item     Value     Moving    Moving    Moving
                  (X)      (Y)      Average   Average   Average
                 ----   -------    -------   -------   -------
                   1       2500
                   2       3467
                   3       4335    3434.00
                   4       6554    4785.33
                   5       2333    4407.33
                   6       5789    4892.00   4163.00
                   7       3445    3855.67   4320.50
                   8       2467    3900.33   4153.83
                   9       4568    3493.33   4192.67
                  10       9777    5604.00   4729.83
                  11       8666    7670.33   5785.33
                  12      10995    9812.67   6653.00   5408.00
                  13      10540   10067.00   7835.50   6078.00
                  14       7656    9730.33   8700.33   6427.08
                  15      10444    9546.67   9679.67   6936.17
                  16      11025    9708.33   9887.67   7308.75
                  17       9555   10341.33  10035.83   7910.58
                  18      10678   10419.33   9983.00   8318.00
                  19      11934   10722.33  10215.33   9025.42
                  20      12450   11687.33  11014.33   9857.33
                  21      11777   12053.67  11236.50  10458.08
                  22      12017   12081.33  11401.83  10644.75
                  23      12698   12164.00  11925.67  10980.75
                  24      13000   12571.67  12312.67  11147.83
              -------   -------
                  300    198670
              =======   =======
```

```
#######################################################################
##########                  SCRATCH PAD                       #########
##########Difference                                           #########
##########   From    Difference                               #########
##########   Mean     Squared   X Times Y X Squared           #########
##########  ---------  ---------  ---------  ---------        #########
##########    -5778   33384321       2500          1          #########
##########    -4811   23144919       6934          4          #########
##########    -3943   15546592      13005          9          #########
##########    -1724    2971889      26216         16          #########
##########    -5945   35342034      11665         25          #########
##########    -2489    6194706      34734         36          #########
##########    -4833   23357084      24115         49          #########
##########    -5811   33766753      19736         64          #########
##########    -3710   13763482      41112         81          #########
##########     1499    2247251      97770        100          #########
##########      388     150609      95326        121          #########
##########     2717    7382542     131940        144          #########
##########     2262    5117021     137020        169          #########
##########     -622     386780     107184        196          #########
##########     2166    4691917     156660        225          #########
##########     2747    7546467     176400        256          #########
##########     1277    1630942     162435        289          #########
##########     2400    5760400     192204        324          #########
##########     3656   13366945     226746        361          #########
##########     4172   17406279     249000        400          #########
##########     3499   12243584     247317        441          #########
##########     3739   13980744     264374        484          #########
##########     4420   19537137     292054        529          #########
##########     4722   22298071     312000        576          #########
##########            --------    -------    -------          #########
##########           321218468    3028447       4900          #########
##########            ========    =======    =======          #########
#######################################################################
```

```
SOLUTIONS                                                           Sheet 2.1
==============================================================================
          Number of Items:                           24
          Maximum Value:                          13000
          Minimum Value:                           2333
          Range:                                  10667
          Mean:                               8277.9167
          Standard Deviation:                 3658.4290
          Linear Regression
            Data Item:                               26
            Estimated Value:                   14676.59


INSTRUCTIONS                                                        Sheet 3.1
==============================================================================

        1) Enter data in column headed "Values" (C16 to C39)
        2) RECALCULATE by typing: !
        3) SAVE by typing: /SSFilename (CR)
        4) PRINT by typing: >A10 (CR) /PPG54 (CR)
```

The formulas used to calculate each number are listed below. They are read from bottom to top and right to left and are referenced by their location in the model.

```
>F68:")
>E68:"/PPG54 (CR
>D68:">A10 (CR)
>C68:"y typing:
>B68:"4) PRINT b
>E67:" (CR)
>D67:"SSFilename
>C67:" typing: /
>B67:"3) SAVE by
>D66:"ping: !
>C66:"LATE by ty
>B66:"2) RECALCU
>G65:"9)
>F65:"(C16 to C3
>E65:" "Values"
>D65:"umn headed
>C65:"ata in col
>B65:"1) Enter d
>G62:/-=
>F62:/-=
>E62:/-=
>D62:/-=
>C62:/-=
>B62:/-=
>A62:/-=
>G61:"Sheet 3.1
>B61:"NS
>A61:"INSTRUCTIO
see formula below
>C54:"d Value:
>B54:"  Estimate
>E53:26
>C53:"m:
>B53:"  Data Ite
>C52:"ression
>B52:"Linear Reg
>E51:(K41/E46)^.5
>C51:"eviation:
>B51:"Standard D
>E50:@AVERAGE(C16...C39)
>B50:"Mean:
>E49:+E47-E48
>B49:"Range:
>E48:@MIN(C16...C39)
>C48:"lue:
>B48:"Minimum Va
>E47:@MAX(C13...C39)
>C47:"lue:
>B47:"Maximum Va
>E46:@COUNT(C16...C39)
>C46:"Items:
>B46:"Number of
>G45:/-=
>F45:/-=
>E45:/-=
>D45:/-=
>C45:/-=
>B45:/-=
>A45:/-=
>G44:"Sheet 2.1
>A44:"SOLUTIONS
>N43:/-#
>M43:/-#
>L43:/-#
>K43:/-#
>J43:/-#
>I43:/-#
>N42:" #########
>M42:"   =======
>L42:"   =======
```

```
>J37:/FI+C37-E50
>I37:/-#
>F37:/F$@AVERAGE(C26...C37)
>E37:/F$@AVERAGE(C32...C37)
>D37:/F$@AVERAGE(C35...C37)
>C37:12017
>B37:22
>N36:" #########
>M36:+B36*B36
>L36:+B36*C36
>K36:/FI+J36*J36
>J36:/FI+C36-E50
>I36:/-#
>F36:/F$@AVERAGE(C25...C36)
>E36:/F$@AVERAGE(C31...C36)
>D36:/F$@AVERAGE(C34...C36)
>C36:11777
>B36:21
>N35:" #########
>M35:+B35*B35
>L35:+B35*C35
>K35:/FI+J35*J35
>J35:/FI+C35-E50
>I35:/-#
>F35:/F$@AVERAGE(C24...C35)
>E35:/F$@AVERAGE(C30...C35)
>D35:/F$@AVERAGE(C33...C35)
>C35:12450
>B35:20
>N34:" #########
>M34:+B34*B34
>L34:+B34*C34
>K34:/FI+J34*J34
>J34:/FI+C34-E50
>I34:/-#
>F34:/F$@AVERAGE(C23...C34)
>E34:/F$@AVERAGE(C29...C34)
>D34:/F$@AVERAGE(C32...C34)
>C34:11934
>B34:19
>N33:" #########
>M33:+B33*B33
>L33:+B33*C33
>K33:/FI+J33*J33
>J33:/FI+C33-E50
>I33:/-#
>F33:/F$@AVERAGE(C22...C33)
>E33:/F$@AVERAGE(C28...C33)
>D33:/F$@AVERAGE(C31...C33)
>C33:10678
>B33:18
>N32:" #########
>M32:+B32*B32
>L32:+B32*C32
>K32:/FI+J32*J32
>J32:/FI+C32-E50
>I32:/-#
>F32:/F$@AVERAGE(C21...C32)
>E32:/F$@AVERAGE(C27...C32)
>D32:/F$@AVERAGE(C30...C32)
>C32:9555
>B32:17
>N31:" #########
>M31:+B31*B31
>L31:+B31*C31
>K31:/FI+J31*J31
>J31:/FI+C31-E50
>I31:/-#
>F31:/F$@AVERAGE(C20...C31)
>E31:/F$@AVERAGE(C26...C31)
```

```
>D27:/F$@AVERAGE(C25...C27)
>C27:10995
>B27:12
>N26:" #########
>M26:+B26*B26
>L26:+B26*C26
>K26:/FI+J26*J26
>J26:/FI+C26-E50
>I26:/-#
>E26:/F$@AVERAGE(C21...C26)
>D26:/F$@AVERAGE(C24...C26)
>C26:8666
>B26:11
>N25:" #########
>M25:+B25*B25
>L25:+B25*C25
>K25:/FI+J25*J25
>J25:/FI+C25-E50
>I25:/-#
>E25:/F$@AVERAGE(C20...C25)
>D25:/F$@AVERAGE(C23...C25)
>C25:9777
>B25:10
>N24:" #########
>M24:+B24*B24
>L24:+B24*C24
>K24:/FI+J24*J24
>J24:/FI+C24-E50
>I24:/-#
>E24:/F$@AVERAGE(C19...C24)
>D24:/F$@AVERAGE(C22...C24)
>C24:4568
>B24:9
>N23:" #########
>M23:+B23*B23
>L23:+B23*C23
>K23:/FI+J23*J23
>J23:/FI+C23-E50
>I23:/-#
>E23:/F$@AVERAGE(C18...C23)
>D23:/F$@AVERAGE(C21...C23)
>C23:2467
>B23:8
>N22:" #########
>M22:+B22*B22
>L22:+B22*C22
>K22:/FI+J22*J22
>J22:/FI+C22-E50
>I22:/-#
>E22:/F$@AVERAGE(C17...C22)
>D22:/F$@AVERAGE(C20...C22)
>C22:3445
>B22:7
>N21:" #########
>M21:+B21*B21
>L21:+B21*C21
>K21:/FI+J21*J21
>J21:/FI+C21-E50
>I21:/-#
>E21:/F$@AVERAGE(C16...C21)
>D21:/F$@AVERAGE(C19...C21)
>C21:5789
>B21:6
>N20:" #########
>M20:+B20*B20
>L20:+B20*C20
>K20:/FI+J20*J20
>J20:/FI+C20-E50
>I20:/-#
>D20:/F$@AVERAGE(C18...C20)
```

```
>D15:"   -------
>C15:"   -------
>B15:"      ----
>N14:" #########
>M14:" X Squared
>L14:" X Times Y
>K14:"   Squared
>J14:"    Mean
>I14:/-#
>F14:"    Average
>E14:"    Average
>D14:"    Average
>C14:"       (Y)
>B14:"        (X)
>N13:" #########
>K13:"Difference
>J13:"    From
>I13:/-#
>F13:"    Moving
>E13:"    Moving
>D13:"    Moving
>C13:"     Value
>B13:"       Item
>N12:" #########
>J12:"Difference
>I12:/-#
>F12:" 12-Period
>E12:"  6-Period
>D12:"  3-Period
>B12:"      Data
>N11:"=#########
>M11:/-=
>L11:/-=
>K11:/-=
>J11:/-=
>I11:/-#
>G11:/-=
>F11:/-=
>E11:/-=
>D11:/-=
>C11:/-=
>B11:/-=
>A11:/-=
>N10:" #########
>L10:" PAD
>K10:"    SCRATCH
>I10:/-#
>G10:"Sheet 1.1
>F10:"2)
>E10:"s to row 4
>D10:" (Continue
>C10:"G AVERAGES
>B10:" AND MOVIN
>A10:"DATA TABLE
>N9:/-#
>M9:/-#
>L9:/-#
>K9:/-#
>J9:/-#
>I9:/-#
>G9:/-=
>F9:/-=
>E9:/-=
>D9:/-=
>C9:/-=
>B9:/-=
>A9:/-=
>C7:">A61
>B7:"TRUCTIONS
>A7:"   3.1 INS
```

GROWTH CAPACITY CALCULATOR

The formulas used to calculate each number are listed below. They are read from bottom to top and right to left and are referenced by their location in the model.

```
>D72:"NTS >A65
>C72:"5.1 CONTE
>E71:"A51
>D71:"UCTIONS >
>C71:"4.1 INSTR
>F70:">A37
>E70:"IVIDENDS
>D70:"NGS AND D
>C70:"3.1 EARNI
>E69:">A22
>D69:"TABILITY
>C69:"2.1 PROFI
>E68:" >A8
>D68:"ALIZATION
>C68:"1.1 CAPIT
>H66:/-=
>G66:/-=
>F66:/-=
>E66:/-=
>D66:/-=
>C66:/-=
>B66:/-=
>A66:/-=
>H65:"Sheet 5.1
>A65:"CONTENTS
>G59:"(CR)
>F59:") /PPH47
>E59:": >A8 (CR
>D59:"by typing
>C59:"4) PRINT
>F58:"ame (CR)
>E58:" /SSFilen
>D58:"y typing:
>C58:"4) SAVE b
>E57:"typing: !
>D57:"ULATE by
>C57:"3) RECALC
>H56:"n D
>G56:" in colum
>F56:"(*) cells
>E56:" starred
>D56:"Data into
>C56:"2) Enter
>F55:")
>E55:"PPH72 (CR
>D55:"g: >A50 /
>C55:"    typin
>G54:"y
>F54:"ONTENTS b
>E54:"ONS and C
>D54:"INSTRUCTI
>C54:"1) PRINT
>H52:/-=
>G52:/-=
>F52:/-=
>E52:/-=
>D52:/-=
>C52:/-=
>B52:/-=
>A52:/-=
>H51:"Sheet 4.1
>B51:"ONS
>A51:"INSTRUCTI
>H47:"   ======
>G47:"   ======
>F47:"   ======
>E47:"   ======
>D47:"   ======
>H46:/F$+H33/H12*100
>G46:/F$+G33/G12*100
>F46:/F$+F33/F12*100
>E46:/F$+E33/E12*100
>D46:/F$+D33/D12*100
>C46:"ty (%)
>B46:"n on Equit
>A46:"Net Retur
>H44:"   ======
>G44:"   ======
>F44:"   ======
>E44:"   ======
>D44:"   ======
>H43:/FI+H33-H41
>G43:/FI+G33-G41
>F43:/FI+F33-F41
>E43:/FI+E33-E41
>D43:/FI+D33-D41
>C43:"d
>B43:"Reinveste
>A43:"Earnings
>H42:"   ------
>G42:"   ------
>F42:"   ------
>E42:"   ------
>D42:"   ------
>H41:/FI+H40*H33/100
>G41:/FI+G40*G33/100
>F41:/FI+F40*F33/100
>E41:/FI+E40*E33/100
>D41:49
>B41:"ds Paid
>A41:"* Dividen
>H40:/FI+G40
>G40:/FI+F40
>F40:/FI8
>E40:/FI+D40
>D40:/FI+D41/D33*100
>C40:"yout (%)
>B40:"vidend Pa
>A40:"Target Di
>H38:" ========
>G38:" ========
>F38:" ========
>E38:" ========
>D38:" ========
>C38:/-=
>B38:/-=
>A38:/-=
>H37:/FR"Year 5
>G37:/FR"Year 4
>F37:/FR"Year 3
>E37:/FR"Year 2
>D37:/FR"Year 1
>C37:"ENDS
>B37:"AND DIVID
>A37:"EARNINGS
>H34:"   ======
>G34:"   ======
>F34:"   ======
>E34:"   ======
>D34:"   ======
>H33:/FI+H28-H31
>G33:/FI+G28-G31
>F33:/FI+F28-F31
>E33:/FI+E28-E31
>D33:+D28-D31
>B33:"ter Tax
>A33:"Profit Af
>H32:"   ------
>G32:"   ------
>F32:"   ------
>E32:"   ------
>D32:"   ------
>H31:/FI+H28*H29/100
>G31:/FI+G28*G29/100
>F31:/FI+F28*F29/100
>E31:/FI+E28*E29/100
>D31:414
>B31:"ense
>A31:"* Tax Exp
>H30:"   ------
>G30:"   ------
>F30:"   ------
>E30:"   ------
>D30:"   ------
>H29:/FI+G29
>G29:/FI+F29
>F29:/FI+E29
>E29:/FI+D29
>D29:/FI+D31/D28*100
>B29:"(Percent)
>A29:"Tax Rate
>H28:/FI+H25-H26
>G28:/FI+G25-G26
>F28:/FI+F25-F26
>E28:/FI+E25-E26
>D28:+D25-D26
>H27:"   ------
>G27:"   ------
>F27:"   ------
>E27:"   ------
>D27:"   ------
>H26:/FI+H18*H13/100
>G26:/FI+G18*G13/100
>F26:/FI+F18*F13/100
>E26:/FI+E18*E13/100
>D26:+D18*D13/100
>B26:"Expense
>A26:"Interest
>H25:/FI+G25/G15*H15
>G25:/FI+F25/F15*G15
>F25:/FI+E25/E15*F15
>E25:/FI+D25/D15*E15
>D25:1700
>B25:"axes
>A25:"    and T
>C24:"terest
>B24:"before In
>A24:"* Profit
>H23:" ========
>G23:" ========
>F23:" ========
>E23:" ========
>D23:" ========
>C23:/-=
>B23:/-=
>A23:/-=
>H22:/FR"Year 5
>G22:/FR"Year 4
>F22:/FR"Year 3
>E22:/FR"Year 2
>D22:/FR"Year 1
>C22:"Sheet 2.1
>B22:"LITY
>A22:"PROFITABI
>H19:"   ======
>G19:"   ======
>F19:"   ======
>E19:"   ======
>D19:"   ======
>H18:/F$11
>G18:/F$12
>F18:/F$13
>E18:/F$14.5
>D18:/F$13
>C18:"ercent)
>B18:"t Rate (P
>A18:"* Interes
>H16:"   ======
>G16:"   ======
>F16:"   ======
>E16:"   ======
>D16:"   ======
>H15:/FI+H12+H13
>G15:/FI+G12+G13
>F15:/FI+F12+F13
>E15:/FI+E12+E13
>D15:+D12+D13
>C15:"on
>B15:"italizati
>A15:"Total Cap
>H14:"   ------
>G14:"   ------
>F14:"   ------
>E14:"   ------
>D14:"   ------
>H13:/FI+H11*H12
>G13:/FI+G11*G12
>F13:/FI+F11*F12
>E13:/FI+E11*E12
>D13:4000
>B13:"ebt
>A13:"* Total D
>H12:/FI+G12+G43
>G12:/FI+F12+F43
>F12:/FI+E12+E43
>E12:/FI+D12+D43
>D12:5000
>A12:"* Equity
>H11:/F$+G11
>G11:/F$1
>F11:/F$+E11
>E11:/F$+D11
>D11:/F$+D13/D12
>C11:"ty Ratio
>B11:"Debt/Equi
>A11:"Accepted
>H9:" ========
>G9:" ========
>F9:" ========
>E9:" ========
>D9:" ========
>C9:/-=
>B9:/-=
>A9:/-=
>H8:/FR"Year 5
>G8:/FR"Year 4
>F8:/FR"Year 3
>E8:/FR"Year 2
>D8:/FR"Year 1
>C8:"Sheet 1.1
>B8:"ATION
>A8:"CAPITALIZ
>H7:/-=
>G7:/-=
>F7:/-=
>E7:/-=
>D7:/-=
>C7:/-=
>B7:/-=
>A7:/-=
>G5:">A65
>F5:"CONTENTS
>C5:"ONS >A51
>B5:"INSTRUCTI
>H3:/-=
>G3:/-=
>F3:/-=
>E3:/-=
>D3:/-=
>C3:/-=
>B3:/-=
>A3:/-=
>H2:"orp. 1983
>G2:"(C) Que C
>F2:"opyright
>E2:"          C
>C2:"LCULATOR
>B2:"PACITY CA
>A2:"GROWTH CA
>H1:/-=
>G1:/-=
>F1:/-=
>E1:/-=
>D1:/-=
>C1:/-=
>B1:/-=
>A1:/-=
/W1
/GOC
/GRA
/GC9
/X>A1:>A7:/TH
/X>A63:>A83:
```

```
=========================================================================
GROWTH CAPACITY CALCULATOR                    Copyright (C) Que Corp. 1983
=========================================================================

        INSTRUCTIONS >A51                     CONTENTS >A65

=========================================================================
CAPITALIZATION    Sheet 1.1  Year 1   Year 2   Year 3   Year 4   Year 5
========================== ======== ======== ======== ======== ========

Accepted Debt/Equity Ratio     0.80     0.80     0.80     1.00     1.00
* Equity                       5000     5717     6495     7411     8551
* Total Debt                   4000     4574     5196     7411     8551
                             ------   ------   ------   ------   ------
Total Capitalization           9000    10291    11691    14821    17103
                             ======   ======   ======   ======   ======

* Interest Rate (Percent)     13.00    14.50    13.00    12.00    11.00
                             ======   ======   ======   ======   ======


PROFITABILITY     Sheet 2.1  Year 1   Year 2   Year 3   Year 4   Year 5
========================== ======== ======== ======== ======== ========
* Profit before Interest
    and Taxes                  1700     1944     2208     2800     3231
Interest Expense                520      663      675      889      941
                             ------   ------   ------   ------   ------
                               1180     1281     1533     1910     2290
Tax Rate (Percent)               35       35       35       35       35
                             ------   ------   ------   ------   ------
* Tax Expense                   414      449      538      670      803
                             ------   ------   ------   ------   ------
Profit After Tax                766      831      995     1240     1486
                             ======   ======   ======   ======   ======


EARNINGS AND DIVIDENDS       Year 1   Year 2   Year 3   Year 4   Year 5
========================== ======== ======== ======== ======== ========

Target Dividend Payout (%)        6        6        8        8        8
* Dividends Paid                 49       53       80       99      119
                             ------   ------   ------   ------   ------
Earnings Reinvested             717      778      915     1141     1368
                             ======   ======   ======   ======   ======

Net Return on Equity (%)      15.32    14.54    15.32    16.73    17.38
                             ======   ======   ======   ======   ======


INSTRUCTIONS                                                   Sheet 4.1
=========================================================================

                  1) PRINT INSTRUCTIONS and CONTENTS by
                       typing: >A50 /PPH72 (CR)
                  2) Enter Data into starred (*) cells in column D
                  3) RECALCULATE by typing: !
                  4) SAVE by typing: /SSFilename (CR)
                  4) PRINT by typing: >A8 (CR) /PPH47 (CR)



CONTENTS                                                       Sheet 5.1
=========================================================================

                  1.1 CAPITALIZATION >A8
                  2.1 PROFITABILITY >A22
                  3.1 EARNINGS AND DIVIDENDS >A37
                  4.1 INSTRUCTIONS >A51
                  5.1 CONTENTS >A65
```

QUEUE ANALYSIS (SINGLE-STATION SERVICE FACILITY)

The formulas used to calculate each number are listed below. They are read from bottom to top and right to left and are referenced by their location in the model.

```
>G48:" (CR)
>F48:"R) /PPH31
>E48:": >A10 (C
>D48:"by typing
>C48:"4) PRINT
>F47:"ame (CR)
>E47:" /SSFilen
>D47:"y typing:
>C47:"3) SAVE b
>E46:"typing: !
>D46:"ULATE by
>C46:"2) RECALC
>E45:"NS (>A10)
>D45:"ASSUMPTIO
>C45:"1) Enter
>H42:/-=
>G42:/-=
>F42:/-=
>E42:/-=
>D42:/-=
>C42:/-=
>B42:/-=
>A42:/-=
>H41:"Sheet 3.1
>B41:"ONS
>A41:"INSTRUCTI
>H31:" %
>G31:/FI((G14/G15)^(D31-1))*100
>D31:5
>C31:"ter Than:
>B31:"  is Grea
>E30:"System
>D30:"umber in
>C30:"ty That N
>B30:"Probabili
>H29:" minutes
>G29:/F$(G28/G14)*60
>E29:"ue:
>D29:"me in Que
>C29:"aiting Ti
>B29:"Average W
>G28:/FI(G14^2)/(G15*(G15-G14))
>D28:" Queue:
>C28:"Number in
>B28:"Expected
>G27:+G14/(G15-G14)
>D27:" System:
>C27:"Number in
>B27:"Expected
>H26:" minutes
>G26:/F$60/G15
>D26:"me:
>C26:"ervice Ti
>B26:"Average S
>H25:" %
>G25:/F$100-G24
>D25:"tage:
>C25:"on Percen
>B25:"Utilizati
>H24:" %
>G24:/F$(1-(G14/G15))*100
>D24:"ge:
>C24:" Percenta
>B24:"Idle Time
>H23:/-=
>G23:/-=
>F23:/-=
>E23:/-=
>D23:/-=
>C23:/-=
>B23:/-=
>A23:/-=
>H22:"Sheet 2.1
>A22:"SOLUTIONS
>G15:30
>E15:"r Hour:
>D15:"pacity pe
>C15:"ervice Ca
>B15:"Average S+
>G14:25
>E14:"per Hour:
>D14:"Arrivals
>C14:"umber of
>B14:"Average N
>H11:/-=
>G11:/-=
>F11:/-=
>E11:/-=
>D11:/-=
>C11:/-=
>B11:/-=
>A11:/-=
>H10:"Sheet 1.1
>B10:"NS
>A10:"ASSUMPTIONS
>H9:/-=
>G9:/-=
>F9:/-=
>E9:/-=
>D9:/-=
>C9:/-=
>B9:/-=
>A9:/-=
>D7:"A41
>C7:"UCTIONS >
>B7:"3.1 INSTR
>G6:"IONS >A22
>F6:"2.1 SOLUT
>D6:"10
>C6:"PTIONS >A
>B6:"1.1 ASSUM
>E4:"ENTS
>D4:"       CONT
>H3:/-=
>G3:/-=
>F3:/-=
>E3:/-=
>D3:/-=
>C3:/-=
>B3:/-=
>A3:/-=
>H2:"orp. 1983
>G2:"(C) Que C
>F2:"ITY)
>E2:"CE FACILI
>D2:"ION SERVI
>C2:"NGLE STAT
>B2:"LYSIS (SI
>A2:"QUEUE ANA
>H1:/-=
>G1:/-=
>F1:/-=
>E1:/-=
>D1:/-=
>C1:/-=
>B1:/-=
>A1:/-=
/W1
/GOC
/GRA
/GC9
/X>A1:>A9:/TH
/X>A1:>A1:
```

```
=========================================================================
QUEUE ANALYSIS (SINGLE STATION SERVICE FACILIITY)      (C) Que Corp. 1983
=========================================================================
                                 CONTENTS

        1.1 ASSUMPTIONS >A10                   2.1 SOLUTIONS >A22
        3.1 INSTRUCTIONS >A41

=========================================================================
ASSUMPTIONS                                                     Sheet 1.1
=========================================================================


        Average Number of Arrivals per Hour:                   25
        Average Service Capacity per Hour:                     30




SOLUTIONS                                                       Sheet 2.1
=========================================================================
        Idle Time Percentage:                               16.67 %
        Utilization Percentage:                             83.33 %
        Average Service Time:                                2.00 minutes
        Expected Number in System:                              5
        Expected Number in Queue:                               4
        Average Waiting Time in Queue:                      10.00 minutes
        Probability That Number in System
          is Greater Than:          5                          48 %




INSTRUCTIONS                                                    Sheet 3.1
=========================================================================


                    1) Enter ASSUMPTIONS (>A10)
                    2) RECALCULATE by typing: !
                    3) SAVE by typing: /SSFilename (CR)
                    4) PRINT by typing: >A10 (CR) /PPH31 (CR)
```

QUEUE ANALYSIS (MULTI-STATION SERVICE FACILITY)

The formulas used to calculate each number are listed below. They are read from bottom to top and right to left and are referenced by their location in the model.

```
>G52:" (CR)
>F52:"R) /PPH38]
>E52:": >A10 (C
>D52:"by typing
>C52:"4) PRINT
>F51:"ame (CR)
>E51:" /SSFilen
>D51:"y typing:
>C51:"3) SAVE b
>E50:"typing: !
>D50:"ULATE by
>C50:"2) RECALC
>E49:"NS (>A10)
>D49:"ASSUMPTIO
>C49:"1) Enter
>H46:/-=
>G46:/-=
>F46:/-=
>E46:/-=
>D46:/-=
>C46:/-=
>B46:/-=
>A46:/-=
>H45:"Sheet 3.1
>B45:"ONS
>A45:"INSTRUCTI
>G44:/F$
>G43:/F$
>G42:/F$
>G41:/F$
>G40:/F$
>H38:" minutes
>G38:/FI(G37/G14)*60
>E38:"ue:
>D38:"me in Que
>C38:"aiting Ti
>B38:"Average W
>H37:/F$
see formula below
>D37:" Queue:
>C37:"Number in
>B37:"Expected
>H36:" minutes
>G36:/F$60/G15
>D36:"me:
>C36:"ervice Ti
>B36:"Average S
>H35:" %
>G35:/F$100-G34
>D35:"tage:
>C35:"on Percen
>B35:"Utilizati
>P34:/-#
>O34:/-#
>N34:/-#
>M34:/-#
>L34:/-#
>K34:/-#
>H34:" %
see formula below
>D34:"ge:
>C34:" Percenta
>B34:"Idle Time
>P33:" ########
>N33:" ========
>K33:/-#
>P32:" ########
>N32:@SUM(N6...N31)
>K32:/-#
>P31:" ########
>N31:" --------
>K31:/-#
>H31:/-=
>G31:/-=
>F31:/-=
>E31:/-=
>D31:/-=
>C31:/-=
>B31:/-=
>A31:/-=
>P30:" ########
>N30:@IF((G16-1)>=L30,((G14/G15)^L30)/M30,0)
>M30:+M29*L30
>L30:25
>K30:/-#
>H30:"Sheet 2.1
>A30:"SOLUTIONS
>P29:" ########
>N29:@IF((G16-1)>=L29,((G14/G15)^L29)/M29,0)
>M29:+M28*L29
>L29:24
>K29:/-#
>P28:" ########
>N28:@IF((G16-1)>=L28,((G14/G15)^L28)/M28,0)
>M28:+M27*L28
>L28:23
>K28:/-#
>P27:" ########
>N27:@IF((G16-1)>=L27,((G14/G15)^L27)/M27,0)
>M27:+M26*L27
>L27:22
>K27:/-#
>P26:" ########
>N26:@IF((G16-1)>=L26,((G14/G15)^L26)/M26,0)
>M26:+M25*L26
>L26:21
>K26:/-#
>P25:" ########
>N25:@IF((G16-1)>=L25,((G14/G15)^L25)/M25,0)
>M25:+M24*L25
>L25:20
>K25:/-#
>P24:" ########
>N24:@IF((G16-1)>=L24,((G14/G15)^L24)/M24,0)
>M24:+M23*L24
>L24:19
>K24:/-#
>P23:" ########
>N23:@IF((G16-1)>=L23,((G14/G15)^L23)/M23,0)
>M23:+M22*L23
>L23:18
>K23:/-#
>P22:" ########
>N22:@IF((G16-1)>=L22,((G14/G15)^L22)/M22,0)
>M22:+M21*L22
>L22:17
>K22:/-#
>P21:" ########
>N21:@IF((G16-1)>=L21,((G14/G15)^L21)/M21,0)
>M21:+M20*L21
>L21:16
>K21:/-#
>P20:" ########
>N20:F((G16-1)>=L20,((G14/G15)^L20)/M20,0)
>M20:+M19*L20
>L20:15
>K20:/-#
>P19:" ########
>N19:@IF((G16-1)>=L19,((G14/G15)^L19)/M19,0)
>M19:+M18*L19
>L19:14
>K19:/-#
>P18:" ########
>N18:@IF((G16-1)>=L18,((G14/G15)^L18)/M18,0)
>M18:+M17*L18
>L18:13
>K18:/-#
>P17:" ########
>N17:@IF((G16-1)>=L17,((G14/G15)^L17)/M17,0)
>M17:+M16*L17
>L17:12
>K17:/-#
>P16:" ########
>N16:@IF((G16-1)>=L16,((G14/G15)^L16)/M16,0)
>M16:+M15*L16
>L16:11
>K16:/-#
>G16:3
>E16:"s:
>D16:"Facilitie
>C16:" Service
>B16:"Number of
>P15:" ########
>N15:@IF((G16-1)>=L15,((G14/G15)^L15)/M15,0)
>M15:+M14*L15
>L15:10
>K15:/-#
>G15:30
```

```
>G37:/FI(((G14/G15)^(G16+1))/((G16*(@LOOKUP(G16,L6...L30))*(1-((G14/G15)/G16)^2)))*G34/100

>G34:/F$(((G14/G15)^G16)/(@LOOKUP(G16,L6...L30)*(1-((G14/G15)/G16)))+1+N32)^(-1)*100
```

```
>E15:"r Hour:
>D15:"pacity pe
>C15:"ervice Ca
>B15:"Average S+
>P14:" ########
>N14:@IF((G16-1)>=L14,((G14/G15)^L14)/M14,0)
>M14:+M13*L14
>L14:9
>K14:/-#
>G14:75
>E14:"per Hour:
>D14:"Arrivals
>C14:"umber of
>B14:"Average N
>P13:" ########
>N13:@IF((G16-1)>=L13,((G14/G15)^L13)/M13,0)
>M13:+M12*L13
>L13:8
>K13:/-#
>P12:" ########
>N12:@IF((G16-1)>=L12,((G14/G15)^L12)/M12,0)
>M12:+M11*L12
>L12:7
>K12:/-#
>P11:" ########
>N11:@IF((G16-1)>=L11,((G14/G15)^L11)/M11,0)
>M11:+M10*L11
>L11:6
>K11:/-#
>H11:/-=
>G11:/-=
>F11:/-=
>E11:/-=
>D11:/-=
>C11:/-=
>B11:/-=
>A11:/-=
>P10:" ########
>N10:@IF((G16-1)>=L10,((G14/G15)^L10)/M10,0)
>M10:+M9*L10
>L10:5
>K10:/-#
>H10:"Sheet 1.1
>B10:"NS
>A10:"ASSUMPTIONS
>P9:" ########
>N9:@IF((G16-1)>=L9,((G14/G15)^L9)/M9,0)
>M9:+M8*L9
>L9:4
>K9:/-#
>H9:/-=
>G9:/-=
>F9:/-=
>E9:/-=
>D9:/-=
>C9:/-=
>B9:/-=
>A9:/-=
8:" ########
>N8:@IF((G16-1)>=L8,((G14/G15)^L8)/M8,0)
>M8:+M7*L8
>L8:3
>K8:/-#
>P7:" ########
>N7:@IF((G16-1)>=L7,((G14/G15)^L7)/M7,0)
>M7:+M6*L7
>L7:2
>K7:/-#
>D7:"A45
>C7:"UCTIONS >
>B7:"3.1 INSTR
>P6:" ########
>N6:@IF((G16-1)>=L6,((G14/G15)^L6)/M6,0)
>M6:+L6
>L6:1
>K6:/-#
>G6:"IONS >A30
>F6:"2.1 SOLUT
>D6:"10
>C6:"PTIONS >A
>B6:"1.1 ASSUM
>P5:" ########
>K5:/-#
>P4:"=########
>O4:/-=
>N4:/-=
>M4:/-=
>L4:/-=
>K4:/-#
>E4:"ENTS
>D4:"      CONT
>P3:" ########
>N3:"LE
>M3:"       TAB
>K3:/-#
>H3:/-=
>G3:/-=
>F3:/-=
>E3:/-=
>D3:/-=
>C3:/-=
>B3:/-=
>A3:/-=
>P2:" ########
>N2:"RIAL
>M2:"     FACTO
>K2:/-#
>H2:"orp. 1983
>G2:"(C) Que C
>F2:")
>E2:" FACILITY
>D2:"N SERVICE
>C2:"LTISTATIO
>B2:"LYSIS (MU
>A2:"QUEUE ANA
>P1:/-#
>O1:/-#
>N1:/-#
>M1:/-#
>L1:/-#
>K1:/-#
>H1:/-=
>G1:/-=
>F1:/-=
>E1:/-=
>D1:/-=
>C1:/-=
>B1:/-=
>A1:/-=
/W1
/GOR
/GRM
/GC9
/X>A1:>A9:/TH
/X>A36:>A45:
```

```
=========================================================================
QUEUE ANALYSIS (MULTISTATION SERVICE FACILITY)           (C) Que Corp. 1983
=========================================================================
                              CONTENTS

      1.1 ASSUMPTIONS >A10                2.1 SOLUTIONS >A30
      3.1 INSTRUCTIONS >A45

=========================================================================
ASSUMPTIONS                                                      Sheet 1.1
=========================================================================


      Average Number of Arrivals per Hour:                   75
      Average Service Capacity per Hour:                     30
      Number of Service Facilities:                           3













SOLUTIONS                                                        Sheet 2.1
=========================================================================


      Idle Time Percentage:                                4.49 %
      Utilization Percentage:                             95.51 %
      Average Service Time:                                2.00 minutes
      Expected Number in Queue:                             4
      Average Waiting Time in Queue:                        3 minutes





INSTRUCTIONS                                                     Sheet 3.1
=========================================================================


            1) Enter ASSUMPTIONS (>A10)
            2) RECALCULATE by typing: !
            3) SAVE by typing: /SSFilename (CR)
            4) PRINT by typing: >A10 (CR) /PPH38 (CR)
```

```
###########################################################
#########              FACTORIAL                   ########
#########                TABLE                     ########
#########==================================================
#########                                          ########
#########       1         1 2.500000               ########
#########       2         2 3.125000               ########
#########       3         6        0               ########
#########       4        24        0               ########
#########       5       120        0               ########
#########       6       720        0               ########
#########       7      5040        0               ########
#########       8     40320        0               ########
#########       9    362880        0               ########
#########      10   3628800        0               ########
#########      11  39916800        0               ########
#########      12 4.7900E8         0               ########
#########      13 6.2270E9         0               ########
#########      14 8.718E10         0               ########
#########      15 1.308E12         0               ########
#########      16 2.092E13         0               ########
#########      17 3.557E14         0               ########
#########      18 6.402E15         0               ########
#########      19 1.216E17         0               ########
#########      20 2.433E18         0               ########
#########      21 5.109E19         0               ########
#########      22 1.124E21         0               ########
#########      23 2.585E22         0               ########
#########      24 6.204E23         0               ########
#########      25 1.551E25         0               ########
#########                   --------               ########
#########                   5.625000               ########
#########                   ========               ########
###########################################################
```

QUICK ANALYSIS [illegible]

[illegible]

[illegible]

ASSUMPTIONS [illegible]

Average [illegible] per Hour
Average [illegible] per Hour
Number of [illegible]

[illegible]

ASSUMPTIONS [illegible]

NEW VENTURE BUDGET

The formulas used to calculate each number are listed below. They are read from bottom to top and right to left and are referenced by their location in the model.

```
>H73:")
>G73:"PH61 (CR
>F73:" (CR) /P
>E73:"ng: >A10
>D73:" by typi
>C73:"4) PRINT
>G72:"CR)
>F72:"lename (
>E72:"g: /SSFi
>D72:"by typin
>C72:"3) SAVE b
>F71:": !
>E71:"y typing
>D71:"CULATE b
>C71:"2) RECALC
>G70:">A35)
>F70:"ection (
>E70:"LES proj
>D70:" UNIT SA
>C70:"3) Enter
>F69:"A22)
>E69:" DATA (>
>D69:" EXPENSE
>C69:"2) Enter
>H68:"10)
>G68:"DATA (>A
>F68:"ND COST
>E68:" PRICE A
>D68:" PRODUCT
>C68:"1) Enter
>I66:/-=
>H66:/-=
>G66:/-=
>F66:/-=
>E66:/-=
>D66:/-=
>C66:/-=
>B66:/-=
>A66:/-=
>I65:"heet 4.1
>H65:"        S
>B65:"IONS
>A65:"INSTRUCTI
>M61:"  ======
>L61:"  ======
>K61:"  ======
>J61:"  ======
>H61:"  ======
>G61:"  ======
>F61:"  ======
>E61:"  ======
>D61:"  ======
>M60:+M58+L60
>L60:+L58+K60
>K60:+K58+J60
>J60:+J58+H60
>H60:+H58+G60
>G60:+G58+F60
>F60:+F58+E60
>E60:+E58+D60
>D60:+D58
>C60:"s
>B60:" Earning
>A60:"Retained
>O59:"  ======
>N59:"  ======
>M59:"  ======
>L59:"  ======
>K59:"  ======
>J59:"  ======
>I59:"  ======
>H59:"  ======
>G59:"  ======
>F59:"  ======
>E59:"  ======
>D59:"  ======
>O58:+N58+I58+D58
>N58:+N48-N56
>M58:+M48-M56
>L58:+L48-L56
>K58:+K48-K56
>J58:+J48-J56
>I58:+I48-I56
>H58:+H48-H56
>G58:+G48-G56
>F58:+F48-F56
>E58:+E48-E56
>D58:+D48-D56
>B58:"me
>A58:"Net Inco
>O57:"  ------
>N57:"  ------
>M57:"  ------
>L57:"  ------
>K57:"  ------
>J57:"  ------
>I57:"  ------
>H57:"  ------
>G57:"  ------
>F57:"  ------
>E57:"  ------
>D57:"  ------
>O56:+N56+I56+D56
>N56:@SUM(N51...N55)
>M56:@SUM(M51...M55)
>L56:@SUM(L51...L55)
>K56:@SUM(K51...K55)
>J56:@SUM(J51...J55)
>I56:@SUM(I51...I55)
>H56:@SUM(H51...H55)
>G56:@SUM(G51...G55)
>F56:@SUM(F51...F55)
>E56:@SUM(E51...E55)
>D56:@SUM(D51...D55)
>C56:"Expenses
>B56:"erating
>A56:"Total Op
>O55:"  ------
>N55:"  ------
>M55:"  ------
>L55:"  ------
>K55:"  ------
>J55:"  ------
>I55:"  ------
>H55:"  ------
>G55:"  ------
>F55:"  ------
>E55:"  ------
>D55:"  ------
>O54:+N54+I54+D54
>N54:@SUM(J54...M54)
>M54:+M43*D32/100
>L54:+L43*D32/100
>K54:+K43*D32/100
>J54:+J43*D32/100
>I54:@SUM(E54...H54)
>H54:+H43*D32/100
>G54:+G43*D32/100
>F54:+F43*D32/100
>E54:+E43*D32/100
>D54:+G32
>B54:"sing
>A54:" Advertis
>O53:+N53+I53+D53
>N53:@SUM(J53...M53)
>M53:(D29+@IF(@SUM(I42...M42)>F30,D30,0))
>L53:(D29+@IF(@SUM(I42...L42)>F30,D30,0))
>K53:(D29+@IF(@SUM(I42...K42)>F30,D30,0))
>J53:(D29+@IF(@SUM(I42...J42)>F30,D30,0))
>I53:@SUM(E53...H53)
>H53:(D29+@IF(@SUM(D42...H42)>F30,D30,0))
>G53:(D29+@IF(@SUM(D42...G42)>F30,D30,0))
>F53:(D29+@IF(@SUM(D42...F42)>F30,D30,0))
>E53:(D29+@IF(@SUM(D42...E42)>F30,D30,0))
>D53:(D29+@IF(@SUM(D42...D42)>F30,D30,0))*4
>B53:"Expenses
>A53:" Office
>O52:+N52+I52+D52
>N52:@SUM(J52...M52)
>M52:(D27/100*M51)
>L52:(D27/100*L51)
>K52:(D27/100*K51)
>J52:(D27/100*J51)
>I52:@SUM(E52...H52)
>H52:(D27/100*H51)
>G52:(D27/100*G51)
>F52:(D27/100*F51)
>E52:(D27/100*E51)
>D52:(D27/100*D51)
>B52:"erhead
>A52:" Wage Ove
>O51:+N51+I51+D51
>N51:@SUM(J51...M51)
>M51:(D25+@IF(@SUM(I42...M42)>F26,D26,0))
>L51:(D25+@IF(@SUM(I42...L42)>F26,D26,0))
>K51:(D25+@IF(@SUM(I42...K42)>F26,D26,0))
>J51:(D25+@IF(@SUM(I42...J42)>F26,D26,0))
>I51:@SUM(E51...H51)
>H51:(D25+@IF(@SUM(D42...H42)>F26,D26,0))
>G51:(D25+@IF(@SUM(D42...G42)>F26,D26,0))
>F51:(D25+@IF(@SUM(D42...F42)>F26,D26,0))
>E51:(D25+@IF(@SUM(D42...E42)>F26,D26,0))
>D51:(D25+@IF(@SUM(D42...D42)>F26,D26,0))*4
>B51:"s
>A51:" Salarie
>C50:"es
>B50:"g Expens
>A50:"Operatin
>O48:+N48+I48+D48
>N48:+N43-N45-N46
>M48:+M43-M45-M46
>L48:+L43-L45-L46
>K48:+K43-K45-K46
>J48:+J43-J45-J46
>I48:+I43-I45-I46
>H48:+H43-H45-H46
>G48:+G43-G45-G46
>F48:+F43-F45-F46
>E48:+E43-E45-E46
>D48:+D43-D45-D46
>B48:"rgin
>A48:"Gross Ma
>O47:"  ------
>N47:"  ------
>M47:"  ------
>L47:"  ------
>K47:"  ------
>J47:"  ------
>I47:"  ------
>H47:"  ------
>G47:"  ------
>F47:"  ------
>E47:"  ------
>D47:"  ------
>O46:+N46+I46+D46
>N46:@SUM(J46...M46)
>M46:(M43*D24)/100
>L46:(L43*D24)/100
>K46:(K43*D24)/100
>J46:(J43*D24)/100
>I46:@SUM(E46...H46)
>H46:(H43*D24)/100
>G46:(G43*D24)/100
>F46:(F43*D24)/100
>E46:(E43*D24)/100
>D46:(D43*D24)/100
>C46:"ense
>B46:"ales Exp
>A46:"Direct S
>O45:+N45+I45+D45
>N45:@SUM(J45...M45)
>M45:+M42*E18
>L45:+L42*E18
>K45:+K42*E18
>J45:+J42*E18
>I45:@SUM(E45...H45)
>H45:+H42*E18
>G45:+G42*E18
>F45:+F42*E18
>E45:+E42*E18
>D45:+D42*E18
>C45:"ld
>B45:"Goods So
>A45:"Cost of
>O43:+N43+I43+D43
>N43:@SUM(J43...M43)
>M43:+M42*D18
>L43:+L42*D18
>K43:+K42*D18
>J43:+J42*D18
>I43:@SUM(E43...H43)
>H43:+H42*D18
>G43:+G42*D18
>F43:+F42*D18
>E43:+E42*D18
>D43:+D42*D18
>B43:"ales
>A43:"Dollar S
>O42:+N42+I42+D42
>N42:@SUM(J42...M42)
>M42:14
>L42:14
>K42:14
>J42:14
>I42:@SUM(E42...H42)
>H42:12
>G42:11
>F42:9
>E42:7
>D42:0
```

```
>B42:"es
>A42:"Unit Sal
>O41:" -------
>N41:" -------
>M41:" -------
>L41:" -------
>K41:" -------
>J41:" -------
>I41:" -------
>H41:" -------
>G41:" -------
>F41:" -------
>E41:" -------
>D41:" -------
>O40:"  Totals
>N40:"  Total
>M40:" 4th Qtr
>L40:" 3rd Qtr
>K40:" 2nd Qtr
>J40:" 1st Qtr
>I40:"  Total
>H40:" 4th Qtr
>G40:" 3rd Qtr
>F40:" 2nd Qtr
>E40:" 1st Qtr
>D40:"  Total
>N39:/--
>M39:/--
>L39:/--
>K39:/--
>J39:" -------
>I39:/--
>H39:/--
>G39:/--
>F39:/--
>E39:" -------
>D39:" -------
>L38:"  Year 3
>G38:"  Year 2
>D38:"  Year 1
>O36:/-=
>N36:/-=
>M36:/-=
>L36:/-=
>K36:/-=
>J36:/-=
>I36:/-=
>H36:/-=
>G36:/-=
>F36:/-=
>E36:/-=
>D36:/-=
>C36:/-=
>B36:/-=
>A36:/-=
>I35:"heet 3.1
>H35:"        S
>B35:"ONS
>A35:"PROJECTI
>I32:" 1
>H32:" in Year
>G32:50000
>F32:"les and
>E32:" % of Sa
>D32:10
>C32:"nse
>B32:"ing Expe
>A32:"Advertis
>G30:" sales
>F30:20
>E30:" after
>D30:2000
>C30:"d by
>B30:"increase
>A30:"  to be
>D29:10000
>B29:"xpenses
>A29:"Office E
>F27:"laries
>E27:" % of Sa
>D27:30
>B27:"rhead
>A27:"Wage Ove
>G26:" sales
>F26:20
>E26:" after
>D26:6250
>C26:"d by
>B26:"increase
>A26:"  to be
```

```
>F25:"rter
>E25:" per Qua
>D25:17000
>B25:"ary
>A25:"Base Sal
>E24:" %
>D24:8
>B24:"mmission
>A24:"Sales Co
>I23:/-=
>H23:/-=
>G23:/-=
>F23:/-=
>E23:/-=
>D23:/-=
>C23:/-=
>B23:/-=
>A23:/-=
>I22:"heet 2.1
>H22:"        S
>B22:"DATA
>A22:"EXPENSE
>G19:"  ======
>F19:"  ======
>E19:"  ======
>D19:"  ======
>H18:" %
>G18:/FI+F18/D18*100
>F18:+D18-E18
>E18:+E15+E16
>D18:+D15+D16
>G17:"  ------
>F17:"  ------
>E17:"  ------
>D17:"  ------
>H16:" %
>G16:/FI+F16/D16*100
>F16:+D16-E16
>E16:1100
>D16:7000
>B16:"nt 2
>A16:" Compone
>H15:" %
>G15:/FI+F15/D15*100
>F15:+D15-E15
>E15:5450
>D15:9745
>B15:"nt 1
>A15:" Compone
>G14:" -------
>F14:" -------
>E14:" -------
>D14:" -------
>G13:" Margin
>F13:" Margin
>E13:"  Cost
>D13:"  Price
>G12:" Percent
>F12:" Gross
>E12:"  Unit
>D12:"  Sales
>I11:/-=
>H11:/-=
>G11:/-=
>F11:/-=
>E11:/-=
>D11:/-=
>C11:/-=
>B11:/-=
>A11:/-=
>I10:"heet 1.1
>H10:"        S
>D10:"ATA
>C10:"D COST D
>B10:"PRICE AN
>A10:"PRODUCT
>I9:/-=
>H9:/-=
>G9:/-=
>F9:/-=
>E9:/-=
>D9:/-=
>C9:/-=
>B9:/-=
>A9:/-=
>I7:" >A65
>H7:"RUCTIONS
>G7:"4.1 INST
>C7:"NS >A35
>B7:"ROJECTIO
```

```
>A7:"   3.1 P
>I6:" >A22
>H6:"NSE DATA
>G6:"2.1 EXPE
>E6:"TA >A10
>D6:" COST DA
>C6:"RICE AND
>B6:"RODUCT P
>A6:"   1.1 PR
>E4:"CONTENTS
>D4:"
>I3:/-=
>H3:/-=
>G3:/-=
>F3:/-=
>E3:/-=
>D3:/-=
>C3:/-=
>B3:/-=
>A3:/-=
>I2:"rp. 1983
>H2:") QUE Co
>G2:"right (C
>F2:"    Copy
>C2:"ET
>B2:"URE BUDG
>A2:"NEW VENT
>I1:/-=
>H1:/-=
>G1:/-=
>F1:/-=
>E1:/-=
>D1:/-=
>C1:/-=
>B1:/-=
>A1:/-=
/W1
/GOR
/GRM
/GFI
/GC8
/X>A1:>A9:/TH
/X>A1:>A1:
```

NEW VENTURE BUDGET

CONTENTS

PRODUCT PRICE AND COST DATA — Sheet 1.1

	Sales Price	Unit Cost	Gross Margin	Percent Margin
Component 1	9745	5450	4295	44 %
Component 2	7000	1100	5900	84 %
	16745	6550	10195	61 %

EXPENSE DATA — Sheet 2.1

Sales Commission	8 %			
Base Salary	17000	per Quarter		
to be increased by	6250	after	20	sales
Wage Overhead	30	% of Salaries		
Office Expenses	10000			
to be increased by	2000	after	20	sales
Advertising Expense	10	% of Sales and	50000	in Year 1

PROJECTIONS — Sheet 3.1

	Year 1	Year 2					Year 3					
	Total	1st Qtr	2nd Qtr	3rd Qtr	4th Qtr	Total	1st Qtr	2nd Qtr	3rd Qtr	4th Qtr	Total	Totals
Unit Sales	0	7	9	11	12	39	14	14	14	14	56	95
Dollar Sales	0	117215	150705	184195	200940	653055	234430	234430	234430	234430	937720	1590775
Cost of Goods Sold	0	45850	58950	72050	78600	255450	91700	91700	91700	91700	366800	622250
Direct Sales Expense	0	9377	12056	14736	16075	52244	18754	18754	18754	18754	75018	127262
Gross Margin	0	61988	79699	97409	106265	345361	123976	123976	123976	123976	495902	841263
Operating Expenses												
Salaries	68000	17000	17000	23250	23250	80500	23250	23250	23250	23250	93000	241500
Wage Overhead	20400	5100	5100	6975	6975	24150	6975	6975	6975	6975	27900	72450
Office Expenses	40000	10000	10000	12000	12000	44000	12000	12000	12000	12000	48000	132000
Advertising	50000	11722	15071	18420	20094	65306	23443	23443	23443	23443	93772	209078
Total Operating Expenses	178400	43822	47171	60645	62319	213956	65668	65668	65668	65668	262672	655028
Net Income	-178400	18166	32528	36765	43946	131405	58308	58308	58308	58308	233230	186236
Retained Earnings	-178400	-160234	-127706	-90941	-46995		11313	69620	127928	186236		

INSTRUCTIONS — Sheet 4.1

1) Enter PRODUCT PRICE AND COST DATA (>A10)
2) Enter EXPENSE DATA (>A22)
3) Enter UNIT SALES projection (>A35)
2) RECALCULATE by typing: !

PRICE-VOLUME ANALYSIS

The formulas used to calculate each number are listed below. They are read from bottom to top and right to left and are referenced by their location in the model.

```
>G48:" (CR)
>F48:"R) /PPH32
>E48:": >A10 (C
>D48:"by typing
>C48:"4) PRINT
>F47:"ame (CR)
>E47:" /SSFilen
>D47:"y typing:
>C47:"3) SAVE b
>E46:"typing: !
>D46:"ULATE by
>C46:"2) RECALC
>E45:"NS (>A10)
>D45:"ASSUMPTIO
>C45:"1) Enter
>H42:/-=
>G42:/-=
>F42:/-=
>E42:/-=
>D42:/-=
>C42:/-=
>B42:/-=
>A42:/-=
>H41:"Sheet 3.1
>B41:"ONS
>A41:"INSTRUCTI
>H32:"   ======
>G32:"   ======
>F32:"   ======
>E32:"   ======
>D32:"   ======
>H31:/FI(H28/H24)*100
>G31:/FI(G28/G24)*100
>F31:/FI(F28/F24)*100
>E31:/FI(E28/E24)*100
>D31:/FI(D28/D24)*100
>C31:"ercent)
>B31:" Sales (P
>A31:"Return on
>H29:"   ======
>G29:"   ======
>F29:"   ======
>E29:"   ======
>D29:"   ======
>H28:+H24-H25-H26
>G28:+G24-G25-G26
>F28:+F24-F25-F26
>E28:+E24-E25-E26
>D28:+D24-D25-D26
>C28:/FR"$
>B28:"e
>A28:"Net Incom
>H27:"   ------
>G27:"   ------
>F27:"   ------
>E27:"   ------
>D27:"   ------
>C27:/FR
>H26:+D13
>G26:+D13
>F26:+D13
>E26:+D13
>D26:+D13
>C26:/FR"$
>B26:"ts
>A26:"Fixed Cos
>H25:+D15*H19
>G25:+D15*G19
>F25:+D15*F19
>E25:+D15*E19
>D25:+D15*D19
>C25:/FR"$
>B25:"Costs
>A25:"Variable
>H24:+H17*H19
>G24:+G17*G19
>F24:+F17*F19
>E24:+E17*E19
>D24:+D17*D19
>C24:/FR"$
>B24:"lar Sales
>A24:"Total Dol
>H23:/-=
>G23:/-=
>F23:/-=
>E23:/-=
>D23:/-=
>C23:/-=
```

```
>B23:/-=
>A23:/-=
>H22:"Sheet 2.1
>A22:"SOLUTIONS
>H19:400000
>G19:625000
>F19:825000
>E19:900000
>D19:920000
>C19:"ume
>B19:"Sales Vol
>A19:"Expected
>H17:/F$2
>G17:/F$1.5
>F17:/F$1.25
>E17:/F$1.1
>D17:/F$1
>C17:/FR"it       $
>B17:"ce per Un
>A17:"Sales Pri
>D16:/FR
>C16:/FR
>D15:/F$.35
>C15:/FR"Costs    $
>B15:"Variable
>A15:"Per Unit
>D13:/FR600000
>C13:/FR"$
>B13:"ts
>A13:"Fixed Cos
>H11:/-=
>G11:/-=
>F11:/-=
>E11:/-=
>D11:/-=
>C11:/-=
>B11:/-=
>A11:/-=
>H10:"Sheet 1.1
>B10:"NS
>A10:"ASSUMPTIO
>H9:/-=
>G9:/-=
>F9:/-=
>E9:/-=
>D9:/-=
>C9:/-=
>B9:/-=
>A9:/-=
>D7:"A41
>C7:"UCTIONS >
>B7:"3.1 INSTR
>G6:"IONS >A22
>F6:"2.1 SOLUT
>D6:"10
>C6:"PTIONS >A
>B6:"1.1 ASSUM
>E4:"ENTS
>D4:"      CONT
>H3:/-=
>G3:/-=
>F3:/-=
>E3:/-=
>D3:/-=
>C3:/-=
>B3:/-=
>A3:/-=
>H2:"orp. 1983
>G2:"(C) Que C
>F2:"opyright
>E2:"         C
>C2:"SIS
>B2:"UME ANALY
>A2:"PRICE VOL
>H1:/-=
>G1:/-=
>F1:/-=
>E1:/-=
>D1:/-=
>C1:/-=
>B1:/-=
>A1:/-=
/W1
/GOC
/GRA
/GC9
/X>A1:>A9:/TH
/X>A1:>A1:
```

```
=========================================================================
PRICE VOLUME ANALYSIS                          Copyright (C) Que Corp. 1983
=========================================================================
                              CONTENTS

        1.1 ASSUMPTIONS >A10                 2.1 SOLUTIONS >A22
        3.1 INSTRUCTIONS >A41

=========================================================================
ASSUMPTIONS                                                    Sheet 1.1
=========================================================================

Fixed Costs                $   600000

Per Unit Variable Costs    $     0.35

Sales Price per Unit       $     1.00     1.10     1.25     1.50     2.00

Expected Sales Volume          920000   900000   825000   625000   400000

SOLUTIONS                                                      Sheet 2.1
=========================================================================
Total Dollar Sales         $   920000   990000  1031250   937500   800000
Variable Costs             $   322000   315000   288750   218750   140000
Fixed Costs                $   600000   600000   600000   600000   600000
                               ------   ------   ------   ------   ------
Net Income                 $    -2000    75000   142500   118750    60000
                               ======   ======   ======   ======   ======

Return on Sales (Percent)           0        8       14       13        8
                               ======   ======   ======   ======   ======



INSTRUCTIONS                                                   Sheet 3.1
=========================================================================

                  1) Enter ASSUMPTIONS (>A10)
                  2) RECALCULATE by typing: !
                  3) SAVE by typing: /SSFilename (CR)
                  4) PRINT by typing: >A10 (CR) /PPH32 (CR)
```